RETURN OF THE DRAGON

Return of the Dragon

China's Wounded Nationalism

Maria Hsia Chang
University of Nevada, Reno

A Member of the Perseus Books Group

Copyright © 2001 by Westview Press, A Member of the Perseus Books Group

Published in 2001 in the United States of America by Westview Press, 5500 Central Avenue, Boulder, Colorado 80301-2877, and in the United Kingdom by Westview Press, 12 Hid's Copse Road, Cumnor Hill, Oxford OX2 9JJ

Find us on the World Wide Web at www.westviewpress.com

Library of Congress Cataloging-in-Publication Data

Chang, Maria Hsia.
  Return of the Dragon: China's wounded nationalism/by Maria Hsia Chang.
    p. cm.
  Includes bibliographical references and index.
  ISBN 0-8133-3856-5 (pbk.)
  1. Nationalism and communism—China. 2. Nationalism—China. 3. China—Politics and government—1976– . 4. China—Economic policy—1976– . I. Title: China's wounded nationalism. II. Title.

HX550.N3 C38 2001
320.54'0951—dc21

The paper used in this publication meets the requirements of the American National Standard for Permanence of Paper for Printed Library Materials Z39.48–1984.

10   9   8   7   6   5   4   3   2   1

To the memory of my friend,
Kathy Petrinovich,
who loved without qualification

Contents

Acknowledgments

The successful undertaking of any sustained endeavor is dependent on the support of many individuals and institutions. This book is no different.

The seedling that grew to become this book was a paper I presented before the 25th Sino-American Conference on Contemporary China in June 1996, in Taipei, which was met with unmitigated opposition and skepticism. Were it not for the encouragement of Professors Jan Prybyla, Michael Kao, James Myers, and Edward Friedman, my efforts might have ended with that paper. Professor Friedman, in particular, graced me with undeserved kindness and counsel.

I also owe my gratitude to several institutions: the Historical Commission of the Kuomintang, under the directorship of Dr. Chin Hsiao-yi, for a grant many years ago; the Chiang Ching-kuo International Foundation for bestowing me with an Individual Research Fellowship in 1995; U.C. Berkeley's Center for Chinese Studies and East Asian libraries for their Chinese collection and helpful staff; and the University of Nevada—Reno, for providing a supportive environment for scholarship, including the able computer assistance of Tony Chedester, Beverly Siegel, and Ken Hull.

I am indebted to the following individuals for providing me with research assistance: Dr. Xiaoyu Chen for the many Chinese-language books he procured for me from the People's Republic; Professors Li Fusheng and Craig Lipman for administering the nationalism questionnaire to their students in Beijing; David Chain and research assistants Dr. Kevin Peek, Jacqui Granville, and Ryan Larson; and Chen Xiaowai and my father, Chang Pao-en, for their thoughts on the etymology of *Huaxia* and *Zhongguo*. I also greatly appreciate the efforts of my two outside referees who gave my manuscript a careful reading and whose encouraging comments and criticisms both inspired and spurred me toward making the final improvements.

Finally, this book would not be completed if I could not draw spiritual sustenance from the interest and support of the following individuals: my colleagues Professors Eric Herzik, Richard Ganzel, Leah Magennis, and Chris Simon; my students Muhammed Begenchev, Angie Wise, Christian Johnson, and Ariela Wagner; and my friends Stephanie Free, Steve Rogers, Joseph Kuo, Herbert Neal, Tanya Berry, Judge Patricia Stephens, and

Deidre Cleek. Most of all, I am grateful to my husband, Professor A. James Gregor, for his unfailing love and wisdom, and to my boys, Gabriel Raphael and Charles Elmo, for their peerless companionship and unspoken devotion.

Maria Hsia Chang

RETURN OF THE DRAGON

1

The Problem

The dawning of a new millennium is bringing closure to the bloodiest hundred years in human history. Not only did the twentieth century witness two cataclysmic world wars, it also gave birth to the phenomenon of totalitarianism, a "historically unique and *sui generis*"[1] form of government that is unparalleled in its systematic and organized brutality. In a totalitarian dictatorship, political rule is "all-embracing"[2] because the state attempts to control every aspect of society, including the individual's private life and thoughts.[3]

Totalitarian systems are conventionally subdivided into those of the right and the left. On the right are Nazi Germany, Fascist Italy, and Imperial Japan—the Axis powers and aggressors in World War II. On the left is the subspecies of communist countries, epitomized by the Soviet Union and the People's Republic of China (PRC).

Although right and left totalitarianism, in the judgment of Carl Friedrich and Zbigniew Brzezinski, "are sufficiently alike to class them together,"[4] they differ in several important aspects. Anti-Semitism, while often cited as one such distinction, does not seem to qualify. Lawrence C. Mayer contended that whereas racism in general and anti-Semitism in particular constituted a key element in Nazi ideology and that, although Marxism preached the brotherhood of an entire economic class that would presumably encompass all races, in practice the Soviet Union became "one of the world's most vociferously anti-Semitic states."[5]

All totalitarian systems are characterized by central control and direction of the entire economy, but in right totalitarianism, state control of the economy is effected through the economic system of corporatism, which retains the private sector with its private property ownership and enterprises. Left totalitarianism, in contrast, abolishes private ownership altogether and replaces it with state ownership and central planning. Right and left also differ in their enemies. Whereas the ideology of left totalitarianism pivots on Karl Marx's notion of class warfare and identifies the domestic and international bourgeoisie as the enemy, right totalitarianism's worldview is not class-based but is animated instead by an aggressive and expansionist nationalism.[6] Right and left totalitarianism also differ in their durability. All three exemplars of right totalitarianism were defeated in World War II and became successfully democratized. The communist left, in contrast, has proven to be more pervasive and enduring.

Russia was the first country to embrace communism, in the Bolshevik Revolution of 1917. From the newly founded Soviet Union, communism ultimately expanded to some 150 countries in almost every continent in the world—in Eastern Europe, Asia, Africa, and Latin America. At its zenith, communism was the ruling system for over one-third of humanity and accounted for more than 40 percent of industrial production in the world.[7]

Communism's inspiration and legitimation was the ideology of Marxism-Leninism, at the heart of which was the promise of universal brotherhood and equality. But "the Devil may appear in the vesture of the Angel of Light."[8] Despite its utopian impulse, the reality of communism proved to be very different. As Brzezinski expressed it, communism, born out of "an impatient idealism" that rejected the injustice of the status quo and sought a better and more humane society, captivated some of the brightest minds and the most idealistic hearts. Despite those benign impulses, communism produced mass oppression and "prompted some of the worst crimes of this or any century."[9] With the clarity of hindsight, Klaus Risse, head of Section A of East Germany's secret police, now could see that communism's basic flaw was that it failed to take into account "the inner *Schweinehund.*" Communism could have worked only if people had been angels.[10]

Instead of utopia, what actually transpired in Marxist states was a dystopic nightmare that took the lives of 85 to 100 million people who perished from misguided economic experiments and deliberate abuse and murder by the state. The People's Republic of China has the dubious distinction of having the greatest human toll, at 45 to 72 million.[11] In the Soviet Union between 1917 and 1987, anywhere from 32 to 62 million people lost their lives;[12] in Lithuania between 1940 and 1955, some 1.2 million were killed or were dispatched to labor camps; in Hungary 15,000 died in Budapest during the 1956 uprising; in Vietnam a minimum of 65,000 were executed after 1975; in Cambodia, in a span of merely three years between 1975 and 1978, the Khmer Rouge regime exterminated a third (2.3 million) of the population.[13] At a minimum, the human costs of communism amounted to 50 million lives, representing "without a doubt" the most extravagant and wasteful experiment in social engineering ever attempted.[14]

It was because of communism that, instead of international peace, the end of World War II was followed by a Cold War. For more than four decades, the world teetered on the brink of nuclear war between the two superpowers that led their respective ideological camps. Only with the abrupt dissolution of the Soviet Union in 1991 did the Cold War end. Until that time, the West had regarded communism with equal measures of loathing and fear. If not immutable, communism was believed to be inherently stable.

As an example, Samuel Huntington wrote in 1970 that he expected "revolutionary" one-party systems like the Soviet Union to evolve through three phases to become "established" one-party systems—their evolution propelled by the political leadership's successes in the earlier phase.[15] There were even those in the West who seemed convinced that communist countries possessed strengths, superior to those of representative democracies, which would ensure not only their enduring survival but their continuous advance in the world.[16] Jean-François Revel, for one, observed that democracies were inherently vulnerable to what he called "the totalitarian temptation," their chief weakness being their disposition to be excessively self-critical about the perceived economic and moral failings of capitalism. Communist countries, in contrast, were impervious to that corrosive self-doubt because of the state's iron control over speech, information, and communication. Once a people came under communist rule, Revel lamented, it would be "too late to escape it should they change their minds." After a generation, their capacity to dream and to think would begin to fail because of propaganda and cultural isolation, rendering them incapable of imagining either past or future. Revel concluded that the transition to totalitarian rule "is by definition irrevocable, except in the case of some cataclysm like a world war."[17]

In the aftermath of the rapid dissolution of the Soviet Union and its satellite states in Eastern Europe, the West's insecurity now seems misplaced. What was, to Revel, the major weakness of democracies turned out instead to be their strength. As a leader of Poland's Solidarity movement put it, "only democracy—having the capacity to question itself—also has the capacity to correct its own mistakes."[18]

The almost overnight disappearance of the Soviet bloc has revealed communism to be far from irrevocable, but inherently flawed and untenable. Although Brzezinski in 1961 was convinced that there was no reason to conclude that the existing totalitarian systems would disappear as a result of internal evolution, the same Brzezinski in 1989 recognized communism to be a "grand" and "historic failure" whose fatal flaws were "deeply embedded in the very nature of the Marxist-Leninist praxis." Possessed of intrinsic shortcomings in every aspect—its operation, institutions, and philosophy—communism "no longer has a practical model for others to emulate."[19]

Since their dissolution, the erstwhile communist states in Russia and East Europe have had varying success at effectuating successful transitions to market-based democracies. Thus far, the more successful cases include Hungary, Poland, and the Czech Republic. For Romania, Russia, and the other constituent republics of the former Soviet Union, the outlook is uncertain. The least effective transitions would have to be those of Albania and Yugoslavia. In the case of Albania, after a spontaneous popular uprising against its corrupt post-communist government, the country dissolved into anarchy that left 2,000 people dead by the end of 1997. For its part, the end of communist rule in Yugoslavia saw the country's descent into the bloodbath of "ethnic cleansing," which was contained only by the forceful intervention and subsequent occupation by NATO troops led by the United States.

The effort to understand, explain, and predict the evolution of communist systems[20] must go beyond the former Soviet bloc countries to take into account the world's remaining communist countries. The latter are subdivided into two distinct groups. A first group is comprised of the unregenerate and unreformed communist states of North Korea and Cuba, the economies of which are in precipitous decline.[21] By introducing market reforms, China pioneered the way for a second group of remnant communist states comprised of China and Vietnam. Unlike the former Soviet Union where Mikhail Gorbachev instituted political reform before (and without) significant economic reform, the Chinese Communist Party (CCP) took an opposite course of action. Beginning in late 1978 under the leadership of Deng Xiaoping, the CCP undertook radical reform of the economic system while eschewing any meaningful political reform.

Reform of the Chinese economy began in December 1978 in the countryside with agricultural decollectivization. Mao's gargantuan communes were dismantled and the unit of farming reverted to China's millennial tradition of the family household, to which the state conferred usufruct rights over land. From the countryside, the economic reform rapidly expanded to the cities. Private and collectively owned businesses and industries began to proliferate in cities, towns, and villages; an "open door" policy toward the West was inaugurated to attract foreign trade and investment.

The results of Deng's economic reforms were quick and impressive. Since 1979, the Chinese economy has grown by an average real rate of 9 to 10 percent a year—a record that is unprecedented in recent world history. If China can sustain that rate of growth, its gross national product (GNP) will double every ten years,[22] catapulting the People's Republic to superpower status by 2025.

By making China stronger and more prosperous, the economic reforms have extended the lifespan of Chinese communism—but at the cost of ideological dilution. Nor is ideological dilution the only tradeoff. Deng's economic reforms have also spawned a host of unintended consequences that are social, economic, demographic, ecological, as well as political. Today, the most serious of those problems threaten not only the CCP's political power but the very integrity and continuity of the People's Republic.[23]

Seymour Martin Lipset once noted that political leaders in developing countries must suffer the brunt of the resentments and problems caused by industrialization, including rapid urbanization and a growing gap between the newly rich and the poor. If the leaders fail to find an effective way to resolve those problems, they lose their hold on the masses. In the case of *socialist* developing countries, where "there is still a need for intense political controversy and ideology," the position of political leaders is even more tenuous. If the leaders were to admit that Marxism is an outmoded doctrine, they would risk becoming conservatives within their own societies, a role that they cannot play and still retain a popular following. Lipset expected the political leadership to adopt a strategy of blaming the ills of development on scapegoats who could be domestic capitalists, foreign investors, Christianity, or "the departed imperialists."[24]

To further complicate the Communist Party's predicament, the ideocratic[25] nature of China's political system demands more than pragmatic legitimacy. From its inception, political rule in the People's Republic was legitimated by the CCP's claim to possess special truths and insights imparted by an absolutist and comprehensive ideology that presumed to know the past and present, as well as predict the course of societal evolution. Given its ideocratic character, the Communist Party is compelled to seek doctrinal legitimation in some overarching ideology. As Marxism-Leninism-Maoism erodes and recedes in relevance and utility, the party must find a suitable replacement—and it seems to have found that in nationalism. In the words of *The Economist*, "With communism discredited and democracy distrusted, China is in search of a new ideology ... [and] nationalism may be filling the gap."[26] All of which would not surprise David E. Apter, who, in 1964, had anticipated China's resort to nationalism when he noted that political leaders in socialist states may turn to "greater nationalism" in order to compensate for weaknesses in solidarity and identity. Nationalism would replace socialism as the dominant ideology in developing countries because, through its ability to incorporate primordial loyalties "in a readily understandable synthesis," it can better provide for the needed identity and solidarity.[27]

There is increasing evidence that post-communist societies and regimes are turning to nationalism as a substitute ideology, as seen in Russia's Chechnya and Yugoslavia's Serbia, Bosnia, and Kosovo. Even newly independent Uzbekistan has made a nationalist hero and symbol out of Tamerlane, the Turkish-Mongol warlord who slaughtered millions. A museum worker in Bukhara gave candid testimony to the need that nationalism fulfills when he admitted that "We don't have Communist idols anymore, so we need our own heroes."[28]

In the case of the People's Republic, nationalism not only is an ideological replacement for an obsolete Marxism, it also provides much-needed identity and solidarity to a society experiencing the disruptive forces associated with rapid development. Beginning in the last decade of the twentieth century, the Chinese Communist Party has actively promoted and encouraged a resurgent nationalism so as to extend its lease on power. The appeal to nationalism may be the Communist Party's last resort and the only fixative that could keep intact the People's Republic.

By turning to nationalism as a panacea, the Communist Party is attempting to carve for itself a third way. Today, communism in China is rapidly mutating into a political species that is neither communist nor capitalist. The People's Republic is still a single-party dictatorship but is no longer utopian or totalitarian. Its government's legitimating ideology is only nominally Marxist but is, in reality, increasingly that of nationalism. China is a political system where government is still the monopoly of a single party, the economy a mixture of capitalism with significant state ownership and controls, and political legitimacy more and more rests on an appeal to nationalism that is increasingly reactive, irredentist, and chauvinistic. Some have called such political systems "fascist."[29]

Whatever its name, Chinese communism is mutating into a virulent nationalism. That development has more than academic interest. The irredentist dimension to contemporary Chinese nationalism carries serious implications for the peace and security in Asia and the Pacific because it transcends mere rhetoric and is manifested in the behavior of the People's Liberation Army (PLA).

Already the largest in the world in manpower (3 million) and with the world's third largest nuclear arsenal, the PLA is a growth industry. Although it decreased in real terms between 1979 and 1988, China's military budget increased after 1990 by about 10 percent each year[30]—despite the end of the Cold War and the crumbling of the Soviet Union, which China had identified as its major threat. At least part of the budget increases went to military purchases that have significantly upgraded China's military capabilities. Those purchases include air refueling kits from Iran; Su-27s (reportedly superior to American F-15 fighter jets in some ways), Su-24s, MiG-29s, Hind assault helicopters, and state-of-the-art *Sovremenny*-class missile destroyers with supersonic anti-ship missiles from Russia; and most recently, an aircraft carrier from Ukraine. In 2000, China is expected to be able to produce modern mobile ICBMs with Russia's help.[31]

Aside from its arms purchases, the PLA's efforts to modernize and upgrade its capabilities are focused in two other areas. Anticipating that post–Cold War conflicts will increasingly be in the arena of regional limited warfare—epitomized by Desert Storm—the PLA has assiduously worked at developing its rapid reaction force, increasing it tenfold to 200,000 troops. At the same time, the PLA is transforming its navy from a coastal force into a blue-water navy. All of which led former U.S. Ambassador to China James Lilley to conclude that the PLA is undertaking a major shift from being a land-based defense force to a military that is "capable of projecting power throughout the Far East and beyond."[32]

Those developments have clearly perturbed China's neighbors, many of whom already have troubled relations with China. Beijing has been explicit in its irredentist objectives regarding Hong Kong, Macao, Taiwan, and the South China Sea. In 1997 and 1999, respectively, former British colony Hong Kong and Portuguese colony Macao were returned to the People's Republic. Regarding Taiwan, Beijing is resolved to reunite with its "rebel province" and has not hesitated to employ force to intimidate and persuade. For a week in March 1996, missiles were "test-fired," landing barely miles from the northern and southern coasts of Taiwan—prompting the United States to deploy two aircraft carrier groups to the waters of the Taiwan Strait. Beijing is no less insistent on its irredentist claim to the South China Sea, and has demonstrated by word and deed that it considers the sea to be Chinese sovereign territory.

All of which has alarmed the United States and has provoked a raging debate on the direction of U.S. China policy. There is increasing talk of a need for Washington to change course by moving away from its policy of constructive engagement, extant since 1979, to a policy of containment. One commentator described China as having become America's "greatest threat" and "most feared nation."[33]

This perception of China as America's "greatest threat" is not due simply to the PRC's growing power. China would not be perceived as a threat if its worldview and ideology were compatible with those of the United States. What makes China problematic is its volatile mix of economic growth, military modernization, territorial expansion, and rising nationalism. In that mix, it is China's spectacular economic growth that funds the PLA's modernization; and it is Chinese nationalism that provides the intent, motive, and legitimation for the PLA's disposition and behaviors. An understanding of China's rising nationalism is thus critical to understanding and anticipating Beijing's present and future behavior.

To better understand the intent and nature of Chinese nationalism, a study of its ideological content recommends itself. Michael Mann, a scholar on nationalism, has identified three groups as most susceptible to nationalist appeals. They are (1) the administrators, teachers, and public-sector workers who depend on the state for their livelihood; (2) the youth who have been and are being educated by the state; and (3) the armed forces, comprised of millions of young men disciplined by a military cadre "into the peculiar morale, coercive yet emotionally attached, that is the hallmark of the modern mass army." Mann observed that it is these three bodies of men and women and their families who provide most of the ranks of fervent nationalists—those "super-loyalists" and "nation-statists" animated by an exaggerated loyalty to their nation-state.[34]

In the case of the People's Republic, given Chinese nationalism's irredentist character, the Chinese armed forces are clearly the most important of Mann's three groups. But the ideas of the two other pivotal groups—China's youth and its academicians who specialize and write on nationalism—should also be examined. To date, no study of contemporary Chinese nationalism has devoted itself to an examination of the nationalist thought of these three groups. The present enterprise seeks to fill that lacuna in contemporary sinology. Through an account of the nationalist ideology of China's academics, youth, and the PLA, this study hopes to provide a better understanding of the ideological content of contemporary Chinese nationalism: its worldview, beliefs, values, and prescriptions. That understanding, in turn, may provide policymakers in Washington a basis to construct an effective China policy.

Before we turn to the particular case of Chinese nationalism, an understanding of the general phenomenon of nationalism would be both useful and necessary. Such an understanding should include an effort at defining key concepts, the provision of a classificatory schema for nationalism, and explanations for this enduring human phenomenon. All that will be the subject of the next chapter.

Notes

1. Carl J. Friedrich and Zbigniew K. Brzezinski, *Totalitarian Dictatorship and Autocracy* (New York: Praeger, 1961), p. 5.

2. Leonard Schapiro, *Totalitarianism* (New York: Praeger, 1972), p. 14.

3. For a more complete definition of totalitarianism, see the descriptive model of totalitarianism in pp. 150–153 of Maria Hsia Chang, "Totalitarianism and China: The Limits of Reform," *Global Affairs* (Fall 1987).

4. Friedrich and Brzezinski, *Totalitarian Dictatorship*, p. 8. For a more detailed account of the similarities between right and left totalitarianism, see A. James Gregor, *Interpretations of Fascism* (Morristown, NJ: General Learning Press, 1974), pp. 204–207, 211.

5. Lawrence C. Mayer, *Redefining Comparative Politics: Promise Versus Performance* (Newbury Park, CA: Sage, 1989), p. 251.

6. Ibid., p. 7.

7. Stephen White, John Gardner, George Schopflin, and Tony Saich, *Communist and Postcommunist Political Systems: An Introduction* (New York: St. Martin's Press, 1990), p. 3.

8. St. Paul, *The Power of Evil*, as quoted by Polish director Krzystof Zanussi in Marilynne S. Mason, "Moral Moviemaker," *World Monitor*, February 1989, p. 68.

9. Zbigniew Brzezinski, *The Grand Failure: The Birth and Death of Communism in the Twentieth Century* (New York: Charles Scribner's Sons, 1989), p. 240.

10. Timothy Ash, "The Romeo File," *The New Yorker* (April 28 and May 5, 1997), p. 170.

11. According to the authoritative 846-page French tome *The Black Book of Communism*, collectively authored by eleven French historians. See the English translation (by Jonathan Murphy and Mark Kramer) of Nicolas Werth, Jean-Louis Panne, Andrzej Paczkowski, Karel Bartosek, and Jean-Louis Margolin, *The Black Book of Communism: Crimes, Terror, Repression* (Cambridge, MA: Harvard University Press, 1999).

12. According to the historian Dmitry Volkogonov, from 1937 to 1938, in a mere two-year stretch at the height of Stalin's Great Terror, nearly 14 million people died. Charles Diggers, "Mass Grave of Stalin Victims Found in Russia," *San Francisco Chronicle*, July 17, 1997, p. A10.

13. According to the Cambodian Genocide Program at Yale University. See *Parade Magazine*, June 22, 1997, p. 18; and *Shijie ribao (World Journal* or *WJ)*,

December 2, 1997, p. 2. *The Black Book of Communism* gives a provisional figure of about a million.

14. Brzezinski, *Grand Failure*, p. 231.

15. Samuel P. Huntington, "Social and Institutional Dynamics of One-Party Systems," in Samuel P. Huntington and Clement H. Moore (eds.), *Authoritarian Politics in Modern Society: The Dynamics of Established One-Party Systems* (New York: Basic Books, 1970), p. 24. For a different interpretation, which emphasizes the evolution of communist systems being governed by their failures instead of successes, see Maria Hsia Chang, "The Logic and Dynamics of the Evolution of Chinese Communism," *Issues and Studies*, 25:9 (September 1989), pp. 27–47.

16. As an example, columnist George Will thought that communist countries had tactical strengths that democracies lacked. The latter were "poker-playing" nations that thought "episodically and short-term," whereas communist countries were "chess players, patient and thinking many moves ahead." George Will, in *Seattle Post-Intelligencer,* December 7, 1987, p. F3.

17. Jean-François Revel, *The Totalitarian Temptation* (New York: Penguin Books, 1978), pp. 27, 28.

18. Adam Michnik was also editor-in-chief of Warsaw's *Gazeta Wyborcza*. As quoted in "The Talk of the Town," *The New Yorker*, December 9, 1996, p. 52.

19. Friedrich and Brzezinski, *Totalitarian Dictatorship*, p. 6; Brzezinski, *Grand Failure*, pp. 241, 232.

20. See, for example, Brzezinski's effort in *Grand Failure*, p. 255.

21. North Korea, in particular, has suffered from consecutive years of crop failure, mass starvation, and political defections.

22. As a point of comparison, during its period of rapid industrialization in the nineteenth century, it took the United States almost 50 years to double its GNP.

23. See chapters 5, 6, and 7 of Maria Hsia Chang, *The Labors of Sisyphus: The Economic Development of Communist China* (New Brunswick, NJ: Transaction, 1998).

24. Seymour Martin Lipset, *Political Man: The Social Bases of Politics* (Baltimore, MD: Johns Hopkins University, 1981), pp. 454–455.

25. For a definition of "ideocracy," see Jaroslaw Piekalkiewicz and Alfred Wayne Penn, *Politics of Ideocracy* (Albany, NY: State University of New York Press, 1995), p. 27.

26. "China: Saying No," *The Economist*, July 20, 1996, p. 30.

27. David E. Apter, "Introduction," in Apter (ed.), *Ideology and Discontent* (NY: Free Press of Glencoe, 1964), pp. 28, 24.

28. Geoffrey York, "Uzbeks' Unlikely Hero: Bloodthirsty Tamerlane," *San Francisco Examiner*, January 11, 1998, p. A–27.

29. Liu Xiaozhu, "Jingti jiduan minzu zhuyi zai dalu qingqi (Beware of the rise of extreme nationalism on the mainland)," *WJ*, April 3, 1994, p. A6.

30. Fareed Zakaria, "Let's Get Our Superpowers Straight," *The New York Times*, March 26, 1997, p. A19.

31. Richard D. Fisher, "Dangerous Moves: Russia's Sale of Missile Destroyers to China," Heritage Foundation Backgrounder Series, February 20, 1997, p. 1.

32. As reported in *The Wall Street Journal*, October 14, 1993.

33. Marc Sandalow, "Fear and Loathing—The Middle Kingdom," *San Francisco Chronicle*, March 23, 1997, p. 9.

34. Michael Mann, "A Political Theory of Nationalism and its Excesses," in Sukumar Periwal (ed.), *Notions of Nationalism* (Budapest: Central European University Press, 1995), p. 55.

2

On Nationalism

Nationalism has proven its potency time and again through history. Even ostensibly universalistic political movements, most notably those self-identified as Marxist, upon coming to power have devolved into parochial nationalism. As one commentator wryly observed, "Whether on the soccer field or on the battlefield, it has almost always proved easier to mobilize popular passions in the national rather than the international cause."[1]

Today, in the aftermath of the Cold War, there are some[2] who maintain that new circumstances and problems are eroding the power and autonomy of sovereign nation-states. Forces of globalization have created interdependent networks of information, culture, trade, and investment that crisscross the world; new problems of environmental degradation, terrorism, biochemical weapons, overpopulation, and the resultant flood of emigrants and refugees are similarly unconfined by national borders. Neither globalization nor the new problems can be effectively managed by traditional nation-states. Instead, it is argued, they can be addressed only by creating regional entities and international regimes that will render nation-states increasingly obsolete.

Despite all that, there are others who believe that transnational entities simply are unable to meet the human need for community and identity. As one writer explains, "A global culture is memory-less, and the attempt to enforce it merely evokes the plurality of memories that compose particular identities the more intensely."[3] Despite the move toward globalization, nationalism not only persists but seems to become more insistent, its passions demonstrated daily in places such as Chechnya and Kosovo, Tibet and Quebec, East Timor and the West Bank. They are among an estimated 37 stateless nations in the world comprised of 100 million dispossessed people who demand international recognition.[4]

Even in Europe, at the same time as old political boundaries soften, new national identities seem to sharpen. The countries of Western Europe have come together in a new union, but the empire of the former Soviet Union dissolved into newly autonomous states. The German nation expands with the reunification of East and West, but Czechoslovakia breaks into two separate republics while Yugoslavia devolves into the nightmare of ethnic cleansing. Despite repeated peace efforts, the Troubles still plague Northern Ireland, while Italy's Northern League aims to repeal the Risorgimento and sever the country in two. A referendum gives Scotland greater autonomy,[5] propelling the United Kingdom further on the road toward federation, if not ultimate disunion. And beneath the polite rhetoric of a united Europe can be heard the "xenophobic growling" by the "pure nationality"[6] parties of Jean-Marie Le Pen's National Front and Gerhard Frey's German People's Union, which have arisen *in reaction* to globalization as the flood of immigrant labor into Western Europe from places such as North Africa, the Middle East, Asia, and East Europe is bringing racially and ethnically alien peoples into increasing contact and conflict with the natives. It appears unlikely that the power of nationalism will diminish. Instead, nation and nationalism will probably continue "to provide humanity with its basic cultural and political identities" well into the twenty-first century.[7]

Definitions

Given its demonstrated potency, it is all the more curious that nationalism as a concept has been poorly defined and understood. The many efforts at illuminating the meaning of this "slippery term"[8] have been described as resembling an "Alice-in-Wonderland world" where slipshod and inconsistent terminology remain the bane.[9]

Slipshod terminology includes definitions that are tautological in that the concept of nationalism is defined by itself or a derivative. As an example, one author conceives nationalism to be "the conscious demand for political expression of the nation."[10] Another maintains that nationalism is "the belief in the primacy of a particular nation" but avers that "nation is far harder to define than is nationalism."[11]

Not only are some of the definitions for nationalism circular, there is little consistency in the literature regarding its meaning. For some, *nationalism* speaks to an organic community in which membership is secured through "shared roots." For others, *nationalism* is the effort to invent nations where they do not exist.[12] For some, *nation* is a biological entity, "a community affirming a distinct ethnic identity"[13] whose members believe they are ancestrally related.[14] For others, *nation* refers to an "imagined community"[15] that has no common race or ethnicity but nevertheless is bound together by authentic sentiments.[16]

Nation and State

The effort at conceptual clarification can profitably begin with the distinction that Max Weber made between *nation* and *nationalism*, on the one hand, and the related but analytically discrete concepts of *state* and *patriotism*. According to Weber, *nation* is a form of *Gemeinschaften*: a community based on sentiments of solidarity. The *state,* in contrast, is an example of *Gesellschaften*: an association developed consciously for specific purposes.[17] As a community of solidarity, *nation* is similar to other human collectivities of families, clans, and tribes—none of which, however, is considered to be a nation. What makes a particular community a nation, according to Weber, is its intimate relation to statehood. It is a community's aspiration to form its own government that distinguishes the nation from the other *Gemeinschaften* of family, clan, and tribe. In making that critical distinction, Weber echoed the thoughts of John Stuart Mill, who, more than a hundred years ago, had already provided a lucid definition for *nation*. According to Mill,[18]

> A portion of mankind may be said to constitute a Nationality if they are united among themselves by common sympathies . . . which make them cooperate with each other more willingly than with other people, desire to be under the same government, and desire that it should be government by themselves or a portion of themselves exclusively.

For the purposes of this exposition, the contributions of both Weber and Mill may be combined to produce the following stipulative definition for nation: *A biologically reproductive*[19] *collection of people who feel that they belong together and constitute a community, and who demand their political expression via the acquisition of statehood, a government that claims authority over a defined territory.* A nation, therefore, is a subjective phenomenon in that its very existence depends on sentiments and perception; but it has an objective foundation in that the feelings of solidarity stem from having certain objective attributes in common. Those attributes may include a common race, territory, language, religion, customs, and history. It was Mill's contention that a common history is the strongest of all bonds because it confers a common memory on the community—recollections of "collective pride and humiliation, pleasure and regret."[20]

Mill rightly observed that each of these commonalities by itself is neither indispensable nor sufficient for nationhood or nationalism.[21] But it is intuitively evident that the greater the number of shared traits, the more likely that feelings of solidarity would be correspondingly enhanced, although the possession of many common traits provides neither guarantee nor certainty toward the formation of nationhood. In the last analysis, subjective sentiments are all that is required, leading one writer to the tautological observation that "people belong to a certain nation if they feel that they belong to it."[22]

The relationship between nation and state is one of symbiosis. A nation can better secure its well-being if it has its own state: its own land and government. The word *state* refers to a political entity, "a corporate actor" concerned with "the realm of power" who makes decisions on behalf of and speaks in the name of the whole society.[23] It is only through possession of territory that a nation can maximally secure its material means of livelihood. And it is only through having its own government that a nation can best protect itself from external aggressors and preserve collective identity and culture. But the state also needs the nation because the state can best survive if it harnesses the solidarity feelings of the national community. The more the state associates itself with the nation and identifies with popular sentiments, the greater the state's reservoir of goodwill and legitimacy.[24]

Nationalism and Patriotism

The sentiments that nation and state elicit can also be analytically distinguished. One feels *patriotism* toward one's state or government, and *nationalism* toward the people who constitute one's national group. In effect, patriotism and nationalism differ only with respect to their target object, but their sentiments of love, empathy, pride, loyalty, commitment, and devotion are the same.

On an affective level, the word *nationalism* thus refers to feelings of love, identification, loyalty, and commitment to the people who constitute one's national group. Those feelings are the product of "the awakening of nations to self-consciousness."[25] *It is that self-consciousness that distinguishes a nation from the comparatively inert ethnicity or people.* To be maximally effective, however, sentiments of nationalism require ideological articulation for their construction and interpretation.[26] Nationalism, therefore, may also be an ideology of self-determination that demands recognition as a separate people.[27] As an ideology, nationalism seeks to promote the group's values and interests "to a position of primacy, subordinating or even excluding from consideration other loyalties or beliefs."[28] In some cases, the nation is conceived as possessing distinct claims to virtue that may be used to legitimate aggressive action against other national groups.[29]

Given the passions that nationalism arouses, it is not surprising that states generally strive to identify themselves with the nation, particularly during times of domestic uncertainty. In the case of multiethnic and multinational states, such as the historical Austro-Hungarian Empire, the Soviet Union, and the contemporary People's Republic of China,[30] the very survival and integrity of the state requires that patriotism, rather than nationalism, be emphasized. The analytic boundaries between nation and state and between nationalism and patriotism are deliberately blurred. Where such efforts by the state are successful, the most fervent nationalists also become the most loyal statists.

The groups that are most susceptible to this blurring include those who have been inculcated with the state's values and ideals, as well as those who are most dependent on the state for their immediate survival and succor. Such fervent patriotic-nationalists have historically come from three bodies of people and their families. A first group comprises the administrators, teachers, and public-sector workers who directly depend on the state for their livelihood. A second group are the youth, educated in state-controlled institutions, whose very tenderness and gullibility render them especially vulnerable to political manipulation. A last group includes those of the national military who are imbued with the distinctive morale, discipline, and outlook of the armed forces.[31]

Explaining Nationalism

If there is any agreement among social science writings on nationalism, it is that nationalism was the product of a distinct time and place, making its first appearance around the eighteenth century in Western Europe, specifically Britain and France.[32] There, forces of modernization broke down the old order and made available the space for the rise of new political attachments and arrangements. At the same time, the dynamics of modernization resulted in the gradual integration—the process of becoming similar—of disparate peoples. In this manner was laid the groundwork for the creation of "imagined communities" based on the idea of the nation.[33]

The process of modernization had religious, political, economic, and social dimensions. Beginning in the sixteenth century, by challenging the Catholic Church's monopoly on interpretation of the Bible, the Protestant Reformation eventually succeeded at disestablishing church authority and loosening its totalistic grip over the European states. As the old order dissolved, new forces moved into the vacuum, integrating societies and fostering a growing sense of commonness among the people. At the same time, European monarchies were transforming into modern bureaucratic states. Their need for ever more revenue to finance the almost constant warfare among the states of Europe led to the creation of rationalized political bureaucracies charged with the function of revenue collection and political administration. As the bureaucracies expanded their activities, they would increasingly interact and become integrated with the people from whom revenue was extracted.

At the same time, the protean forces of industrialization began to link disparate peoples and communities together, ultimately transforming them into a single nation. In effect, nations were produced as a result of the peculiar functional requirements of the industrial economy.[34] It is said that the logic of modern industry necessitated a common culture and language. Unlike the preindustrial agrarian society—where the economic units were small, isolated, self-sufficient villages of face-to-face relations—the industrial economy required a communication and transportation infrastructure that could connect geographically separated communities. The effective operation of that infrastructure, in turn, required a common language and cultural code so that parochial communities of local dialects and cultures could communicate in an abstract manner over space with strangers. Where a common language was absent, the state would have to impart that common tongue—and common culture—through a public school system. At the same time, the new industries attracted increasing numbers of migrants from the countryside to the cities. As people left their villages and farms for cities, they also left behind many of their previous attachments and became receptive to new identities.[35]

The transformative effects of industrialization were magnified by the rise of civil society, given impetus and justification by the philosophers of the Enlightenment. As ideas of self-government through political representation spread, previously unconnected masses began to identify with each other. More and more, new horizontal linkages replaced the feudal vertical relations between monarch and subject, eventually culminating in a collective consciousness and identity that congealed into nationalism. In this manner, European states became European nations.

In addition to the historical explanation for the rise of nationalism in Western Europe, there is also a more general explanation that transcends the particular time and place of eighteenth-century Europe. This more general explanation aims at explicating the universal human disposition to identify with a group.

As the term is used here, *nationalism* is, at its roots, a type of groupism, or what anthropologist Sir Arthur Keith called "group spirit."[36] It is distinct from other *esprits de corps* only because of its political expression and demand for statehood. As Keith articulated it, the problems of nationality "are by no means new, but in their modern form they are new."[37] Similarly, Régis Debray also recognized the universality of nationalism when he referred to the nation as "only one modality" of the primary invariable of human nature itself.[38]

In effect, there need to be two levels of explanation for nationalism: a historical explanation for the rise of nationalism in Western Europe, and a more general explanation that reaches back to "the immensity of man's unwritten history"[39] to account for humankind's disposition to form groups and group identity. In the parlance of the philosophy of science, the first type of explanation is of the middle-level theory variety, whereas the second type of explanation is an effort toward constructing a grand theory.

Such a grand theory—on "the nature of the inward forces which group mankind into races and nations"[40]—might begin with Keith, who conceived human history as divided into two distinct phases. The first phase was one of "natural subsistence" that stretched over a million years or more when humankind was scattered in a mosaic of isolated small groups in separated territories, each surviving on a sparse, uncertain, and coarse sustenance from the natural produce of "shore and stream, moorland and woodland." There then followed a second shorter phase spanning 10,000 or 12,000 years of "artificial subsistence" when humans conquered nature. It was during that enduring first phase of human history, before the dawn of civilization, when "an elaborate mental machinery" evolved for binding small groups into social units.[41]

That elaborate mental machinery was mainly devoted to the formation and maintenance of group spirit—"a disposition . . . in every man which leads him to extend his sympathy, his goodwill, and fellowship to the members of his group." It is the "consciousness or recognition of kind," an "instinctive or inborn urge" of all social animals, be they ants or apes, which keeps members of a group together and, at the same time, keeps them apart from surrounding territorial groups. It is an extension of the "family spirit," the disposition that leads the members of a family—that first and most basic human group—to be prejudiced in favor of one another.[42]

As conceived by Keith, group spirit has certain distinguishing attributes, one of which is "territorialism": the primeval tendency of all animals to cling to their homelands. Maintaining that a sense of territory is common to all animals, Keith noted that only humans surround their territory by a delimited frontier. Humankind's group ownership of homeland—"the home of the living spirits of the ancestors"—is a matter of life and death, regarded with a deep affection "almost religious in its intensity." For land is essential for group subsistence and solidarity, without which the group "could not work out its evolutionary destiny."[43]

Aside from territorialism, another hallmark of group spirit is a "dual code of morality," believed by Keith to have been essential to human evolution. Underlying this duality is a fundamental amoralism: Actions are judged good or bad solely as they obviously affect the welfare of the tribe—not that of the species nor that of an individual member of the tribe. It is this underlying amoralism that accounts for the code's duality of in-group amity and out-group enmity. Toward one's own group is applied "the code of love": the warm emotional spirit of amity, sympathy, loyalty, and mutual help. Toward outside groups is applied another code: "one of antagonism, of suspicion, distrust, contempt, or of open enmity."[44] Both codes of morality, when not overly developed or unbalanced, work toward the enhancement of the survival of the group. The code of amity helps to strengthen the social bonds of a group, whereas the code of enmity compels the group to maintain its powers of defense as well as offense. As Keith explained:[45]

> Every species is divided into small tribes. . . . [Competition and survival] involve a struggle, not between species, but between groups of the same species . . . . [Human evolution] was, and is, a process of team production and team selection. . . . [Those] men who were arranged in groups or teams, each dominated by a spirit of unity, would conquer and outlive men who were not thus grouped.

Although Keith maintained that the moral duality of group spirit is a "predominantly innate," genetic, inborn disposition, it is also a learned behavior that is susceptible to change by example and practice. While it is "an aptitude born in us," the direction that aptitude takes is a matter of education and can be overcome by discipline and reason.[46]

For Keith, nationalism and patriotism are expressions of group spirit at the third stage of human "evolutionary units." The first stage was that of small local "inbreeding groups" of 50 to 150 individuals, a size determined by the natural fertility of the land. These were the original teams engaged in the intergroup struggle for survival. Keith was convinced that evolutionary change proceeded most quickly when the competing units were small in size and of great number, as evidenced by the rapid structural changes suggested by human fossil remains from the Pleistocene Age. During the second stage in the development of human groupings, these small local groups were federated into larger, though still isolated, tribes. The third and last stage transpired when men forgot their tribal loyalties and began to work for the common destiny of still larger and more powerful units. In this manner, tribes melded into "national units," the enlarged scale sustained by a new economy of agriculture and allied arts.[47]

According to Keith, nationalism and patriotism are thus the group spirit of the third stage of human evolutionary units. Both are "an exaggerated and prejudiced form of affection" for one's group and everything connected with that group—its welfare, prosperity, safety, good name, and fame. In particular, humanity's territorial instinct makes the sentiments of patriotism especially compelling. Being the special bonds of affection between a group and its homeland, patriotism causes the individual "to defend it, to fight for it, and, if need be, to sacrifice his life to save it."[48]

Keith's thesis is affirmed by more contemporary scholars. As an example, Régis Debray maintained that the nation comes after "a historically determined series of other modes of collective existence"—those of clans, tribes, lineage-systems, ethnic groupings, and peoples. Like Keith, Debray thought that an explanation for the "nation phenomenon" must be sought within "general laws" regulating the survival of the human species. Humankind created nations in a continuous struggle to triumph over death. Every society, according to Debray, is distinguished by two fundamental needs. The first is a need to delimit society in time by fixing a point of origin, even if that assignation is mythic. "This zero point or starting point is what allows . . . the ritualization of memory, celebration, commemoration"—the stuff of group spirit. A second need is to delimit society in space with a fixed territory. Debray concluded that there can be no cultural identity for social individuals without distinction from and opposition to a neighboring environment, "without the drawing of lines."[49]

Echoes of Keith's dual code of morality can also be found in Joseph Campbell, who observed that the brotherhood in most myths was confined to an in-group of "bounded community" and that the myths of participation and love "pertain only to the in-group." The out-group is the alien other, and the target of aggression.[50] For his part, psychologist Martin L.

Hoffman expresses Keith's dual moral code as a "paradox of empathy." According to Hoffman, people tend to empathize most readily with those who are similar to themselves in appearance, social circumstances, behavior, and the like. Empathy encourages group identification, but groups often persist by pitting themselves against other groups. Hoffman's conclusion was that, "To the degree that one is very empathic toward one's own group, that may mean one is very hostile toward another group."[51]

Most recently, Steven Pinker has proposed an underlying law of human caring that is also reminiscent of Keith's dual code of morality. According to Pinker, people in all cultures feel that they are members of a group and feel animosity toward other groups. The group bound with the most powerful affective ties is that of kinship: "The love of kin comes naturally, the love of non-kin does not." Pinker explains this duality with a kind of cognitive Darwinism: An organism will care more about another organism the more genetic overlap there is between them, other things being equal, since genes build organisms with propensities that are apt to favor their replication. Because blood relatives share genes to a greater extent than nonrelatives, any gene that makes an organism benefit a relative has a good chance of benefiting a copy of itself. With that advantage, genes for helping relatives will increase in a population over the generations. Thus the vast majority of altruistic acts in the animal kingdom benefit the actor's kin. This explains why "parents love their children above all others, cousins love each other but not as much as siblings do," and why human beings care not terribly much about strangers. For, as Pinker put it, "Blood really *is* thicker than water, and no aspect of human existence is untouched by that part of our psychology." Non-kinship groups, such as nations, are simply efforts to mimic, manipulate, and extend the relations and feelings people have for kin to those who are non-kin in the interest of group solidarity.[52]

Pinker's "law of human caring" is simply the latest reiteration of sociobiology's concept of "inclusive fitness." Van Den Berghe maintained that animals can be expected to behave cooperatively, and thereby enhance each other's fitness to the extent that they are genetically related. Altruism is directed mostly at kin, especially close kin, and represents "the ultimate form of genetic selfishness." Ethnic groups are breeding populations of "inbreeding superfamilies" that maintain clear territorial and social boundaries from other ethnic groups. The extended kinship, real or putative, of the ethnic group is the basis for the "powerful sentiments we call nationalism, tribalism, racism, and ethnocentrism."[53]

Classifying Nationalism

The philosopher of science Ernest Nagel once wrote that typologies are an "indispensable stage" in the development of scientific knowledge.[54] Typologies involve the grouping of things "because they resemble one another." Every effort at classification, at constructing typologies, "serves some purpose or other," the most important of which is to create some sense of order out of the chaotic profusion of sensory phenomena. Beyond that basic purpose are other reasons for building taxonomies. We classify phenomena in a certain way (versus other ways) because we think our particular taxonomy can yield "significant correlations" and insights. Since classification involves the grouping of things by their similarities and dissimilarities, implicit within each taxonomic effort are generalizations about distinguishing traits and/or behaviors. It is for this reason that every taxonomy is also "a provisional and implicit theory."[55]

In the case of nation and nationalism, both concepts yield various typologies, depending on one's particular interest and purpose. As an example, nations can be classified into ethnic or civic in accordance with the criteria of admission or membership. *Ethnic nations,* such as Israel and Japan, are those whose membership is determined by *jus sanguinis,* the law of blood—the biological ascriptive criteria of race and heredity. In contrast, admission into *civic nations,* such as the United States of America, depends on the fulfillment of achievement criteria—the performance of specified behaviors that qualify the individual for citizenship, which may include having been born in that country or, in the case of those not native-born, passing tests of citizenship.

Nations can also be classified in accordance with how the role of the individual vis-à-vis society is conceived. *Lockean liberal nations* of the Anglo-American variety are founded on the conviction that the nation is equal to the sum of its individual members. In the contest between the individual and the collectivity, it is the individual who has preeminence, to whom the state, circumscribed in power, is servant. Then there are the *collectivist Rousseauist nations* where the nation is conceived as something greater than the mere sum of its individual parts. The collectivity has the prior and greater claim to importance to which the interests of individuals must be subordinated. The sovereign state has transcendent power because it is the manifestation of the nation and the embodiment of its "general will."[56]

Nationalism, for its part, can be classified according to its stimulus and genesis. *Organic nationalism* arises naturally as a result of time, inbreeding, and geographic isolation—which, over the course of generations, create the common bonds of "spontaneous patterns of allegiance"[57] that make nations out of mere peoples. In contrast is the *constructed (or artificial) nationalism* of nations that are the deliberate and conscious creations by the state from above, via the systematic mass dissemination and inculcation of a nationalist ideology. An example was Meiji Japan, whose ultranationalist ideology of emperor worship and racial superiority came out of the "national study" *(kokugaku) of samurai* scholars in the late Tokugawa period, on Japan's myths of origins and its native Shinto religion. During the Meiji period, the ideology was widely disseminated to the Japanese people through the mass media and schools, successfully transforming a feudal people into a unified nation.

Organic nationalism can also be distinguished from *reactive nationalism*. The latter is a nationalism, the coming to consciousness, of a group that suffered mistreatment, discrimination, and abuse at the hands of another group. The more powerful group, by systematically discriminating against all members of the victimized group, inadvertently binds the victims together, creating a nation out of a previously inert people. The victims realize they belong together because of their common fate: that of being abused solely because of who they are. Historically, some of the most potent instances of reactive nationalism were in response to European imperialism and colonialism.

To successfully overcome the challenge of Western imperialism, many reactive nationalisms have economic development as a primary objective. *Developmental nationalism* involves the efforts to utilize or create nationalist solidarity in the interest of rapid industrialization. It has been argued that Italian Fascism should be understood to be a form of developmental nationalism.[58] Likewise, the ultranationalism of Imperial Japan.

Nationalism can also be classified depending on its intensity into mild or extreme nationalism. *Mild nationalism* is peaceable toward outsiders, whereas *extreme or ultra nationalism* is aggressive and xenophobic. Given aggressive nationalism's destructive potential, some special attention to this subject is warranted.

Aggressive Nationalism

Although nationalism can be a positive force when it is used chiefly to enhance group unity and solidarity, the layman's impression about nationalism is largely negative, conceiving it to be almost "a synonym of intolerance."[59] In large part, that negative conception is due to the unspeakable acts of cruelty committed in the name of racial nationalism by Nazi Germany during the Second World War. The dual nature of nationalism places it "among the noblest as well as the most destructive of human impulses."[60] Nationalism has inspired individuals to undertake heroic feats of great courage and sacrifice, but it has also perpetrated the Nazis' "final solution" and Japan's Rape of Nanjing, as well as the bloodbath of ethnic cleansing in post-communist Yugoslavia.

In effect, nationalism seems to have a dual nature and potential of "herbivore" and "carnivore." Whereas herbivore nationalism is mainly characterized by love of one's own, that love becomes inseparable from hatred, intolerance, and aggression toward others in the case of carnivore nationalism.[61] Like the mythic Janus, nationalism has two faces: peaceable and aggressive. The latter is described as "self-righteous and self-centered from the inside, arrogant and hypocritical from the outside." Compared to the peaceable self-sacrificing nationalism, this other face of Janus seems like "a fall from grace."[62]

The literature on nationalism identifies a number of attributes that are associated with collective aggression. Acts of aggression may be defined as behaviors that intend to or result in inflicting injury and harm to others. Participation in wars is considered to be "probably the most aggressive and certainly the most destructive of all human activities."[63]

A Preoccupation with Power

Among nationalism's many attributes, a preoccupation with power has been found to be strongly correlated with measures of individual aggression such as a readiness to support war. The preoccupation with power includes feelings of national superiority, of competitiveness with other nations, and of the importance of power over other nations. In contrast, it is maintained, gentler attributes of nationalism—those of love for one's nation and pride in one's national identification—are not significantly correlated with aggression.[64]

Narcissistic Nationalism

Aggression toward others is invariably accompanied by intolerance. As early as Freud, it was suggested that narcissism is associated with intolerance. As one scholar put it, "The root of intolerance seems to be found in our tendency to overvalue ourselves." Narcissistic nationalism acts as "a distorting mirror" wherein believers see their simple ethnic, religious, or territorial attributes turned into "glorious qualities." This systematic overvaluation of the self leads to the systematic devaluation of strangers and outsiders.[65] It is in this manner that narcissistic nationalism breeds and feeds xenophobia: the intolerance and hatred of those considered alien to one's national community. Narcissistic and intolerant nationalists are described as "fundamentally incurious" and uninterested in the groups they despise except insofar as their behavior confirms their prejudices. What matters to them is the particular constitution of the "primal opposition" between "them" and "us."[66]

Insecurity, Wounded Pride, and National Humiliation

Another characteristic of narcissistic nationalists is their insecurity, uncertainty, and weakness of identity. Narcissistic nationalism functions as "a leap into collective fantasy" that enables threatened or anxious individuals to avoid the burden of thinking for themselves. The source of their collective insecurity is usually a history of domination by a more powerful group that left a legacy of wounded pride and resentment in the subjugated group.[67] The "trauma of defeat" leaves an open festering wound that is a breeding ground for virulent reactive nationalism.[68]

This collective sense of insecurity renders the nation especially vulnerable to paranoia and intolerance. Its people become prone to a siege mentality and "to a demagoguery that insists that nobody understands them but themselves." There is the conviction that all outsiders, particularly the great powers who have presided over and witnessed their humiliation, are suspect and can never be true or reliable friends.[69]

Cultural-Moral Relativism

Typically, intolerant nationalists also proclaim their belief in an extreme cultural and moral relativism. They reject the notion that morality is universal, insisting that each ethnic group must have the right to follow its separate development. It is asserted that group identities are so comprehensive in nature that they create an "epistemological closure": moral worlds so unintelligible to each other that different groups are incapable of living together in peace within the same territorial and political space.[70]

Ethnic Nationalism

The disposition to be intolerant of outsiders is intensified in ethnic nations. Although civic nations are not immune to intolerance, it is claimed they can "more easily return to the practice of toleration" than nations that are defined by the biological criteria of race and ethnicity.[71]

Historically, those nations whose membership is defined by blood have been more prone to prejudicial intolerance against ethnic aliens, Nazi Germany being the most egregious example. Ethnic or race-based nationalism alone, however, may be insufficient to instigate collective aggression and may require historical experiences of national humiliation to turn simple "ethnic consciousness into ethnic paranoia."[72] In the German case, those supplementary conditions were provided by its defeat in World War I and the onerous Versailles peace settlement that followed.

Political Authoritarianism and Illiberalism

Nationalism does not have to be ethnic-based in order for it to become virulent. Nations whose political systems and worldviews are authoritarian and illiberal also tend to be intolerant of outsiders because toleration depends on a civic order in which the rights of the individual are held to be prior to and constitutive of the social order.[73]

As one scholar of nationalism put it, "Mild nationalism . . . is democracy achieved, aggressive nationalism is democracy perverted." It is political authoritarianism, the failure to institutionalize representative institutions, that creates the conditions for "exclusionist nationalism"—that particular brand of nationalism that is able to commit atrocities against all persons conceived to be beyond the pale. Historically, it is said, societies that successfully institutionalized representative government experienced comparatively little nationalist violence even when beset by deeply rooted interethnic disputes.[74]

Race and ethnicity are not the only criteria for exclusive nationalism. Instead, authoritarian regimes historically have employed class, religion, ideology, behavior, and other discriminatory criteria to deny national membership to domestic opponents and, in so doing, have legitimized their suppression and selective killing.[75] This was amply demonstrated in Maoist China when Chinese who did not display the prescribed "correct" thinking became identified as "enemies of the people" and were targeted for criticism, torture, and extermination.

Political authoritarianism is typically accompanied and exacerbated by a particular view of human nature and of the world. The individual is regarded as subordinate to the nation and denied inalienable rights. The world is conceived to be an arena where nations are engaged in a struggle for survival and universalism is a "febrile myth." Instead, "one should think with one's blood"—a mentality that can cause nationalist quarrels to devolve into Darwinian zero-sum struggles.[76]

Frustration

Another contributing factor toward aggressive nationalism is frustration. Psychological studies consistently have found that individuals who feel frustrated have a higher propensity to become aggressive, especially if they believe they have been unfairly treated.[77] At a collective level, nations that believe they are thwarted by others from their expected goal attainment may lash out in violence.

Territorial Expansionism and Irredentism

A final correlate of nationalist aggression is territorial expansionism, especially irredentism. The latter refers to political movements that seek to retrieve lost territories and ethnic kin.[78] Irredentism is the attempt by an existing state to annex adjacent lands and the people who inhabit them in the name of historical, cultural, religious, linguistic, or geographic affinity.[79] Although ethnic populations often are a consideration, it is territory more than population that is important—a feature that distinguishes irredentism from pan-ethnic movements.

Irredentism can be understood to be "a poststate phase of nationalism" in which a sovereign power base is already in existence. It appears at a time when the fulfillment of national goals has generated a confidence in the need and the right for further territorial objectives,[80] and when the retrieving state has become strong enough to articulate and press its claims. The acquisition of territory is justified on the grounds of historic right and the restoration of national heritage.[81]

As such, irredentist nationalism has a number of distinctive attributes, including "the denigration of the present state in comparison with the Great Dream," the mystical invocation of "hallowed ground," the claim to revive an ancient civilization, and rapaciousness.[82] It is also observed that, historically, irredentist impulses have been associated with an atmosphere of domestic ambiguity and ideological reexamination within the retrieving nation.[83] This suggests that irredentist nationalism is susceptible to being used as a tool by vulnerable regimes confronted with domestic problems in times of uncertainty.

It is irredentism's primeval appeal that makes possible its manipulation by political authorities. Irredentism has been described as a "call of the wild" because it springs from an instinctive, emotional urge of human beings to define their territory—an urge that activates all the protean biological and territorial sources of nationalism.[84] But since irredentist claims invariably clash with those of others—and if peaceful conflict-resolution methods fail—what remains is the use of force to settle contested claims. Border skirmishes and outright war may result.[85]

Conclusion

In this chapter, an effort was made to provide an unsystematized theory of nationalism comprised of definitions, explanations, and typologies. The propositions contained in such a theory include the following:

- All human beings have an instinctive urge to identify with a group.
- Humankind's "group spirit" is comprised of territorialism and a dual code of morality.
- Human groups range in size and degrees of kinship, from families and clans, to tribes and nations.
- Nations are groups that demand political expression in the form of statehood.
- Nationalism and patriotism are the group spirit at the nation-state unit level.

It is said that Chinese nationalism is a relatively recent phenomenon that arose in reaction to the incursions of foreign imperialism that began with the Opium War of 1840. Chinese reactive nationalism first appeared in the late nineteenth century among the intelligentsia, maturing to full consciousness in the May Fourth Movement of 1919. The intellectuals' nationalism later expanded to the masses when the Chinese common people suffered hardship, torture, abuse, and murder at the hands of the Imperial Japanese army during the 1930s and 1940s.

Today, the resurgent nationalism in the People's Republic of China is still reactive. More than that, contemporary Chinese nationalism carries all the traits that point to an aggressive potential, most notably that of irredentism—a theme that will be more fully discussed and developed in the chapters to follow. But that effort should be preceded by a discussion of who exactly are the Chinese, as well as their origins and formation as a distinct people.

Notes

1. Simon Schama, "Mr. Europe," *The New Yorker*, April 28 and May 5, 1997, p. 211.

2. See, for example, Peter Drucker, *Post-Capitalist Society* (New York: HarperBusiness, 1993), pp. 10–11; Anthony D. Smith, "The Supersession of

Nationalism?" *International Journal of Comparative Sociology*, *XXXI*:1–2 (January–April 1990), pp. 6–7; and Jean-Marie Guehenno, *The End of the Nation-State* (Minneapolis: University of Minnesota, 1995).

3. Smith, "The Supersession of Nationalism?," p. 9.

4. Frank Viviano, "World's Wannabe Nations Sound Off," *San Francisco Chronicle*, January 31, 1995, p. A1.

5. On September 11, 1997, seven hundred years after the Scottish hero William Wallace routed England's forces at the Battle of Stirling Bridge, Scotland voted to establish a legislature of its own—the first since 1707. The new legislature will exercise a range of powers over every aspect of Scotland's domestic affairs.

6. Schama, "Mr. Europe."

7. Smith, "Supersession," p. 24.

8. Peter Mentzel, "Nationalism," *Humane Studies Review*, 8:1 (Fall 1992), p. 8.

9. Walker Connor, "The Nation and its Myth," in Anthony D. Smith (ed.), *Ethnicity and Nationalism* (Leiden, The Netherlands: E. J. Brill, 1992), p. 48.

10. John Armstrong, "Towards a Theory of Nationalism: Consensus and Dissensus," in Sukumar Periwal (ed.), *Notions of Nationalism* (Budapest: Central European University Press, 1995), p. 35.

11. John A. Hall, "Nationalisms, Classified and Explained," in Periwal, *Notions of Nationalism*, pp. 11, 9.

12. Ernest Gellner, "Introduction," in Periwal, *Notions of Nationalism*, p. 4; and Gellner, *Thought and Change* (London: Weidenfeld & Nicolson, 1964), p. 169.

13. Michael Mann, "A Political Theory of Nationalism and Its Excesses," in Periwal, *Notions of Nationalism*, p. 44.

14. Connor, "The Nation and Its Myth," p. 48.

15. An expression coined by Benedict Anderson in *Imagined Communities* (London: Verso, 1991).

16. Gellner, "Introduction," p. 4.

17. Kenneth Thompson, *Beliefs and Ideology* (Chichester, England: Ellis-Horwood Limited, 1986), p. 59.

18. J. S. Mill, "Nationality," in Stuart Woolf (ed.), *Nationalism in Europe: 1815 to the Present* (New York: Routledge, 1996), p. 40. Emphasis supplied.

19. This criterion would exclude mimetic "nations" of nonreproductive groups such as the "Queer Nation" or the "feminist nation."

20. Mill, "Nationality."

21. Ibid.

22. Mentzel, "Nationalism," p. 9.

23. Thompson, *Beliefs and Ideology*, p. 58.

24. Ibid., pp. 59, 60.

25. Hall, "Nationalisms, Classified and Explained," p. 11.

26. Thompson, *Beliefs and Ideology*, p. 61.

27. Arthur Keith, "Nationality and Race: From an Anthropologist's Point of View," a lecture to the Oxford University Junior Scientific Club (London: Oxford University Press, 1919), p. 6.

28. Robert Tombs, "Introduction," in Tombs (ed.), *Nationhood and Nationalism in France* (New York: HarperCollins*Academic*, 1991), p. 3.

29. Mann, "A Political Theory of Nationalism and its Excesses," pp. 44, 55.

30. The Chinese today also distinguish between nation *(minzu)* and state *(guojia)* and between nationalism *(minzu zhuyi)* and patriotism *(aiguo zhuyi)*. This will be explored in detail in Chapter 8.

31. Mann, "A Political Theory," p. 55.

32. Hall, "Nationalisms, Classified and Explained," p. 12.

33. Mentzel, "Nationalism," pp. 9, 12.

34. See, for example, Ernest Gellner, *Nations and Nationalism* (Oxford: Basil Blackwell, 1983) and Karl Deutsch, *Nationalism and Social Communication* (Cambridge, MA: Massachusetts Institute of Technology Press, 1953).

35. Mentzel, "Nationalism," p. 12.

36. An expression coined by Arthur Keith in *A New Theory of Human Evolution* (New York: Philosophical Library, 1949).

37. Keith, "Nationality and Race," p. 5.

38. "Marxism and the National Question," interview with Régis Debray, *New Left Review*, no. 105 (1977), p. 28.

39. Keith, "Nationality and Race," p. 6.

40. Ibid., p. 5.

41. Ibid., pp. 3, 6–7.

42. Keith, *A New Theory of Human Evolution*, pp. 37, 38, 39, 44.

43. Ibid., pp. 29–34.

44. Ibid., pp. 43, 53, 38, 6.

45. Ibid., pp. 43, 6, 39.

46. Ibid., pp. 42, 43, 41, 50.

47. Ibid., pp. 3–5.

48. Ibid., p. 46–47.

49. Debray, "Marxism and the National Question," pp. 28, 27.

50. Joseph Campbell, *The Power of Myth* (New York: Doubleday, 1988), p. 22.

51. See the discussion of Martin L. Hoffman's *Empathy, Justice and Moral Internalization* in Natalie Angier, "Scientists Mull Role of Empathy in Man and Beast," *New York Times*, May 9, 1995, p. B9.

52. Steven Pinker, *How the Mind Works* (New York: W. W. Norton, 1997), pp. 509, 429–430, 431, 432, 438.

53. Pierre Van Den Berghe, "A Socio-Biological Perspective," in John Hutchinson and Anthony D. Smith, *Nationalism* (Oxford: Oxford University, 1994), pp. 96, 98. The essay originally appeared in 1978 in *Ethnic and Racial Studies*. More than any account, Van Den Berghe's thesis is striking in its near-total identity with Keith's, although the former, writing in 1978, seems not to have been aware of his predecessor as no reference to Keith appeared in Van Den Berghe's treatise.

54. Ernest Nagle, *The Structure of Science* (New York: Harcourt, Brace, and World, 1961), p. 31.

55. Abraham Kaplan, *The Conduct of Inquiry* (Scranton, PA: Chandler, 1964), pp. 50, 51, 53.

56. See Mentzel, "Nationalism," p. 10.

57. Schama, "Mr. Europe."

58. See Chapter 6 of A. James Gregor, *Interpretations of Fascism* (New Brunswick, NJ: Transaction, 1997).

59. Michael Ignatieff, "Nationalism and Toleration," in Richard Caplan and John Feffer (eds.), *Europe's New Nationalism: State and Minorities in Conflict* (New York: Oxford University, 1996), p. 218.

60. Seymour Feshbach, "Nationalism, Patriotism, and Aggression," in L. Rowell Huesmann (ed.), *Aggressive Behavior: Current Perspectives* (New York: Plenum Press, 1994), p. 278.

61. Ignatieff, "Nationalism and Toleration," p. 218.

62. Hedva Ben-Israel, "Irredentism: Nationalism Reexamined," in Naomi Chazan (ed.), *Irredentism and International Politics* (Boulder, CO: Lynne Rienner, 1991), p. 32.

63. Feshbach, "Nationalism, Patriotism, and Aggression," pp. 275, 276.

64. See R. Kosterman and S. Feshbach, "Toward a Measure of Patriotic and Nationalistic Attitudes," *Political Psychology*, 10 (1989), pp. 257–274.

65. Ignatieff, "Nationalism and Toleration," p. 215.

66. Ibid., p. 216.

67. Ibid., pp. 216, 218.

68. Hall, "Nationalisms, Classified and Explained," p. 19.

69. Ignatieff, "Nationalism and Toleration," p. 220.

70. Ibid., p. 217.

71. Ibid., p. 219.

72. Ibid., p. 219.

73. Ibid., p. 221.

74. Mann, "A Political Theory," p. 62. The emphasis is on the word "comparatively," as democratic nations have had their share of ethnic violence. One needs only recall the history of violence committed by the "white" population against African Americans, Native Americans, and Asian immigrants.

75. Ibid., p. 59.

76. Hall, "Nationalisms, Classified and Explained," p. 18.

77. See Leonard Berkowitz, *Aggression: Its Causes, Consequences, and Control* (Philadelphia: Temple University, 1993), chapter 2, pp. 30–47.

78. Naomi Chazan, "Approaches to the Study of Irredentism," in *Irredentism and International Politics*, p. 1.

79. Naomi Chazan, "Irredentism, Separatism, and Nationalism," in *Irredentism and International Politics*, p. 139.

80. Ben-Israel, "Irredentism: Nationalism Reexamined," pp. 32, 34.

81. Chazan, "Irredentism," pp. 145, 147.

82. Ben-Israel, "Irredentism," p. 25.

83. Chazan, "Irredentism," p. 150.

84. Ben-Israel, "Irredentism," pp. 33, 32.

85. Chazan, "Approaches," p. 6.

3

Children of the Dragon

Conventional wisdom within the field of sinology maintains that the Chinese, despite being an ancient people, were neither a nation nor possessed of nationalist sentiments for much of their history. Instead, it is said, what the Chinese had was a "civilization."[1] Accordingly, Chinese nationalism is a fairly recent phenomenon, its inception dating to the mid-nineteenth century as a reaction against foreign predation and mistreatment.

That being said, it would be a mistake for the study of Chinese nationalism to simply begin with the mid-nineteenth century. For if it is *ethnie* and people who precede and give birth to the self-conscious nation, then an understanding of the origins and formation of the Chinese as a distinct people will be helpful. Such an effort might also illuminate the centrality of family, clan, and lineage in China's millennial culture. More than their origins and formation, the Chinese people can claim the distinction of having the world's oldest continuous civilization, unlike the peoples of ancient Egypt, Babylon, Rome, India, and Central and South America, whose civilizations were neither as ancient nor continuous. And it was precisely their duration as a people and civilization that made the arrival and impact of Western imperialism especially traumatic for the Chinese.

The Land and Its Peoples

According to Arthur Keith and other social scientists, an important component of group spirit is territorialism: the primeval disposition of all animals, including humans, to cling to their homelands, for which is felt a deep affection almost religious in its intensity.[2] In the case of the Chinese, their evolution as a people and a civilization was played out on a geographic stage that is "at once massive and isolated."[3]

Situated in the eastern part of the continent of Asia, the People's Republic of China is a continental country rich in natural resources but burdened by an oppressive population size and density. Slightly larger, at 3.7 million square miles, than the United States, China is the third largest country in the world.[4] It shares its borders with North Korea, Russia, the Republic of Mongolia, Kazakhstan, Kirghizstan, Tajikistan, Afghanistan, Pakistan, India, Nepal, Sikkim, Bhutan, Burma, Laos, and Vietnam. More than 5,000 islands are scattered over China's territorial waters that stretch from the Bohai Bay and the Yellow Sea in the north, to the East and South China Seas in the south.

China has the second largest river in the world, the Yangzi *(Changjiang)*. Other major rivers are the Yellow *(Huanghe)*, the Pearl, *Heilongjiang*, *Haihe*, and *Huaihe*. There are 370 sizable salt and freshwater lakes. While water resources abound, their geographical distribution is very uneven: Northwestern China is a vast arid region where the only sources of water are glaciers and melted snow. And while China has the world's richest hydroelectric resources, they remain largely untapped. Its mineral resources include rich petroleum deposits with low sulfur content,[5] huge quantities of coal deposits (albeit of the "dirty" sulfurous variety), widely distributed iron-ore deposits, and a variety of nonferrous metals.

From the air the country resembles a west–east staircase that begins from one of the largest plateaus in the world, the Qinghai-Tibet Plateau, to the basins and plains in the east. The frigid, inaccessible highlands of western China are sparsely populated, in contrast to the densely populated central plains and river valleys of eastern China. Blessed with fertile soil, abundant water resources, and a favorable climate, eastern China is the country's principal farm area.

Although China accounts for only 7 percent of the earth's surface, it must sustain 22 percent of the world's population.[6] To compound the problem, being a mountainous country, only 7 percent of China is arable, with little land left that can be reclaimed. Human activities have adversely affected the natural environment and ecological balance, further exacerbating the paucity of arable land.[7] Forests account for less than 13 percent of the land surface and are diminishing by the day. Deserts are expanding, and the amount of cut timber now exceeds that of new growth.

China's population, much of which remains rural, exceeds 1.215 billion and is expected to reach 1.55 billion by the year 2050.[8] Over 90 percent of the Chinese population inhabit the southeastern half of the country, with the greatest population density along the coast, averaging 312 people per square kilometer—a figure similar to those of the most densely populated countries in the world.[9]

Just as China had been during the days of dynasties, the present People's Republic is a multiethnic state. At 93.3 percent, the Han nationality group makes up the vast majority of the population. The remaining 55 minority peoples inhabit the border regions and include the Zhuang, Hui, Uigur, Yi, Miao, Manchu, Tibetan, and Mongolian ethnicities. Historically, the Han people regarded being Han as synonymous with being Chinese.[10] But the present Communist regime has taken considerable pains in specifying that "Chinese" denotes all the ethnic groups of China. Despite that, the perception of Han as Chinese persists. Who, then, are the Chinese? Where and when did they originate? The answers to some of those questions may be found in Chinese mythology.

Myths of Origin

The Chinese term for myth is *shenhua*, "spoken word of the gods." Joseph Campbell, the great scholar of mythology, called myths "the world's dreams"—"archetypal" dreams that deal with great human problems.[11] Anthropologists regard myths as culturally important "imaginal" stories[12] that should be taken seriously because they can yield important information about a people, much as one can sometimes approach the truth more clearly through dreams than through rational thought. Often, the most interesting and revealing myths are a people's myth of origin, which psychologist Carl Jung called "the unconscious of the race."[13]

Chinese mythology came from a prehistoric oral tradition. Unlike the Greeks of antiquity who had Homer, Hesiod, Herodotus, and Ovid to recount their myth for posterity, Chinese mythology persisted for more than 3,000 years as "an amorphous, untidy congeries of archaic expression."[14] It was not until the Han dynasty (206 B.C.–A.D. 220) that Confucian scholars undertook the first significant efforts to reconstruct and record old legends in written form, the most notable of whom was Sima Qian, author of a general history of China ca. 100 B.C., entitled *Shiji (Records of the Historian)*. But the scholars' reconstruction of ancient myths was highly selective: What was recorded tended to reflect the cultural ideals of the prevailing Confucian orthodoxy. As a consequence, the surviving Chinese mythology contains many gaps or unresolved problems and queries.[15]

Creation of the World

A third century A.D. Chinese text contained an anthropomorphic account of creation, believed to be Central Asian in origin.[16] It described the beginning as a time when neither heaven nor earth existed; instead, there was only Chaos, in the form of a hen's egg, from which Pan Gu, the dwarf, was born. As the parts of the egg separated, its heavy elements became the earth, its light and pure elements the sky. As Pan Gu grew in the mesocosm between earth and sky—the first *yin* and *yang*—he increased the distance between the two by ten feet a day. After 18,000 years of growth, Pan Gu died. The various parts of his body metamorphosed into the multiple forces and elements of nature: the sun, moon, stars, wind, clouds, rain, lightning, thunder, rivers, seas, mountains, fields, soil, animals, and plants.[17]

Predating the Pan Gu myth is an impersonal account of cosmogony from the fourth to the second century B.C. that, unlike some other cultures and religious traditions, has neither prime cause nor first creator. Instead, in the beginning there was nothing but a primeval vapor in a shapeless, dark expanse, "a gaping mass." The vapor was the embodiment of the cosmic energy *Taiji* (the Great Ultimate) that governed matter, time, and space. At the moment of creation, the misty vapor underwent a transformation and differentiated into the dual elements of heaven and earth, male and female, hard and soft matter, and other binary *yin-yang* phenomena. The world was a square area of land, above which was the round sky suspended like a dome by eight giant pillars from the earth (or in other accounts, by four great mountains). The interaction of *yin* and *yang* produced the building blocks of the universe, comprised of the five elements of water, fire, metal, wood, and earth. Their continuous interaction and endless permutations in an eternal cycle constitute *dao* (the Way): the unity that is the universe.[18]

Creation of Human Beings

In the impersonal myth of cosmogony, human beings emerged from the purer parts of the primeval vapor. In the Pan Gu myth, humans had a more humble origin. When Pan Gu died, it was said, the mites on his body became the human race: "All the mites on his body were touched by the wind and were turned into the black-haired people."[19] Another account has Pan Gu fashioning humans from modeled clay figurines. As these embryonic men and women dried in the sun, storm clouds gathered. Pan Gu carried the figurines indoors—but the rain fell before he could get all of them to safety. Those damaged by the storm became the lame and the crippled.[20]

Predating Pan Gu in classical mythology is a goddess account from the fourth century B.C. in which humans were the creation of the primeval goddess Nu Wa, who had a human head and a snake's body. Nu Wa kneaded soil into a cord, drew the cord in a furrow through mud, then lifted it out to make human beings from the blobs that fell off: Rich aristocrats were those made from yellow earth, while poor commoners were wrought from mud. Not only was Nu Wa the creator of humanity, she was also their protector for, when the sky fell, she patched it together with five-colored stone. A later myth from A.D. 846–874 demoted Nu Wa from the status of creator-goddess to that of a mortal Eve. In this account, Nu Wa and her brother Fu Xi were the first mortals who wed and became the progenitors of humankind.[21]

The Mythic Sage-kings

Sociologist Émile Durkheim maintained that a major function of mythology is to express the collective ideas of a social group.[22] For the Chinese, some of their most important ideals concerning political leadership are embodied in their stories about the legendary sage-kings—the Three Sovereigns *(San Huang)* and Five Emperors *(Wu Di)* who ruled before the first Chinese dynasty of Xia. Fu Xi (ca. 2953–2838 B.C.), Shen Nong, and Yan Di were the Three Sovereigns; the Five Emperors were Huang Di (the Yellow Emperor, whose reign began ca. 2697 B.C.), Zhuan Xu, Ku, Yao, and Shun.[23]

Not only were they wise and benign rulers, the sage-kings are credited with having created Chinese civilization. Fu Xi is said to have invented writing, fishing, divinatory trigrams, measuring instruments, and the calendar. (His sister-wife, Nu Wa, invented marriage.) Shen Nong discovered agriculture, herbal medicine, and invented animal husbandry. Emperor Yao regulated the winds with the help of the archer Yi. Emperor Shun invented the writing brush and helped control the flood by putting the Great Yu to the task, who succeeded Shun as the last of the Five Emperors. At the end of Yu's reign, he broke with the sage-kings' tradition of meritocracy when he selected his eldest son to succeed him, thereby initiating China's system of primogeniture as well as its first dynasty.[24]

Among the sage-kings, it is the Yellow Emperor who stands preeminent as the first and foremost god, "the fountainhead" of Chinese civilization and cultural history.[25] He is credited with having innovated some hundred technologies and handicrafts (including housing, clothing, the written script, porcelain, the compass, chariot wheel, potter's wheel, ships, armor), as well as the code of human relations that became the moral foundation of Chinese society. His wife invented silk through her discovery of silk-worms.[26]

In these legends can also be found the enduring Chinese preoccupation with water control. A Chinese version of the near universal story of the great flood recounted how Yu labored for years to control the waters, refusing even to take the time for family visits, eventually succeeding by piercing gaps in the mountains for drainage. It is for that reason that Shun made Yu emperor because "But for Yu we should all have been fishes."[27] Another account had the Yellow Emperor dispatch his daughter, Ba, a goddess of dryness, to stop the flood. But Ba only caused plants and animals to wilt in her path. To repair the damage, the Yellow Emperor carried her away from the inhabited world to the great desert north of the Red Waters, then returned to resow the ground and instruct men to cultivate the fields.[28]

As the creators of Chinese civilization, the sage-kings are also conceived to be the actual biological ancestors of the Chinese people. A contemporary PRC scholar insists that "The Han people are the descendants of the Yellow Emperor."[29] More than that, as the sage-kings were not hereditary monarchs, having ascended to leadership by dint of talent, they also signify the importance of virtue over birth in the determination of political leaders. To illustrate, Emperor Yao anointed Shun as successor because of the latter's wisdom. Shun, in turn, chose Yu for his prowess at flood control. As the collective embodiment of "the most typical activities and cherished values of Chinese civilization,"[30] the sage-kings are the touchstone for subsequent generations of Chinese who would recall, with enduring nostalgia, their admittedly mythic reign as a lost golden age.

The Myth of the Dragon

A collective symbol of the Chinese and their millennial culture is the dragon, a mythological creature that has served as the Chinese people's "collective object of worship"[31] for over 6,000 years. The dragon, for whom the Chinese have a "special affection," has had a profound effect on nearly every aspect of Chinese society, including its religion, customs, politics, economy, and art.[32]

Contemporary Chinese scholars speculate that the dragon most probably began as the totem[33] of First Sovereign Fu Xi's tribe, worshipped as its genesis and god. That "tribe" *(buluo)* was formed by amalgamating eleven "dragon clans" *(long shizu).*[34] Anthropologists maintain that dragon images were probably first employed by primitive pre-Neolithic matriarchal tribes in what became China, although the earliest archaeological evidence is from the Neolithic period some five to six thousands years ago, in the form of dragon paintings on pottery. The fact that the pottery was discovered in a variety of regions suggests that by the Neolithic Age, instead of being the exclusive symbol of one tribe, the dragon had become the common symbol of many clans and tribes "as a result of cultural exchange over a long period."[35]

The dragon, of course, is a fantasy that never actually existed. One PRC account has the snake as the inspiration of the dragon image, as dragon paintings on Neolithic pottery have the body of a snake.[36] Other accounts maintain that the crocodile might have inspired the dragon legend because of their many similar characteristics and behaviors.[37] In Chinese mythology, the dragon is described as a scaly beast with a large head, round eyes, hairy ears like those of an antelope, a wide-open mouth with sharp bared teeth and a mustache above its lips, a beard, horns, a long slender neck above a thicker body with fins, four sturdy legs ending in claws, and a long tail. It is a ferocious but graceful creature that can turn dark or bright, large or small, long or short. It rises to the sky at the spring equinox and dives into the depths at the autumn equinox.[38]

The dragon is a much-loved and benevolent assistant to both gods and humans in the ceaseless struggle with nature. Dragons are always depicted as the appendages of goddesses in China's goddess shrines; Yu the Great used a dragon to conquer the floods; dragon oracles were also used for divination in the *Book of Changes (Yi Jing)* to guide the actions of princes and "great men." Chinese lore describes the dragon as a changeable creature possessed of magical power over the wind, rain, thunder, and lightning—making it a particularly potent god for an agricultural society. Studies of ancient bone and tortoise-shell oracles[39] reveal that the dragon was consulted for weather predictions; both dragon paintings and "dragon jade" (a kind of jade with dragon carvings) were regularly used to pray for rain.[40]

The earliest dragon designs were simple and crude, resembling lizards and snakes. By the Han dynasty (206 B.C.– A.D. 220), the dragon design had become fully realized and was appropriated by the dynasty's founder, Liu Bang, as his exclusive symbol. Born to a humble family amid the confusion of wars, Liu concocted a tale of divine birth to elevate himself above commoner status. As recounted by historian Sima Qian:[41]

> Liu's mother was sleeping one day on the slope of a marsh and met a god in her dream. The sky was overcast, and there was thunder and lightning. When her husband came looking for her, he saw a dragon mounting her. She subse-

quently became pregnant and gave birth to Emperor Gaozu. When he grew up to be a man, he had the regular features of a dragon and a beautiful beard. . . .

According to a recent PRC account, from then on, the dragon became directly linked with the emperor, "a ploy devised by the ruling class" to consolidate its rule. Reported dragon sightings signified the reigning emperor's virtuous rule. Despite rulers' efforts to forbid commoners from using the dragon design, the prohibition was widely ignored, except for some minor restrictions on the dragon's color and the number of claws. The emperor had exclusive use of the five-clawed yellow imperial dragon; ministers and lower-rank officials were allowed dragons with four or three claws; those for commoners presumably would have even fewer claws.[42]

In effect, originating as the totem of First Sovereign Fu Xi's tribe, the dragon was embraced by the Chinese people as their collective symbol by the time of the Han dynasty. Despite Emperor Gaozu's attempt to appropriate the dragon for the exclusive use of the Son of Heaven, he and subsequent emperors managed to impose only minor restrictions on the popular employment of the dragon image. The evolution of the dragon is thus both a microcosm as well as a metaphor for the gradual evolution and integration of the Chinese people.[43]

The Beginning

E. T. C. Werner once wrote that the origin of the Chinese people is undetermined, for "We do not know who they were nor whence they came."[44] Chinese themselves traditionally have maintained that their earliest ancestors were migrants from western Asia.[45] Whatever their point of origin, fossil remains indicate that the earliest human presence in the area now identified as China dates to the Pleistocene period that began some 2 or 3 million years ago.[46]

It has been the mainstay of Western anthropology that human beings originated in Africa, from which *Homo erectus* departed to the other continents a million years ago. That belief is now being challenged by recent archaeological findings in China that point to the presence of hominids in Asia some 2 million years ago.

In 1921, a series of archaeological findings culminated in the discovery of the first hominid fossils near Beijing in Zhoukoudian—those of the *Homo erectus* Peking Man (actually, woman), estimated to be about 400,000 years old. Since that time, more than a hundred Paleolithic sites have been uncovered in China, spanning the later portions of the Pleistocene period.[47] In the late 1980s, a team of Chinese archaeologists uncovered hominid bones and stone tools from Longgupo Cave in Sichuan Province estimated to be 1.7 million to 1.9 million years old.[48] In 1985, hominid fossils (dubbed Wushan Man) were discovered in the Three Gorges area of the Yangzi River, determined by scientific tests conducted in 1998 to be more than 2 million years old[49]— making Wushan Man the oldest human remains discovered to date in China.

Both the Longgupo and Wushan fossils appear to belong to a hominid species that resided somewhere between *Homo habilis* and *Homo erectus* on the human evolutionary tree. *H. habilis* appeared 2.5 million years ago in Africa and was the first toolmaker; *H. erectus* was the species to which Peking man belongs and the first human ancestor thought to have left Africa.[50] Both Longgupo and Wushan Man resemble more closely the primitive *H. habilis* than the later *H. erectus*, suggesting that the conventional view that *H. habilis* evolved into *H. erectus* only in Africa, then wandered into the Mideast and Asia, might have to be modified. Although humankind's deepest evolutionary roots are sunk in the African soil, the branches of the family tree may not be confined to a single continent. Some early *Homo* species might have left Africa and evolved into *H. erectus* in Asia.[51] *H. erectus* thus could have been an Asian side branch of the hominid evolutionary tree, rather than part of the African lineage that led to modern humans.[52]

Those earliest humans in what became China began as hunters, fishers, and gatherers, some of whom discovered agriculture in the lush, fertile, and temperate central valley of the Yellow River about 13,000 to 10,000 years ago. That valley would become the cradle of Chinese civilization.

These early cultivators lived in villages of about 50,000 square meters in area, shifting from one locale to another after a short period of occupancy because of their slash-and-burn farming technique. Houses and animal pens were clustered in the center of each oval-shaped village, with the village cemetery located north of the dwelling area. The villages were organized according to membership in unilinear clans, a form of social organization that would persist and expand into later stages of Chinese history.[53]

From that core region of the Yellow River, which the Chinese call *zhongyuan* (central source or central plains), human settlements gradually radiated out to encompass nearby regions. By 5000 B.C., a number of distinctive, though cross-fertilizing, Neolithic cultures had sprung up in different regions. Two such cultures were those of Yangshao and Longshan. The former, regarded by some to be northern China's primary Neolithic culture, occupied the middle Yellow River valley from today's central Honan to Gansu and Qinghai.[54] The Yangshao culture is distinguished by its red pottery with painted black designs, polished stone axes and knives, the use of domesticated animals, as well as agriculture. East of Yangshao, in today's Shandong, was the parallel culture of Longshan, with its distinctive thin, lustrous, black pottery.[55]

Over the course of time, as a result of interaction and cross fertilization among the regional cultures, a geographic sphere of increasing integration was formed. That prehistoric sphere became the geographic stage for the transition to civilization by 3000 B.C., a process in which all the regional cultures "played a part".[56]

The Beginning of Civilization

By the early part of the second millennium B.C., the process of cultural integration had culminated in a qualitatively new stage of Chinese history. The transition to civilization was characterized by the following attributes: the passage from Stone to Bronze Age; the development of a new type of settlement (urban); a new form of government (the state); the introduction of written language (ideograms); and a new quality of life (civilization). Gradually hundreds of small city-states *(guo)* developed, each ruled by a warrior hegemon who wielded power over his clan and other clans. Despite a common culture and, often, a common legendary ancestor, neighboring states engaged in incessant competition and warfare. Inevitably, one state would be subjugated by another. Around 2000 B.C., one such city-state succeeded in vanquishing "ten thousand" other states and installed China's first dynasty (Xia) in the middle Yellow River valley.[57]

The Xia dynasty, spanning today's Shanxi, Shaanxi, and Henan provinces, would persist for more than 400 years. Its last king was the brutal and despotic Jie, who provoked a rebellion led by Tang that succeeded, ca. 1750 B.C., in supplanting the Xia with the Shang[58] dynasty in the lower Yellow River valley. Tang's uprising set the template for subsequent dynastic changes—the characteristic peasant rebellion against despotic and corrupt rule that has punctuated China's millennial history.

It is said that hard archaeological evidence of an organized cultural and political order begins with the Shang dynasty. The Shang were the ruling tribe among a large number of tribes, both friendly and hostile. Each tribe occupied and controlled a specific area of territory. The supreme figure in Shang society was the king *(wang)*, a lineal descendant of the founder of the Shang tribe, who was more like a nomadic chief than the all-powerful Chinese emperors of later periods. Below him were the shamans and nobles. The latter had their own states *(guo)* and were either related by blood or allegiance to the Shang ruling house, or were at war with the Shang. Below the nobility were the commoners, comprised of artisans, a free peasantry organized into the "well-field" *(jingtian)* system[59], and slaves. The latter were prisoners taken in military expeditions who were pressed into court service or as soldiers.[60]

The Shang dynasty is considered by historians to be the political prototype and "point of departure" for Chinese history because it exemplifies for the first time the full cycle from dynastic succession to dynastic succession. The dynasty began as a populist rebellion against a corrupt monarch and ended in like manner. After 29 successive kings, the last Shang ruler (Shouxin) was another monster who "ripped up pregnant women" and incited Wen Wang to rise up in rebellion. Wen Wang's uprising was completed by his son, Wu Wang, who founded the Zhou dynasty in 1100 B.C.[61]

It was during the Zhou dynasty that feudalism became institutionalized in China when the embryonic feudalism of the Shang dynasty was formalized into a system of permanent control—the *fengjian* system of enfeoffment. North China was divided into four types of some 100 domains. There was the personal domain of the Zhou king, which stretched from modern Shaanxi down the Yellow River into Honan. There were domains to the east and south of the king, which were given to members of the Zhou royal family and their closest allies. There were domains situated farther to the east in Honan, enfeoffed to members of the defeated Shang royal family. Surrounding the potentially hostile Shang domains were appanages granted to Zhou family members to counterbalance and prevent Shang insurrection.[62]

The lords of these hundred or so domains made up the nobility of the Zhou dynasty. At the bottom of society were the peasants who went with the land, although they had some claims on its produce. Each lord had complete political and economic control over his domain and was assisted by appointed officials, many of whom were his collateral kinsmen. Anchoring the entire society was the lineage system *(zongfa)* of clans, with the line of descent passed down from generation to generation through the eldest son. Families and descendants of the eldest sons comprised the main lineage *(dazong);* those of the younger brothers made up the minor lineage *(xiaozong).*[63]

The three dynasties of Xia, Shang, and Zhou constitute China's classical period or antiquity that lasted almost two thousand years. The dynasties formed "a system of parallel and interrelated regional developments with shifting centers of gravity"[64]—subgroups that vied for political dominance within a single cultural tradition. Many shared traits point to the three dynasties' membership in a single cultural tradition. All three were agrarian societies with domesticated animals and identical architecture and urban design, employing utensils, weapons, and ritual paraphernalia made of bronze. In all three dynasties, society and state were hierarchically organized along clans and lineages, with each clan maintaining a careful record of its ancestors who were worshipped as spirits *(gui)* and deities *(shen)*. In all three dynasties, shamans were important figures who mediated between heaven and earth by communicating with deceased ancestors and performing divinations about great undertakings such as military expeditions, harvest forecasts, and the political fortunes of kings and princes. In all three dynasties, the kings called themselves *Tianzi* (Son of Heaven), holders of magical powers that could be transmitted to their successors. The king was not only political sovereign but also chief shaman who alone offered sacrifices to the supreme heavenly deity *(di)* in state rituals.[65]

It was also during the three dynasties that the collective identity of the Chinese people became solidified. By the Zhou dynasty, its people were informed by a distinctive worldview that divided the world into five peoples. The first were the Huaxia people of the three dynasties, who inhabited the Central Plains *(Zhongyuan)*—an area between the Yellow River and the Lohe River of some 200,000 square miles. Surrounding the Huaxia people were the four peoples in the four corners with whom the Huaxia interacted.[66] The nucleus and locus of culture was the Central Plains, whose inhabitants clearly felt themselves to be different from and superior to the four peripheral peoples. The Huaxia people in the Central Plains were literate; the peripheral peoples were not. The Central Plains had cities, palaces, royal tombs, and a ritual art in bronze and jade; the peripheral peoples enjoyed none of this, except for their copies of bronze vessels.[67] Most importantly, by the middle half of the first millennium B.C., the Central Plains alone witnessed a burst of creativity unmatched by any subsequent period in Chinese history. This was the original "blooming of the Hundred Flowers" when Confucius, Laozi, and Zhuangzi founded China's major philosophies of Confucianism and Daoism, and left their lasting imprint on society and statecraft.

In effect, it was the culture of the Central Plains that defined the Huaxia people, instead of vice versa. The people of the Central Plains came to regard themselves as the bearers of civilization; the peoples on the margins and beyond were viewed as uncultured barbarians. Joseph E. Spencer observed that such ethnocentrism "is a common human tendency, but Chinese culture eventually developed this feeling into a very strong self-centeredness." Chinese ethnocentrism, however, did not prevent their selective assimilation of many "barbarian" customs. Despite that assimilation, the stable nucleus of the Chinese cultural hearth remained fundamentally unaltered. Any feature that threatened the balance of Chinese culture was met with a "strong reaction."[68]

As the culture of the Central Plains expanded, assimilation into that culture, more than race or ethnicity, became the defining criterion of "Chineseness." As an example, the inhabitants of the coastal lowlands of South China in the past and present include a Negrito strain; similarly, "a backwash of proto-Malay" people are found along the whole South China littoral.[69] Although both are racial varieties unlike the Mongoloid peoples of inland China, they nevertheless are considered Chinese. Through the process of acculturation, ethnically foreign conquest peoples could always aspire to be, and many in fact became, Chinese.[70]

Zhongyuan, the Central Plains, would be the source from which came the name of the later unified Chinese state—that of Zhongguo (Middle State or Kingdom).[71] Huaxia was the earliest name for the Chinese people until it was supplanted by Hanren (Han dynasty people) and Tangren (Tang dynasty people).[72] Today, *Huaxia* denotes a cultural identity; whereas *Han* has a strong ethnic flavor and is used to distinguish the Han Chinese from the ethnic minorities in the People's Republic. As PRC scholars insist, "The Chinese culture, with Huaxia as its core . . . includes the cultures of all the members of the big family of the Chinese nation,"[73] but the "Han race (*Hanzu*)" is China's "mainstream or host *(zhuti)* nation."[74] Contemporary Chinese call themselves Huaren (Hua people), including even the overseas diaspora Chinese who call themselves Huayi (Hua posterity). The combination of Zhongyuan and Huaxia produces Zhonghua (China or Chinese), a word that is common to both contemporary Chinese states: the government on the mainland is Zhonghua renmin gongheguo (Chinese People's Republic); its counterpart on Taiwan is Zhonghua minguo (Chinese Republic or the Republic of China).

China's third dynasty of Zhou lasted almost a millennium, for 900 years. In 771 B.C., the dynasty began to decline and was increasingly besieged by nomads from the north.[75] As the power of the Zhou court waned, the nobles in the various domains or states grew more independent. At the same time, new states arose on the dynasty's periphery and absorbed some of the Zhou appanages. This was the period of the Warring States (771–221 B.C.)—a time of increasing bloody conflict, but also remarkable material progress and philosophical creativity.

As the long reign of the Zhou dynasty drew to a close, so did the formative years of Chinese antiquity. With the end of antiquity came the beginning of Imperial China, which would persist for the next 2,000 years until it was brought to an ignominious conclusion by the forces unleashed by Western imperialism.

Unification and the Beginning of Imperial China

In the year 221 B.C., Qin Shihuang, ruler of one of the warring states, vanquished and unified the other states and brought a formal conclusion to the moribund Zhou dynasty. Emperor Qin abolished feudalism, centralized political power, and unified all the territories into a single state. Thus began the enduring centralized bureaucratic state that history identifies as Imperial China.

While it was brute force that enabled Qin to conquer and unify, historians argue that his feats were the culmination of antecedent historical forces, both cultural and political. To begin with, Qin's unification was "a political follow-up" of a process of cultural unification that had gone on for some 4,000 years and resulted in the formation of the Huaxia people. Politically, it is maintained, over the course of several centuries, some of the contending Zhou states were already moving in the direction of centralization.[76]

In effect, Qin Shihuang's unification might be regarded as the logical conclusion of a long process. To say this, however, is not to diminish his historical significance. Whatever the preceding conditions, Qin's territorial and political integration created China and transformed an already culturally homogeneous people, the Huaxia, into Chinese. As Anthony Christie observed,[77]

> The point in time at which it is possible to identify a given group or aggregation of groups as being the Chinese ... is difficult to determine, but it is perhaps reasonable to do so at the moment when the Qin dynasty (221–207 B.C.) brought about the first unification of China.

Qin is credited with having established the system that would characterize China for the next 2,000 years: a multiethnic empire governed by an extensively bureaucratized and centralized authoritarian elite. It was Qin who assured central dominance over the enormous expanse of Imperial China by institutionalizing prefectural and county-level appointments, standardizing weights and measures, and imposing a uniform currency, a universal calendar, and a common script that bridged across diverse regional dialects. In order to reduce dissidence, Qin suppressed unorthodox schools of opinion: Education and ideological instruction came under the control of the state; private libraries and unauthorized texts were destroyed by fire; and scholars who resisted those measures were executed. In one instance, 460 scholars were buried alive for having objected to the state's censorship. Qin Shihuang also embarked upon massive public works projects that included the first constructions of the Great Wall, and the building of palaces, garrison fortifications, a mausoleum, and a network of roads connecting the major regions of the empire to the capital.[78] To do all that, hundreds of thousands of peasants, as well as convicts and political criminals, were compelled into corvée labor.

Although the formal apparatus of the state extended only to the county level, state power nevertheless penetrated to the villages through the local gentry—a landowning literati class who acted as the emperor's intermediary by collecting and remitting taxes from the peasants to the center. It is estimated that this elite class, on whom the emperor depended for local administration and the maintenance of social stability, comprised but 2 percent of the total population.[79]

Thus, long before the modern era, a system of population management practices were introduced into China that would persist into the twentieth century. A control apparatus, staffed by government functionaries with collateral support from the local gentry, was cast over the broad expanse of the Middle Kingdom. The people across that empire were bound to the center by prescriptions of loyalty and obedience inculcated by an educational system predicated on conformity and submissiveness.

As described by Étienne Balazs, state power in Imperial China was near totalitarian in that "No private undertaking nor any aspect of public life could escape official regulation." In addition to a whole series of state monopolies,[80] "the tentacles of the state Moloch . . . superintended, to the minutest detail, every step its subjects took from the cradle to the grave."[81] The only exceptions to the all-encompassing state were the religions of Daoism and Buddhism, which thrived in spite of the prevailing Confucian orthodoxy, and popular groups that the state was unable to appropriate. The latter included secret societies, criminal gangs, clan associations, and separatist ethnic minorities along the empire's borders.[82]

The entire economic substructure of China rendered such arrangements eminently functional. Not only was traditional Chinese agriculture labor intensive, it was hydraulic in nature, relying heavily on irrigation supplied by the major rivers. In a primitive preindustrial environment, the harnessing, control, and maintenance of those long and fragile river systems required a powerful centralized political authority that could mobilize whole populations into conscript labor for flood control and irrigation construction.[83]

Sustaining the entire system were ideological convictions that were systematically inculcated into the populace, then buttressed and reinforced by a homogeneous class of gentry-officials. Those convictions had been articulated by Confucius, Laozi, Mozi, Mencius, and Han Feizi in the first millennium before Christ. With some minor exceptions, almost all the political thought of this period was devoted to the principles of stable governance. Society was conceived as a set of interrelated patterns of human obligation. Man was understood to be a social animal, sustained in a web of relations governed by rules of appropriate conduct or propriety. Filial piety and its political corollary, submission to the political ruler, became the normative ideal for an entire society. Before a ruler who was virtuous and just, the people were to be content and obedient, each in his/her proper place.

The proper place of the educated class was somewhat ambiguous. On the one hand, the gentry-officials upheld the state ideology because Confucian scholarship, as tested by the national civil service examination, was their route of upward mobility into the elite stratum. On the other hand, the intellectuals were also expected to be China's conscience because only they had the education and critical faculties to correct and remonstrate an errant or immoral emperor. Those few who dared to speak out, however, did so at their own peril, for they could depend on neither man nor institution to check the emperor's power and contain his wrath.

Reinforcing the social-control function of the Confucian state ideology was the powerful adhesive of family and clan. The importance of blood and kinship was generalized to all social relations, so that a premium was placed on personal connections *(guanxi)* in business and politics. Biologically unrelated Chinese with the same surname pretended to kinship in a common lineage *(tongzong)*. Natives of the same village or county were *xiao tongxiang;* those from the same province were *tongxiang;* those from neighboring provinces were "extended fellow natives" *(da tongxiang).* Chinese who passed the imperial examinations in the same year were *tongnian;* colleagues would forever remain *tongshi,* even when they no longer worked together. At its most expansive, the web of biological commonality includes every Chinese, even the overseas ethnic Chinese, who are siblings from the "same womb" *(tongbao).*[84]

The Celestial Chinese Empire

The Qin dynasty was also the beginning of empire. In the northeast, its reach extended beyond the confines of the Zhou dynasty to embrace modern Liaoning and Kirin in Manchuria. In the south, the dynasty absorbed the "barbarian" peoples in modern Hunan, Jiangxi, and Guangdong. During the 427 years of the Han dynasty, the Chinese empire was further enlarged. In the northeast, it included most of modern North Korea; in the south and southwest, the Middle Kingdom absorbed modern Guangxi, Guizhou, Yunnan, and the northern part of Vietnam; in the north, a tentacle was extended westward into the upper region of today's Qinghai and western Gansu.

In the 2,000 years after Qin's unification, China alternately expanded or contracted like an amoeba, its borders ebbing and flowing, peaking especially during the two alien dynasties of Yuan (1206–1294) and Qing (1644–1911). The Chinese, as a consequence, never had a firm conception of national boundaries that were fixed by international treaties, unlike the European conception of national boundaries, which is a complex product of fairly recent history. The extent of the Chinese empire depended entirely on the reigning emperor's ambition and power.

Whatever its size, Imperial China was a hegemonic power in Asia, its known world, without peer or rival among its neighboring states. Not surprisingly, China's view of its place was quite different from that of the states in Europe.

Traditionally, the Chinese Empire was conceived to comprise China Proper, Outer China, and the tributary territories. China Proper is the cultural heart of China and the core of Han Chinese settlement. Outer China is comprised of buffer territories ruled directly from China Proper but inhabited almost entirely by non-Han peoples. This buffer zone historically included all or parts of Xinjiang, Inner and Outer Mongolia, Manchuria, Tibet, and, at times, northern Korea and northern Vietnam.

During the Yuan dynasty, Outer China expanded to include all of Korea, Central Asia, Ukraine, Iraq, Iran, Burma, and Vietnam. Outside the buffer regions were China's tributary client states, considered to be voluntary parts of the Chinese Empire who were allowed to have their own rulers as long as their foreign policies were in accord with China's. Among Imperial China's traditional clients were the peoples of Southeast Asia, Taiwan, Korea, the islands in the South China Sea, the East China Sea, and most of the Bay of Bengal. At the height of China's last dynasty, the Qing, its borders included today's Russian Far East, Sakhalin Island, the western half of the Sea of Japan, the Korean peninsula, the Yellow Sea, the East China Sea, the Ryukyu Islands, Taiwan, Hong Kong, the South China Sea, Vietnam, Laos, Thailand, Cambodia, Burma, Malaysia, the Andaman Sea and Island, Nepal, Bhutan, Kirghizstan, the eastern half of Kazakhstan, Russia's Altay and Sayan Mountains, and Mongolia.[85]

In China's ancient theory of tributary relations, the Middle Kingdom was the center of civilization. Its Son of Heaven represented all mankind in his functions as a moral and ceremonial intermediary between human society and the unseen forces of nature. In effect, the Chinese state was conceived as a universal empire. Foreign rulers who wished contact or trade with the Celestial Empire must enroll as China's tributaries, accept its investiture, send envoys to *kowtow* before the Son of Heaven, and "otherwise obey the regulations for tributary intercourse."[86]

The "barbarian" peoples in the areas of Chinese colonization were either allowed to reside in their native territory or were forcibly transplanted into ethnically Han areas. In both cases, the "barbarians" were eventually absorbed into the Chinese mainstream through intermarriage or acculturation. So powerful was Chinese civilization that both the Mongols and Manchus who conquered China and installed, respectively, the Yuan and Qing dynasties, eventually became assimilated. Manchuria today is Chinese in blood, culture, and economics.[87]

Some of the "barbarians," however, managed to resist assimilation by continuously retreating southward ahead of Chinese colonization, eventually into southeastern Asia. Along the Tibetan frontier, Chinese colonization was somewhat stalled by the frigid temperatures and the rugged terrain. Along the central Asian corridor, the standard Chinese technique of making Chinese of all other peoples was also ineffective because the alien cultures held strong against the Chinese, who, despite in-migration and resettlement, have remained a numerical minority. Repeated efforts over the centuries to absorb and acculturate the non-Han peoples of Xinjiang have achieved only bitterness, unrest, and internal distress. There are some who maintain that Chinese colonization and frontier expansion are ongoing, as "there is no indication that activity has ceased."[88]

Conclusion

Although the dynasty founded by the first Qin emperor proved to be short-lived, lasting only 49 years, the centralized-bureaucratic-despotic state that he created would endure into the twentieth century. By A.D. 220 at the end of the Han dynasty, the system that Qin Shihuang founded had become entrenched, working "reasonably well for all concerned."[89]

Through 2,000 years, the political rhythm of China displayed a curious cyclical quality. Periods of unity would alternate with episodes of fragmentation.[90] Dynasties were born, flourished, and decayed; each gave way to a successor in a convulsion of populist insurrection. Some dynasties had a short life span: The Later Jin lasted 11 years, the Later Zhou nine, the Later Han only four. Others were long-lived: The Tang, Ming, and Qing each persisted for nearly 300 years. The peasant rebellions that overthrew dynasties were oddly lacking in ideology or class consciousness in that the rebels opposed the ruling dynasty but not the system of government itself. The problem was understood to be one of personality rather than system—it was the reigning emperor's vices that had led heaven to withdraw its mandate. What was needed was to replace the morally bankrupt dynasty with a new one, founded by a man of virtue who was also the leader of the rebellion.

The dénouement of every dynasty was marked by a series of increasingly intractable crises and disasters. These included a precipitous decline in the availability of revenue, disintegration of the hydraulic system, and a corresponding failure of agricultural production. All of this would be attended by an increase in banditry that took on more and more organized forms until active resistance threatened the very continuity of the dynasty. The mass migration of peasants, no longer able to sustain themselves through their traditional pursuits, brought recruits to peasant armies. Communication from the provinces to the center could no longer be sustained; more and more local revenue failed to reach the capital. Corruption increased and further undermined the effectiveness of government, which was no longer capable of ensuring order and of responding to even relatively minor natural dislocations and disasters. It was said that heaven had withdrawn its mandate to rule.

Despite the periodic peasant upheavals, Imperial China displayed an impressive stability and a stubborn conservatism. Any political system such as dynastic China that could persist for 2,000 years must possess an internal consistency and logic that acted as a powerful "fixative" *(ningju li)*.[91] That which held Imperial China together were the bonds of culture, territory, language, political institutions, the millennial system of clans and lineages, and an elite class who depended on the Confucian state ideology for its very raison d'être. For such a system to break irreparably would take a force of calamitous proportions. In the words of James T. C. Liu,[92]

[I]t seems that no force . . . could possibly emerge from within that society . . . to tear apart the integration so formed over many centuries. The only force capable of causing a disintegration had to come from the outside. . . . Even then, the process of disintegration took at least half a century.

Notes

1. See Jonathan Unger (ed.), *Chinese Nationalism* (Armonk, NY: M. E. Sharpe, 1996).

2. Arthur Keith, *A New Theory of Human Evolution* (New York: Philosophical Library, 1949), pp. 29–34.

3. Kwang-chih Chang, *The Archaeology of Ancient China* (New Haven: Yale University Press, 1986), p. 7.

4. The United States is 3.6 million square miles. Only Russia and Canada are larger than China. The People's Republic is three times the size of India, 18 times the size of France, and 26 times larger than Japan.

5. These include the recently discovered oil reserves in the seabed of China's offshore waters.

6. Frank Leeming, *The Changing Geography of China* (Oxford: Blackwell, 1993), p. 11.

7. It is estimated that, each year, China is losing to soil erosion an area equivalent in size to the state of Maine.

8. *San Francisco Chronicle*, April 20, 1988, p. A13.

9. The population density figures for The Netherlands, Belgium, and Japan are 346, 323, and 316 people per square kilometer.

10. See, for example, the definition of Hanzu as "the Chinese race" in *Matthews' Chinese-English Dictionary* (Taipei: Guohuang Books, 1975), p. 303.

11. Joseph Campbell, *The Power of Myth* (New York: Doubleday, 1988), p. 15.

12. Anne Birrel, *Chinese Mythology: An Introduction* (Baltimore, MD: Johns Hopkins University Press, 1993), p. 4.

13. Marianne McDonald, *Tales of the Constellations: The Myths and Legends of the Night Sky* (New York: Smithmark, 1996), pp. 16, 10–13, 15.

14. Birrell, *Chinese Mythology*, pp. 17–18.

15. Anthony Christie, "China," in Richard Cavendish (ed.), *Mythology: An Illustrated Encyclopedia* (New York: Barnes and Noble, 1993), pp. 58–59.

16. Birrell, *Chinese Mythology*, p. 31.

17. Anthony Christie, *Chinese Mythology* (New York: Barnes and Noble, 1996), pp. 54–55.

18. Birrell, *Chinese Mythology*, pp. 32, 25, 23–24; and Christie, *Chinese Mythology*, pp. 37, 40.

19. Birrell, *Chinese Mythology*, p. 33.

20. Christie, "China," p. 64.

21. Ibid., p. 64; Yang Xin, "The Development of Dragon Imagery in Chinese Art," in Yang Xin, Li Yihua, and Xu Naixiang, *The Art of the Dragon* (Boston: Shambhala, 1988), p. 11; and Birrell, *Chinese Mythology*, pp. 33–35.

22. McDonald, *Tales of the Constellations*, p. 14.

23. *Matthews' Chinese-English Dictionary* has Shen Nong and Yan Di as the same person (Yan Di was Shen Nong's dynastic title). Another account has Zhu Rong (aka Sui Ren), the inventor of fire, as the Third Sovereign. Kwang-chih Chang, *Archaeology of Ancient China*, p. 305. The reigning dates of Emperors Zhuan Xu, Yao, and Shun are ca. 2513–2435 B.C., 2357–2255 B.C., and 2255–2205 B.C., respectively.

24. Christie, "China," p. 61. According to historian Sima Qian in *Shiji*, Yu was the great-great-grandson of the Yellow Emperor himself. See Yang Xuechen, *Zhongguo minzu shi (History of the Chinese People)* (Taipei: Wenjin, 1994), pp. 1–2. Although this book was published in Taiwan, its author is a researcher at the Chinese Academy of Social Sciences' Nationalities Institute.

25. Birrell, *Chinese Mythology*, pp. 19–20.

26. Deng Luoqun, "Dangdai yanhuang wenhuare di xingqi jiqi shidai yiyi (The Revival and Historical Relevance of the Culture of Emperors Yan and Huang)," in *Dangdai sichao (Contemporary Thought)* (Beijing), no. 6 (1994), pp. 57, 59. Deng's account credits Yandi, the Third Sovereign, instead of Shennong, with the discovery of medicine and farming.

27. Joseph R. Levenson and Franz Schurmann, *China: An Interpretive History* (Berkeley, CA: University of California Press, 1975), p. 5.

28. Ibid.

29. Yang Xuechen, *History of the Chinese People*, p. 1.

30. Ibid., p. 7.

31. He Xingliang, "Long: Tuteng-sheng (Dragon: Totem-God)," *Minzu yanjiu* (*Nationality Studies*) (Beijing), no. 2 (1993), p. 38.

32. Wang Liquan, "Longsheng zhimi (The mystery of the dragon)," *Dangdai sichao*, no. 5 (1992), p. 22.

33. Totems are creatures (such as a bear) or natural phenomena (such as the wind) believed to possess magical powers for bringing disaster or good fortune.

34. He Xingliang, "Long: Tuteng-sheng," pp. 38–39. Chinese mythology recounts that the dragon, cloud, fire, water, and bird were the respective totems of the clans of Tai (or Da) Hao, Huang Di, Yan Di, Gong Gong, and Shao Hao. This would make the dragon the totem of First Sovereign Fu Xi's tribe, as Tai Hao was Fu Xi's reigning title. See Yang Xin et al., *Art of the Dragon*, p. 11.

35. Yang Xin et al., *Art of the Dragon*, pp. 10–11.

36. Ibid., p. 11.

37. See Wang Liquan, "Mystery of the Dragon," pp. 23–25. This view is lent some credence by the discovery in China in the 1960s of a short-snouted, long-legged, long-tailed 100-million-year-old fossil that paleontologists recently identi-

fied to be a plant-eating crocodilian living in southern China during the Cretaceous Period. "Weird and Wonderful: Chinese Cretacean Fossil Identified As a Vegetarian Crocodilian," *Discover,* December 1995, p. 16.

38. Yang Xin et al., *Art of the Dragon,* pp. 15–16.

39. Oracle bones were tortoise shells and ox and sheep scapulas used for divination purposes. The bone fragment was heated on one side by fire to produce a pattern of cracks, the meaning of which would be interpreted by a shaman. The shaman's interpretation of the omen would be inscribed on the other side in Chinese characters.

40. Ibid., pp. 12–14, 17.

41. Ibid., pp. 12–13, 15.

42. In the Qing dynasty (A.D. 1644–1911), the rulers attempted to further appropriate the use of the dragon symbol by calling only the imperial five-clawed dragon a dragon; those with four or fewer claws were demoted to being called pythons. Ibid., pp. 15, 18.

43. Ibid., p. 18.

44. E. T. C. Werner, *Myths and Legends of China* (New York: Benjamin Blom, 1971), p. 13.

45. Levenson and Schurmann, *China: An Interpretive History,* p. 9.

46. If one were to imagine the accounts of China's legendary sage-kings to be factual, their purported cumulative chronology would place them "well within the Pleistocene period." Chang, *Archaeology of Ancient China,* p. 22.

47. Ibid., pp. 22–23.

48. Elizabeth Culotta, "Asian Hominids Grow Older," *Science,* vol. 270 (17 November 1995), p. 1116.

49. *Shijie ribao (World Journal),* April 6, 1998, p. A8.

50. Sharon Begley, "An Ancient Wanderlust: A Find Suggests Humans Left Home Early," *Newsweek,* November 27, 1995, pp. 78–79.

51. Ibid.

52. Culotta, "Asian Hominids Grow Older."

53. Chang, *Archaeology of Ancient China,* pp. 71, 114, 116, 119.

54. Levenson and Schurmann, *China,* p. 9.

55. Other regional cultures included the Dawenkou Culture of northern Jiangsu, the Xinluo, Hongshan, and Fuhe Cultures of the lower Liao River valley, the Majiabang Culture of the southern Huai River and lower Yangzi valleys, the Hemudu Culture of northern Zhejiang, the Daxi Culture of western Hubei and eastern Sichuan, and the Qujialing Culture of eastern and central Hubei. Chang, *Archaeology of Ancient China,* pp. 108–109, 112–113, 156, 107–108.

56. Ibid., pp. 236, 242.

57. Ibid., pp. 295, 304, 305, 307.

58. Legend traces the Shang (aka Yin) dynasty to a remote ancestor named Xie, said to be the son of mythic Third Emperor Ku, who gave Xie a fief in the Shang district of what is now Shaanxi Province. That fief no doubt was the origin of the name of the later Shang dynasty, whose capital was initially located at Bo in eastern

Honan, but moved five times, the fifth and last time to Anyang. Levenson and Schurmann, *China,* p. 11.

59. Fields were divided into nine squares, the produce of eight of which went to the peasants, and that of the ninth to the lord. The "well-field" system would persist for centuries.

60. Levenson and Schurmann, *China,* pp. 10, 18–19, 22–23.

61. Ibid., pp. 12, 28–30. Legend has it that the Zhou were the descendants of Ji Houji, a minister of Yu, the founder of Xia dynasty. Ji's son lost his position at court and fled northwestward to the land of the Yi and Di barbarians. As time passed, his descendants began moving eastward while, at the same time, the Shang dynasty expanded westward—bringing the Zhou and Shang peoples into increasing contact.

62. One such appanage was Lu, given to the descendants of the Duke of Zhou, which later became the home state of Confucius.

63. Levenson and Schurmann, *China,* pp. 31–33.

64. Chang, *Archaeology,* p. 361.

65. Ibid., pp. 362–366; Levenson and Schurmann, *China,* p. 4.

66. They were the Yi in the east, the Man in the south, the Rong in the west, and the Di in the north. Joseph E. Spencer, "General Characteristics of Chinese Geography," in James T. C. Liu and Wei-ming Tu (eds.), *Traditional China* (Englewood Cliffs, NJ: Prentice-Hall, 1970), p. 28.

67. Chang, *Archaeology,* pp. 368–369, 409.

68. Spencer, "General Characteristics of Chinese Geography," pp. 30, 36–37.

69. Ibid., p. 30.

70. Levenson and Schurmann, *China,* p. 14.

71. Yang Xuechen, *History of the Chinese People,* p. 2.

72. Of the two, the more common expression has been *Hanren* or *Hanzu* (Han race). The expression *Tangren* is rarely used today, except in reference to Chinatowns *(Tanren jie)* in the United States.

73. Liu Ruzhong and Li Zhefeng, "Preface," in Liu Zhiqin and Wu Tingjia, *Zhongguo wenhuashi gailun (A Summary of the History of Chinese Culture)* (Taipei: Wenjin, 1994), p. 1.

74. Yang Xuechen, *History of the Chinese People,* p. 16.

75. The Zhou capital was moved to Loyang in the east, thereby initiating the Eastern Zhou dynasty (as distinct from the earlier Western Zhou dynasty). Chang, *Archaeology,* pp. 317, 339, 341.

76. Ibid., p. 410; James T. C. Liu, "Integrative Factors Through Chinese History: Their Interaction," in James Liu and Wei-ming Tu (eds.), *Traditional China,* p. 17.

77. Christie, *Chinese Mythology,* p. 6.

78. According to Chinese archeologists, one of these roads was 457 miles long, stretching from Shaanxi to Inner Mongolia. Construction began in 212 B.C. and took only two and a half years. *World Journal,* April 20, 1998, p. A10.

79. Andrew L. March, *The Idea of China: Myth and Theory in Geographic Thought* (New York: Praeger, 1974), p. 13.

80. The state monopolies included large trading monopolies in goods for mass consumption (salt, iron, tea, wines, and spirits); monopoly in foreign trade, education, and literature. There were also regulations concerning many aspects of daily life: dress, the colors of clothing, the dimensions of public and private buildings, festivals, music, birth, death.

81. Étienne Balazs, *Chinese Civilization and Bureaucracy* (New Haven: Yale University Press, 1964), pp. 10–11.

82. March, *The Idea of China*, p. 21.

83. See Karl A. Wittfogel, *Oriental Despotism: A Comparative Study of Total Power* (New Haven: Yale University Press, 1967).

84. Liu, "Integrative Factors Through Chinese History," p. 22.

85. "The Dragon Awakes," *Browning Newsletter* (an investment newsletter for stockbrokers, published in the United States), 20:2 (February 21, 1996), pp. 5, 4.

86. Ssu-yu Teng and John K. Fairbank, *China's Response to the West: A Documentary Survey 1839–1923* (New York: Atheneum, 1973), pp. 18–19.

87. Spencer, "General Characteristics of Chinese Geography," p. 34.

88. Ibid., pp. 35–36.

89. Ibid., p. 32.

90. From the time of Qin Shihuang's unification to the Revolution of 1911 that ended dynastic rule, China's periods of unification and of fragmentation totaled 1,700 years and 900 years, respectively. Zhu Songbo (ed.), *Fenlie guojia di hudong guanxi* (*Mutually Interactive Relationship of Divided States*) (Taipei: Institute of International Relations, 1989), pp. 1–6.

91. Liu Zhiqin and Wu Tingjia, *A Summary of the History of Chinese Culture*, p. 56.

92. Liu, "Integrative Factors Through Chinese History," pp. 22–23.

4

One Hundred Years of Humiliation

Accurate scholarship can
Unearth the whole offence
From Luther until now
That has driven a culture mad . . .
—W. H. Auden, September 1, 1939

The centralized bureaucratic state created by Emperor Qin Shihuang endured for 2,000 years. Despite cyclical upheavals marking the transition from dynasty to dynasty, the fundamental pattern of Chinese political institutions was remarkably stable. In 1644, the Ming dynasty succumbed to nomadic invaders from Manchuria who installed what would be China's last dynasty: the Qing.

The invaders soon discovered that although military prowess enabled them to vanquish the Chinese, governing them was another matter altogether. Like the Mongols who founded the Yuan dynasty, the Manchus succeeded only in imposing themselves as an alien elite over an implacable Chinese state and society. To govern the empire's vast expanses, the political bureaucracy, staffed by Chinese mandarins and animated by the Confucian state ideology, was retained. In effect, China simply absorbed its conquerors, who, in due course, became almost completely assimilated.

The Qing proved to be one of China's most enduring and glorious dynasties. Its long lifespan of 267 years, together with its political stability and economic prosperity, created the environment for a great flowering of arts and culture. The Qing was also one of those periods in which the Chinese

Empire was the most expansive. On the eve of the Opium War in 1840, the empire stretched over some 13 million square kilometers of land, exceeding the present People's Republic by 3.4 million square kilometers.[1]

By the beginning of the nineteenth century, however, the dynasty had begun to display some of the characteristic symptoms of a sunset regime. Were it not for the arrival of the Western Europeans, China's inimitable dynastic cycle would undoubtedly have been replicated. Once again, peasant rebellions would have engulfed the country, eventually overthrowing the dynasty and replacing it with another. But the Western Europeans were a new breed of foreign "barbarians" who, unlike those whom the Chinese encountered in the past, could be neither pacified, deflected, nor assimilated. Not only were they equipped with powerful armaments produced by modern industry, the Westerners were convinced of their superiority in culture, morality, and civilization. Their arrival at the shores of China marked the crest of Europe's outward expansion. Unlike China's traditional neighbors and vassals, the "barbarians" from the West did not come as tributaries, allies, or supplicants. Awed neither by the magnificence nor the size of Imperial China, they came as conquerors to bring progress to a retrograde civilization.

Western Imperialism

Few events in history had as significant an impact on the world as the outward expansion of Western Europe in the eighteenth and nineteenth centuries. That impact was particularly acute on the peoples of the non-Western world. Not only did they suffer immeasurably from the effects of European expansion, new social and political formations would be forged from that crucible. Confronted with the extinction of their traditional communities, the inhabitants awakened to a newfound nationalism. Marshaling their collective energies and resources to meet the challenge of the West, they were ushered into the modern era.

Although imperialism usually involves "the geographical expansion of states into other territories," it is not synonymous with colonialism but encompasses instead "the gamut of state-centred relations of military, political, economic, and cultural domination."[2] Imperialism is "the extension of sovereignty or control, whether direct or indirect, political or economic, by one government, nation or society over another."[3] Outright colonization is only one means to effectuate control.

Imperialism is not a uniquely European or modern undertaking. In the past, Assyrians, Phoenicians, Ottoman Turks, Huns, Tartars, Romans, Napoleonic French, Zulus, Aztecs, and Chinese—among others—all created empires through conquest. No other imperialism, however, equaled that of Western Europe in either scope or impact.

There were two stages to Western imperialism. The first, dominated by Spain and Portugal, began in the waning years of the fifteenth century and resulted in the colonization of Central and South America until independence in the first half of the nineteenth century. In the eighteenth century, a second more rapacious stage of imperialism began under the auspices of the Dutch and the British. By then, the Industrial Revolution provided both the impetus and means for colonization. The urge to colonize came from European manufacturers' searching for ever more export markets, and from missionaries intent on converting heathens to Christianity. At the same time, new science and technology created Europe's superior military capabilities. In the last analysis, it was military might that enabled the Europeans to pursue their interests and impose their will over the less developed peoples of the world. Once territory was conquered by force, political dominance was exercised through a colonial administrative apparatus, ensuring the continual exploitation and subjugation of the inhabitants.

A century later, an entire roster of new players joined the quest for a place in the colonial sun. The list of imperialist powers expanded beyond Britain and Holland to include France, Germany, Belgium, Russia, the United States, and Japan. Their colonial possessions spanned the globe. To illustrate, in 1800, the imperialist powers staked out claims to 55 percent of the earth's surface, totaling some 28 million square miles.[4] By the time World War I broke out, 84.4 percent of the earth's surface, totaling 43,125,000 square miles, had been colonized.[5]

Every continent, except Antarctica, fell prey to the imperial appetite. In Europe, Britain colonized Gibraltar, Malta, and Cyprus. In the Middle East, Syria became a French mandate, Palestine a British mandate, and Kuwait a British protectorate. In North America, Canada was colonized by Britain, Greenland by Denmark, Wrangel Island by the Soviet Union, and Alaska and the Aleutian Islands by the United States. In Central America, Honduras, Bahamas, and Jamaica became British colonies; the Panama Canal, Puerto Rico, and the Virgin Islands were U.S. possessions; Martinique and Guadeloupe were acquired by France; Curaçao Island became Dutch. In South America, although ten Spanish colonies eventually broke free of their Iberian master, Britain retained British Guiana and

Trinidad Island. In the Pacific, France claimed Tahiti and New Caledonia, Britain had Australia, the United States had Samoa and Hawaii. The impulse to colonize was particularly egregious in Africa. Before the great rush of the 1880s, only one-tenth of Africa was colonized; by 1936, however, the entire continent (except Egypt and Liberia) was partitioned among France, Britain, Belgium, Portugal, Italy, and Spain.[6]

Asia, bruited to be "the source of all wealth and therefore power," was the last continent to be colonized.[7] Portugal was the pioneer, acquiring from China the tiny island of Macao in 1557. The British and Dutch followed. British colonies in Asia ultimately included India, Ceylon, Burma, Hong Kong, and Malaya. Holland acquired Sumatra, Java, the Celebes, Moluccas, Bali, Borneo, and the Timor Archipelago—collectively known as the Dutch East Indies. France amalgamated Cochin-China, Annam, Cambodia, Tonking, and Laos into the colony of Indochina. Sakhalin Island came under the control of Russia, while control of the Philippines changed hands from Spain to the United States after the Spanish-American War of 1898–1899. The last colonial power in Asia was Imperial Japan, whose possessions on the eve of World War II encompassed the southern half of Sakhalin Island (wrested from Russia after the war of 1905), the Kurile Islands, Korea, the Liaodong Peninsula, Manchuria, the Ryukyu Islands (including Diaoyutai or Senkaku), and Taiwan.[8]

Imperialism and Racism

The intellectual rationale that facilitated the West's subjugation and colonization of other peoples was predicated on the notion of race, in particular the belief in the innate superiority of the Caucasian race. Some maintain that without racism as its "base logic," imperialism would never have worked. Simply put, "imperialism was racism plus capitalism."[9]

Although anthropologists today recognize that the taxonomic construct of "race" is of dubious validity, in the past, they unquestioningly accepted races as fixed entities or types of humans, equivalent to animal subspecies. Each race was believed to be pure and distinct, possessing defining physical attributes that clustered together in a predictable fashion. Even then, the taxonomic scheme was riddled with problems in that the racial categories were neither pure nor distinct; the contents in each racial basket would spill over the rims into another. To illustrate, among the defining traits of the Mongolian race is the epicanthic eyefold that presumably characterizes all the peoples of Northeast Asia. (Other defining attributes are yellow skin, wide flat cheekbones, straight black hair, sparse body hair, and shovel-shaped incisor teeth.) But while it is true that many Northeast Asians indeed have epicanthic folds, some do not. At the same time, there are non-Asians (such as the Bushmen of southern Africa) who do have the folds. In identifying epicanthic folds as a distinctively Mongolian racial attribute, Western taxonomists had mistaken what is, at most, a central or modal trait for a defining attribute. Yet another problem is that the defining characteristics do not cluster together, as there are no traits that are inherently, inevitably associated with one another. While morphological features vary from region to region, they do so independently, not in packaged sets. It turns out that the vast majority of human genetic variation occurs *within* races, rather than *between* them. A study by Harvard geneticist Richard Lewontin found that only some 6 percent of human genetic variation can be accounted for by race.[10]

Compounding the already dubious taxonomic validity of race was the contamination of the classificatory enterprise by normative and subjective criteria. That contamination originated from the work of Johann Friedrich Blumenbach (1752–1840), a German anatomist and naturalist. Blumenbach divided all humans, by geography and appearance, into five groups—Caucasians, Mongolians, Ethiopians, (native) Americans, Malays—and arranged them in a hierarchy of worth based upon their perceived beauty. Caucasians were at the apex of that hierarchy because Blumenbach judged them to be the most beautiful and most probably the first humans. In effect, Blumenbach changed "the geometry of human order"—what should properly be a classification governed by strictly objective physical criteria—into a system based on putative worth. Regrettably, his taxonomy became canonical, the most influential of all racial classifications, and the foundation of much that continues to influence and disturb us today.[11]

Blumenbach's subjective typology rapidly devolved into a moral taxonomy in which the white race alone was assumed to possess moral excellence.[12] As an example, in 1602 John Brereton maintained that no nation was as "fit" as England for being a colonial power.[13] Brereton's views reflected those of his fellow Britons who shared his belief that the "clearly superior ability, knowledge, and virtue" of the English made them deserving of the role of "hegemonic exploiter" over the peoples and natural resources of the globe.[14]

Moral superiority justified Europe's domination over the inferior races of the world. Speaking before the Ethnological Society of London in 1861, John Crawfurd described the native aborigines of Australia as "the feeblest ... hordes of black, ill-formed, unseemly, naked savages," while in Africa, "the races of man . . . correspond with the disadvantages of its physical geography."[15] There, according to George Gliddon, were "some of the most inferior types of Men."[16] Sir Rudolph Slatin described "the nigger" as "a lazy beast" who must be compelled with a stick to work. Popular belief was that Africans remained childlike because their "obsession with sex" had arrested their mental development.[17] As late as 1914, Ellsworth Huntington still portrayed the "morally degraded" tropical races as sexually indulgent, drunken, and lacking in will power and industry.[18] Griffith Taylor concluded that racial evolution had left the Negro "far behind."[19]

Judgments about the moral and cognitive retardation of nonwhite peoples had direct implications for their future in a new imperialist world economy. British ambassador James Bryce proposed in 1892 that, excepting the Chinese who had a native civilization, the "tropical peoples" were not "fitted to play any part in history . . . in any way, save as producers by physical labour of material wealth." Only under the "tutelage" of Western colonial powers could they hope to develop toward any higher condition.[20]

The Impact of Imperialism

While the non-Western peoples no doubt derived benefits from being colonized, including their development toward a "higher condition" of culture and civilization, they did so at considerable costs, one of which was loss of life. In the Americas, as an example, an immediate effect of colonization was that the native population fell catastrophically from exposure to foreign diseases, abuse, and massacre by Spanish and English settlers.[21]

More than their physical extermination, colonization also led to the political extinction—the loss of sovereignty, independence, and self-determination—of whole communities. The colonized were reduced to subjects, without the rights of modern citizens. Kept away from the exercise of political power, neither voting nor bearing the responsibility for community affairs, the colonized forgot "how to participate actively in history."[22] In effect, colonialism made children out of entire peoples.

Loss of political sovereignty enabled the systematic exploitation of the native economy. The colony became a source of cheap labor and raw materials, as well as a market for Europe's excess commodities. Flooded by Western manufactured goods that were cheaper and of better quality than those produced by traditional cottage industries, the native economy became impaired or collapsed altogether. Although the Europeans funneled commercial and industrial investments into the colonies, the investments were calculated more to serve the interests of the imperial power than those of the natives.

Then there are the more intangible effects of imperialism that had a truly insidious effect on the psychology of the colonized. Colonization was more than the political extermination of a society, it also involved the colonization of its indigenous culture. As Frantz Fanon maintained, "the systematic destruction of a culture is necessary for colonialism to prevail."[23] Under the sustained impact of colonialism, the native culture begins to atrophy, degenerating into a "closed culture" that is stunted, incapable of organic growth and of "flowering from its own traditional base."[24] Prevented from natural development, the colony can only deify and ape the culture of its master.

The destruction of the native culture is effected through the agents of socialization and communication, beginning with the schools. The native is taught the language of the colonial power rather than his own. All the important affairs of the colony are conducted in that foreign tongue, including the inscriptions on street, railroad station, and highway signs—all of which make "the colonized feel like a foreigner in his own country."[25]

Language becomes one of the yardsticks by which social status is calibrated. It was said that "a native who can speak eloquent French is thought to be more sophisticated than the native who can speak only Creole, the patois."[26] In the linguistic conflict that takes place within the native, it is the mother tongue that is crushed and devalued. Hoping to gain admission into the elite world of the colonial master, the native discards his "infirm" language at incalculable costs to his self esteem—for the mother tongue is "that which is sustained by his feelings, emotions and dreams, that in which his tenderness and wonder are expressed . . . that which holds the greatest emotional impact."[27] By devaluing the mother language, the colonized devalues herself. Nor will the native, by abandoning her native language, be able to realize her vainglorious ambition of being admitted into the colony's elite stratum. Not only is it difficult for her to acquire proficiency in an alien tongue, even if she were successful, mastery of language alone is no guarantee for full admission into the elite "when a basis for discrimination is color differentiation."[28]

There is another problem still: Achieving proficiency in the master's language is also to accept his worldview as more valid than one's own.[29] More insidious than the adoption of the colonizer's language is the concomitant assimilation of that language's substantive contents: the culture, values, and historical memories of the oppressor. Thus, we have the curious phenomenon of brown and yellow children in Africa and Asia who merrily sing songs of "silverbells and cockleshells in the English country garden," and read with silent rapture of freshly baked hot cross buns and meadows of heather in the Scottish highlands—all of which they are unlikely ever to see, taste, smell, or touch. In the words of Albert Memmi:[30]

> The memory which is assigned him is certainly not that of his people. The history which is taught him is not his own. . . . The books talk to him of a world which in no way reminds him of his own; the little boy is called Toto and the little girl, Marie; and on winter evenings Marie and Toto walk home along snow-covered paths, stopping in front of a chestnut vendor.

In effect, at the critical point in an individual's development, rather than prepare the native to form an authentic identity, the colonial educational system creates an ersatz self, a "void."[31] By depicting Westerners as the normative ideal, the colonial schools and mass media impart to the natives "a permanent duality,"[32] a "double consciousness"—"the sense of always looking at one's self through the eyes of others, of measuring one's soul by the tape of a world that looks on in amused contempt and pity."[33] As an example, the double consciousness for Africans is that of "black skin, white mask." For all colonized peoples, their double consciousness can lead to psychological disorders.[34]

What began as a feeling of cultural and linguistic inadequacy is generalized into a pervasive sense of racial inferiority. To be a white European is to be a member of the superior race. Caucasian physical attributes, especially those of the Nordic, become the embodiment of the aesthetic ideal: "A blonde woman, be she dull or anything else, appears superior to any brunette."[35] The native's own physiognomy suffers in comparison, transformed in her eyes into something unspeakably ugly and inferior. She grows to hate her very reflection in the mirror: the African's dark pigmentation, platyrrhine nose, and everted lips; the Asian's flat face and epicanthic eyefolds. The profound depths of that self-hatred account for its persistence in the contemporary world, despite the fact that the sun has long set on the West's colonial empires.[36] How else can one explain the nagging sense of inadequacy that still haunts the non-Western peoples of the world? Witness the enduring popularity of cosmetic surgery in Hong Kong, Japan, and other parts of Asia to alter facial features to better accord with "white" standards of beauty. Even the People's Republic of China, notwithstanding decades of proclamations by Chairman Mao that "the Chinese people had finally stood up," is not immune. When Deng Xiaoping's economic reforms opened the country to interaction with the West, Chinese women promptly sought to curl their hair, lift their nasal bridges, inflate their breasts with implants, and surgically excise their epicanthic eyefolds.

For some, the question of whether the colonized, if left alone, would have advanced at the same pace as other peoples "has no great significance."[37] It is possible that they might not, for we have no way of knowing. What is more important is that each society travels according to its own pace and along its own path—a course that is closed to a subjugated people. Along with the loss of political sovereignty and independence, European imperialism and colonialism also laid waste to native languages, cultures, and ways of life. Arguably, most damaging of all was that the non-Western peoples were imbued with an abiding sense of inferiority that continues to fuel an inchoate rage. As Nadel and Curtis so eloquently observed:[38]

> In the volatile area of race relations the expansion of Europe has had lasting repercussions. The smoldering resentment of non-white people throughout the world for having been instilled with a sense of inferiority based on pigmentation is part of the price white men must continue to pay for the ascendancy enjoyed by Western Europe. . . .

Western Imperialism in China

If Asia was thought to be the source of all wealth and power, China was "the primary target"[39] in Asia for imperialist penetration. The British, who followed the Portuguese and Dutch to China, were convinced that access to exotic Cathay, rumored to be the land of unicorns, would assure them great wealth and prestige, thereby confirming "the special place which God gave to the English nation."[40] Unlike the other non-Western countries that must borrow from Europe in order to purchase its manufactured goods, China was comparatively more developed and represented a potentially vast market. The difficulty in China was its government's "hostile attitude" to free trade—an opposition that would have to be overcome "by force and threats."[41]

European traders came to China with expectations of a highly advanced and prosperous civilization—expectations that were molded by Marco Polo's chronicle of a society far more sophisticated than that of fourteenth-century Europe. Those expectations were reinforced by later Jesuit reports of a secular polity governed wisely and well, without benefit of the

Church—accounts that were used by Enlightenment philosophers to buttress their case for the separation of Church and state in Europe.

Instead of an advanced civilization, what the traders found was quite different. By the time they reached China via a sea passage discovered by the Portuguese, Europe had experienced a revolution in science, technology, economics, and philosophy. From the Industrial Revolution came capitalism and a level of prosperity unprecedented in human history. At the same time, West Europe was in a philosophical and political ferment of new ideas and values concerning the human capacity for reason, the sanctity of the individual, the rule of law, and democratic self-government. Compared to the new Europe, China, caught in the aspic of its static history, seemed "oddly puerile" and "no more than the shadow of a shade." Instead of awe and respect, Western traders came to regard all things Chinese with "amused contempt."[42]

Their contempt was abetted by racist popular literature, such as the stories of W. H. G. Kingston, which depicted Chinese pirates in the Yellow Sea as having "hideous" faces, flat noses, grinning mouths, and "queer twisted eyes."[43] Reports by Western missionaries in China were no better, one of which attributed the "principal difficulty" in introducing the gospel to the Chinese to their debased character. Lamenting that the "hardness of a Chinese heart is great" because a "lying spirit is implanted and cherished in them from their childhood," the writer concluded that China was nothing less than "the empire of the prince of darkness."[44] A book by American missionary A. H. Smith, who based his claim to expertise on 22 years of residence in China, described Chinese as having a disregard for time and accuracy, a talent for misunderstanding and indirection, "flexible inflexibility," and an absence of public spirit. They knew how to struggle for an existence and nothing else; their lives consisted of only "two compartments, a stomach and a cash-bag." Even the Chinese language was impaired in that it "cannot be made to convey human thought" but only "invites to intellectual turbidity," much as "the incandescent heats of summer gently woo to afternoon repose." Admitting that he had "extreme difficulty" in comprehending their language, Smith solipsistically concluded that neither could the Chinese. Unable to understand each other's incoherent blabber, Chinese people communicated by sheer happenstance: "It is remarkable what expert guessers long practice has made most Chinese. . . ." They lived as frogs in a well, "to which even the heavens appear only as a strip of darkness."[45] Evidently, Smith's long residence in China was entirely misspent, as he succeeded in learning nothing.

The Clash of Civilizations

It is difficult to imagine two civilizations more dissimilar than those of China and the West. Continental in proportion, agrarian China was insular and self-sufficient; industrial Western Europe was driven to export and championed free trade. Chinese culture deified authority and the group; Western civilization was rooted in individualism. Europeans were Judeo-Christians who regarded the Chinese, with their ancestor worship, as benighted pagans. Westerners believed in the rule of law, due process, and innocence until proven guilty; Chinese long opted for rule by Confucian ethics, in which the courts were a last recourse where the accused was presumed to be guilty until proven innocent. Although East and West were each other's complete opposite, both were great and proud civilizations. The Chinese, an ancient people with a 5,000-year history, still thought they were the center of the world; whereas Westerners, with a civilization that reached back to Greco-Roman antiquity, found only confirmation of their superiority in their excursions across the globe. It does not take the gifts of a prophet to predict that contact between two such disparate civilizations could only lead to deadly conflict. Indeed, a British trader, writing in 1833 on the miserable trade conditions in China, ominously concluded that "war with the Chinese cannot be doubted."[46]

Eager to engage in productive trade relations with China, Europeans found only disinterest. In 1655, the Dutch were the first to attempt a diplomatic solution to the impasse when they dispatched an emissary to the Qing court to request that a port be opened to trade. Although the mission was initially a failure, in 1685 Emperor Kangxi (1662–1722) opened the southern port of Guangzhou (Canton) to trade, in what he thought to be a magnanimous gesture. Mindful of the enormous differences in culture between China and the "barbarians" and wary of the potentially disruptive effect that foreigners and their ideas could have on the Middle Kingdom, he imposed restrictions on that trade. Foreign merchants were confined to a compound—a virtual ghetto—outside of the city walls, where they would live and conduct business. Even thus confined, the traders could reside in the compound for only half of the year, departing in autumn to pass the winter on Macao, and returning to Guangzhou with the arrival of spring. More than that, foreign women were forbidden in the ghetto—a prohibition that effectively consigned the traders to a monkish existence. Westerners were proscribed from traveling in China and mingling with the natives, who were barred from giving language instruction to the "foreign devils." The traders' only contact was with a monopolistic group of Chinese merchants, the Thirteen Hongs, who were appointed by the emperor to conduct all foreign business, including official transactions of tariff collection and the receipt of complaints and petitions.

As time passed and the volume of trade grew, the Westerners increasingly chafed at the trade restrictions. Most of them could do little but submit to the Chinese, except the British, "the proudest, stiffest" of all the Westerners and, by then, the most powerful nation in the world, whose navy ruled the seas. More and more, they found the restrictions imposed at Guangzhou "tiresome, insulting, and stultifying."[47]

The China trade had become important for both British consumers and their government. Until 1830, when India began the commercial cultivation of tea, tea could be bought only from China. In 1785, some 15 million pounds of Chinese tea a year were purchased by the British East India Company; tax on that tea accounted for a tenth of the British government's total revenue. In 1795, and again in 1816, envoys were sent from London to prevail upon the Chinese emperor to improve trade conditions by lifting the restrictions in favor of a modern commercial treaty. Both missions, like the earlier Dutch effort, returned empty handed. To add fuel to fire, the emperor treated the representatives of the British monarch with customary imperiousness, sublimely oblivious that he was dealing with a new breed of "barbarians." That arrogance was only too evident in the letter to King George III from Emperor Qianlong (1736–1795), in response to the Macartney mission of 1795:[48]

> My capital is the hub and centre about which all quarters of the globe revolve. . . . Our Celestial Empire possesses all things in prolific abundance . . . [and has] no need to import the manufactures of outside barbarians. . . . But as the tea, silk and porcelain which the Celestial Empire produces, are absolute necessities to . . . yourselves, we have permitted, as a signal mark of favour, that foreign *hongs* should be established at Canton, so that . . . your country thus participate in our beneficence.

What the Chinese did not realize was that Britain had the power to force them into making trade concessions. But before force could be resorted to, a *casus belli* had to be found.[49] That pretext was opium.

The Opium War (1840–1842)

Until the Macartney mission, the balance of trade between Britain and China had been overwhelmingly in the latter's favor. Beginning in 1800, however, a new commodity increasingly tilted the balance to Britain's advantage. By that time, the British East India Company secured a monopoly on the production of opium from the poppy fields in the northern part of British colonial India. The opium would be sold at auctions to British and other Western merchants, who, in turn, smuggled it into China.[50]

Opium was banned by the Chinese government as early as 1729 when a law forbade its sale and made the operating of opium dens punishable by strangulation. Despite that prohibition, which was followed by some 16 imperial edicts and as many provincial edicts against the smoking, importation, or sale of opium,[51] Western traders continued to smuggle it into China in increasing quantities. To illustrate, in 1750, about 200 chests[52] of opium a year were brought into China mainly for medicinal purposes; by 1821, the contraband had increased to 5,000 chests annually. In 1804, enough opium entered China so that trade between Europe and China began to shift in favor of the former. In 1830, the opium trade had become "probably the largest commerce of its time in any single commodity, anywhere in the world."[53] By 1835, one out of every 150 Chinese, totaling over two million, were addicted, the majority of whom were from the political, economic, and military elite. On the eve of the Opium War in 1839, the amount of opium entering China had exploded to 40,000 chests a year—an increase of 800 percent in just 18 years. The opium was paid for with 100 million ounces of silver, which constituted one-fifth of the total amount of silver in circulation in China.[54] The hemorrhage of silver, in turn, led to the debasement of China's domestic copper currency, which was pegged to silver. The devaluation of domestic currency, in turn, led to steep rises in land taxes and the increasing emiseration of the Chinese peasantry.

Motivated by greed, Westerners rationalized their complicity in the illicit trade by pointing to the corrupt Chinese provincial and local officials who not only consumed the opiate but actively participated in its smuggling. As expressed by an agent of the British Bible Society at the time:[55]

> Opium . . . has this one good . . . inasmuch as it shows of what stuff a mandarin is made. . . . Here are the men who promulgate the law, that opium shall not be imported; here are the men who break the law . . . by doing the very deed themselves . . . in the broad eye of daylight . . . in boats belonging to the government. . . . [T]he Chinese mandarins are the last men in the world to be entrusted with any public function. . . .

Repeated attempts by the central government to enforce its prohibition met with scant success. As an example, in 1821, Chinese opium dealers were threatened with fines, imprisonment, and exile; Western traders had their tea trade suspended for two months. In 1839, the emperor renewed the effort by appointing Lin Cexu, a righteous mandarin with no experience dealing with foreigners, to be imperial commissioner in charge of putting an end to the illicit trade. Arriving in Guangzhou with armed soldiers, Commissioner Lin, upon the refusal of the British to surrender their opium, installed a blockade on the foreign compound and confiscated more than 20,000 chests of opium valued at over 10 million silver dollars. The opium was mixed with quicklime, salt, and water, and flushed into the sea. The British, along with the other Western traders, retreated to their refuge on Macao and sent word to London for help.

Help came the following year in June, when a British battle fleet arrived at the mouth of the Canton River. Thus began the Opium War, which ended two years later with China's defeat and Commissioner Lin's recall and exile to Ili. On August 29, 1842, the Qing dynasty signed what became the first of a series of "unequal treaties" that China signed under duress because of war or the threat of war. The Treaty of Nanjing (Nanking) between China and Britain ceded Hong Kong (specifically Victoria Island) to Britain in perpetuity; opened Xiamen (Amoy), Fuzhou, Ningbo, and Shanghai to foreign trade; and abolished the Hong system, freeing British merchants to deal directly with their Chinese counterparts. The Treaty of Nanjing also required that the Chinese pay the British an indemnity of 21 million silver dollars—which led Emperor Daoguang (1821–1850) in 1838 to offer political promotions for sale to the highest bidder. A fourth-class mandarin could be bought for 30,000 taels of silver. In 1845, the treaty was amended to enable the British to rent, in perpetuity, a plot of land in Shanghai for foreign settlements.

Thereafter, the political integrity of China began to unravel. In 1844, without fighting a war, treaties were concluded with the United States and France that had effects more far-reaching than the Treaty of Nanjing. The Treaty of Wangxia with the United States introduced the most-favored-nation clause and the right of extraterritoriality, both of which had devastating impact on China's well-being and sovereignty. The most-favored-nation clause extended all bilateral treaties between China and a foreign country to all other interested powers, thereby enabling the United States to obtain all the benefits that Britain had derived from the Treaty of Nanjing (excepting Hong Kong and the indemnity). The right of extraterritoriality, for its part, gave foreigners in China immunity from its laws and criminal justice system. Foreigners suspected of having committed crimes in China would be handed over to their consuls for trial in accordance with their own country's laws—which was rarely followed through in practice. More than that, the right of extraterritoriality was not mutual: Chinese immigrants in Western countries enjoyed no reciprocal legal immunity.

France followed the United States by concluding the Treaty of Huangpu, which promptly invoked the most-favored-nation principle, thereby gaining for France every erstwhile concession obtained by Britain and the United States. Additionally, the Chinese agreed to lift their ban on Christianity, opening China to proselytization by French and other Western missionaries.

The Second Anglo-Chinese War (1857–1860)

After Britain's triumph in the Opium War, its manufacturers expected that they would gain full access to China's enormous market. As Sir Henry Pottinger put it to cotton traders at Manchester, the war "opened up a new world . . . so vast that all the mills in Lancashire could not make stocking stuff sufficient for one of its provinces."[56] To their disappointment, however, Chinese continued to wear their homespun cotton, purchasing the same quantity of British cotton in 1850 as in 1843. Making matters worse was that, during the same period, Chinese silk exports to Britain actually increased fivefold! Silver was no longer bleeding out of China, and the balance of trade swung again in its favor. As an example, in 1857, the British incurred a deficit of 4.5 million pounds in their China trade, with 15 million pounds of imported Chinese tea and silk, but exported only 10.5 million pounds' worth of opium, raw Indian cotton, and assorted British manufactured products. All of which led the Manchester Chamber of Commerce in 1854 to propose to the Foreign Secretary that British traders must gain access to China's interior so as to increase cotton sales. That, in turn, required that China's internal custom duties, the *likin,* be abolished. To do all that, the Chamber concluded, "it would be necessary to conquer and take possession of the entire country."[57]

Adding to Britain's discontent was the failure on the part of the Chinese government to enforce its treaty commitments. Instead, the Chinese authorities had been deliberately elusive, avoiding diplomatic contact with Westerners and contriving ways to make the treaties unenforceable. A French diplomat, in 1854, wryly observed that, "With all their guns, the English cannot get their treaties executed and are worse off at Canton today than before the war."[58]

The Arrow Incident[59] of October 8, 1856 was the immediate provocation for a second Anglo-Chinese War. Sixteen British warships were brought into Guangzhou from Hong Kong, joined by the French, who were unhappy with China's arrest and decapitation of a French priest, Father Chapdelaine. In May 1858, the Anglo-French forces invaded Tianjin. By October, Beijing was occupied and the Imperial Summer Palace burnt and looted.[60] The emperor had long fled to Jehol, leaving the defense of the palace's 80 square miles of park and buildings to 480 hapless eunuchs.

The Treaty of Tianjin that concluded the war in 1860 mandated Chinese payment of 4 million silver dollars in indemnity. Diplomatic relations between the two countries were put on terms of equality;[61] henceforth, a British envoy would reside in the capital instead of a treaty port. Kowloon, the tip of the peninsula across the Hong Kong harbor from Victoria Island, was given to Britain. (In 1897, an amendment to the Treaty of Tianjin leased the rest of the peninsula, New Territories, to London for a period of 99 years. It was that lease that expired on July 1, 1997, when Britain returned all of Hong Kong—comprising Victoria Island, Kowloon, and the New Territories—to China.) Cities along the Yangzi River up to Hankou were opened to foreign trade, thereby exposing China's heartland to foreign penetration. France obtained the right to have its missionaries travel within China. Foreign warships would be permitted in all treaty ports—which made possible the Great Powers' subsequent resort to gunboat diplomacy. As if all this were not enough, Westerners would take over the administration of China's maritime customs, inflicting a mortal blow to its sovereignty.

Through the defeat of China in a second war, British manufacturers finally realized their commercial objectives. By 1864, the British nearly monopolized all foreign trade in China, accounting for seven-eighths of that commerce. British cotton exports to China increased by almost 400 percent between 1856 and 1880, from 113 to 448 million yards. Opium exports from British India, most of which went to China, rose by 180 percent from 58,681 chests in 1859 to 105,508 chests by 1879.[62]

China's Descent into Disarray

With each defeat, the European powers exacted more concessions from an increasingly inert dynasty. More and more, China was exposed to foreign trade and missionary activities, with deleterious consequences. The opening of coastal ports to foreign trade rendered obsolete the traditional inland route from the Yangzi valley to Guangzhou—and with it, the ancient livelihood of Chinese porters. At the same time, foreign imports increasingly displaced native workers engaged in the production of cotton, ironworks, and coastal junks. The enormous sums of war indemnities exacted on the Chinese government resulted in increased taxation on the commonfolk. Added to all that was the occurrence in the 1840s of a series of natural disasters, the traditional harbingers of a dynasty's loss of the mandate of heaven. Repeated breaks in the dikes of the Yellow River, the flooding of the lower Yangzi River, drought, storms, and infestation devastated crops and took millions of lives. In the midst of the chaos, all that was needed was a charismatic leader who could articulate popular discontent into a call to revolution.

The Taiping Rebellion

That individual was Hong Xiuquan, a frustrated aspirant to the mandarin elite who had twice failed at the imperial civil service examination. Hong devised an ideology that combined elements of traditional dynastic uprisings with radical new ideas. Under the veneer of a banal and superficial Christianity was an eclectic mix of anti-Manchu nationalism, an incipient economic developmental plan, communism, asceticism, gender and class egalitarianism, and a political system of elected officials led by an aristocratic elite with Hong, the Heavenly Prince, at its pinnacle.

With the objective of creating a Heavenly Kingdom of Peace *(Taiping tianguo)* on earth, the Taiping Rebellion erupted in 1850. The rebels were composed of poverty-stricken peasants, jobless coolie porters, opium smugglers, pirates, and secret society members who were anti-Manchu Ming loyalists. Beginning in the mountains of Guangxi, the rebels advanced rapidly northward. Three years later, they declared the installation of a new kingdom at Nanjing. For fourteen years, the greatest revolution of the nineteenth century engulfed half of China's provinces, laid waste to 600 cities, and took 20 million lives. Only with the greatest effort was the rebellion suppressed and the dynasty preserved. Departing from its practice of having only ethnic Manchus as soldiers, the dynasty permitted Han Chinese governors to form provincial armies. Those armies, along with a small force of Western mercenaries, finally ended the uprising—with some assistance from the Taipings' own dissolution into internal rivalry and corruption.

The suppression of the Taipings gave the moribund dynasty a new lease on life and convinced the dynasty under Emperor Tongzhi (1862–1874) to reform. From 1864 to 1890, the Tongzhi Restoration attempted to modernize China by retaining "Chinese learning as the fundamental structure" while adapting "Western learning for practical use." Although the pace of reform slackened after the first decade, the Restoration could claim some modest but nonetheless significant achievements. They included the establishment in 1867 of a naval shipyard in Fuzhou and a naval academy in Tianjin in 1885; military arsenals staffed by foreign engineers and mechanics in Tianjin, Jiangnan, Nanjing, and Shanghai; an engineering school in Shanghai; a coal mine in 1878; the creation of the Beiyang naval fleet in 1888; an iron foundry in 1890; Chinese translations of Western books on science, technology, and law, including Euclid's 15-volume *Elements of Geometry*; foreign-language schools, including one in Beijing to train interpreters; diplomatic missions to foreign countries; and the dispatch of army officers to study in Germany, as well as other students to Western countries.

In the end, however, the reforms were inadequate to surmount the depths of China's backwardness. To begin with, the reforms should have begun sooner. As Teng and Fairbank explained, the country being vast and slow to change, "the rulers of China had wasted twenty years in refusing to face the problems created by Western contact."[63] Even when the reforms were initiated, their pace was slow and their scope circumscribed. As an example, in 1897, some 35 years after China's first school to study Western learning was established, its student body numbered only 120.[64] In the judgment of some, "China's slowness in self-strengthening was due in part to the fact that the officials concerned were more interested in profit to themselves than in progress for their country." Other reasons included the anti-foreign conservatism of the Chinese educated class and court officials who opposed every proposal at Westernization.[65] The ultimate failure of the reform movement to modernize and industrialize China became painfully evident in the Sino-Japanese War of 1894–1895.

The Beginning of Japanese Imperialism

Like China, Japan also suffered humiliation at the hands of Western imperialist powers, beginning in 1854 when its Tokugawa government capitulated to U.S. Admiral Matthew Perry's peremptory demand that Japan open itself to interaction with the West. Until then, for some 200 years, Tokugawa Japan was in a self-imposed cocoon of *sakoku*—that is, isolation from the rest of the world. Like China, Japan had been defeated by the West: the Satsuma clan by the British navy in 1862; the Choshu clan by the

United States, Britain, France, and Holland in 1864. Like China, Japan had been subjected to the indignities of unequal treaties.[66]

Unlike China, however, Japan quickly rallied itself to meet the challenge, first, by replacing the ineffective Tokugawa regime, followed by a program of rapid industrialization. In 1867, an alliance of southwestern clans overthrew the Tokugawa shogunate and installed young Emperor Meiji as the charismatic figurehead of a new nation. The feudal system that had existed for 700 years was replaced by an authoritarian centralized state, the traditional samurai warriors by a modern conscript army. Meiji Japan molded feudal loyalties into an emperor-worshiping patriotic nationalism—all for the purpose of industrialization. In a matter of two to three decades, Japan was transformed into Asia's first and only industrial power, with dreams of empire.

Korea became the first target of Japan's imperialist ambition—but China stood in the way. Korea was a vassal of China, a relationship in which the former acceded to the latter's will, especially over matters of foreign policy, in exchange for Chinese protection of the Korean monarch from external invaders and internal unrest. In 1876, China agreed in a treaty with Japan that Korea would be an independent state no longer under Chinese suzerainty. That treaty was put to the test in January 1894, when the Qing dynasty, responding to an appeal for help by the Korean monarch, dispatched 3,000 soldiers to suppress a rebellion by the Tonghak, a Korean secret society. Japan reacted to China's action with a force of 10,000 and, on August 1, 1894, declared war against China.

To China's utter dismay and humiliation, the Imperial Japanese army quickly overran the Chinese forces, even the vaunted Beiyang naval fleet. The Sino-Japanese War ended in April 1895 with the Treaty of Shimonoseki, which declared Korea's independence (a condition that proved to be short-lived); required that China pay Japan an indemnity of 200 million silver dollars; opened four inland cities, including Chongqing (Chungking), to foreign trade; and ceded to Japan, in perpetuity, Taiwan (Formosa), Penghu (Pescadore Islands), and the Liaodong Peninsula in Chinese Manchuria.

It was one thing for China to be defeated in the Opium War by the greatest power in the world. It was quite another matter for China to be overcome by its small neighbor across the sea—the same Japan that once looked to China as its mentor, whose inhabitants Chinese had traditionally dismissed as the "dwarfs to the east." Defeat in the Sino-Japanese War not only humiliated the Chinese, it thoroughly exposed to the world the hollowness of the once mighty Middle Kingdom. More damaging still were the reverberations that rippled from the defeat.

The Scramble for Concessions

The significance of the 1894 Sino-Japanese War transcended the defeat of China—it signaled the end of the great Chinese Empire. China lost not only Korea but all its other tributary states *(fanshu)* as well, which promptly became the targets of acquisition by the imperialist powers.[67]

There were other reverberations still. By this time, the Qing dynasty was bankrupt—its treasury depleted by wars and indemnities, internal rebellions,[68] and efforts at reform. For its indemnity to Japan, the dynasty turned to borrowing from the Western powers: from France and Russia a combined loan of 400 million francs; from Britain, two loans totaling 20 million pounds; and from Germany, two loans totaling 17 million pounds. In return for the loans, each lender obtained special concessions from a supine China. Between 1895 to 1898, the Western powers carved out their respective "spheres of influence": areas in China that were proto-colonies in intention and effect, in which the lending country enjoyed exclusive economic rights and privileges, including those of trade, mining, and railroad construction. France obtained Yunnan Province as a sphere, as well as a 99-year lease of Guangzhouwan (harbor) in southern Guangdong; northern Manchuria became Russia's sphere of influence through the extension of the trans-Siberian railroad to Vladivostok (Haisanwei) and a 25-year lease of Port Arthur (Luda or Dairen) and Dairen Bay; Germany acquired a 99-year lease over Shandong peninsula;[69] and Britain obtained as its sphere the lower Yangzi River area, as well as a 99-year lease of the New Territories.

Were it not for the diplomatic initiative of the United States—its proposal in 1899–1900 to the Great Powers to maintain an "open door" to China by preserving its "territorial and administrative integrity"—China would probably have been partitioned among the colonial powers like a lamb before the slaughter. A Chinese official at the time described the imperialist powers as "glaring at China like tigers," seeking "to find a plump spot to bite into us."[70] The U.S. Open Door policy succeeded in convincing the Great Powers in China to refrain from actual colonization, so that China was saved from political extinction. Aside from that, little else that was good came from the Open Door initiative. Once again, the moribund Qing dynasty was preserved, too weak either to reform itself or resist imperialist predations.

Aborted Reform and the Boxer Rebellion

The 1894 Sino-Japanese War was a turning point: From there, China rapidly descended into disarray. In 1898, a last-gasp effort at reform by constitutional monarchists around young Emperor Guangxu (born in 1871, he reigned from 1875 to his death in 1908) was sabotaged by the aged Dowager Empress Cixi and court conservatives. As it turned out, the aborted Hundred Days' Reform was China's last chance at peaceful change.

Though not an actual colony, China had become instead a "hypo-colony": a country that suffered from all the ills and disabilities of colonialism without being formally colonized. By the beginning of the twentieth century, not only had China lost all its vassal states, it had ceded to the various imperialist powers Macao, Hong Kong, Taiwan, and the Penghu Islands; leased off Kowloon, New Territories, Jiazhou Bay, Lushun, Dalian, Weihaiwei, and Guangzhou Bay; opened 82 coastal and inland ports to foreign trade; and marked off areas in 16 cities as concessions. Through their spheres of influence, the Great Powers in China enjoyed all the privileges and perquisites of colonizers without any of the attendant obligations and responsibilities, setting up instead "a many-tiered structure of exploitation to fleece the Chinese people."[71]

As expressed by Zeng Guofan in 1867: "Since the hostilities, the Chinese people have been for a long time in deep suffering, as if immersed in water or fire." The treaty ports along the coast and the Yangzi River had made their livelihood more and more difficult. "The common people are impoverished, have no one to appeal to, and are as oppressed as if they were hanging upside down."[72] As V. G. Kiernan put it, "China's misery was great," and although some of it had been self-inflicted, Western imperialism significantly contributed to the fact that far more Chinese than ever before in history were struggling for bare existence. To assuage themselves of complicity in China's emiseration, Westerners advanced the curious notion that the Chinese were a unique people impervious to pain. Just as "Anglers like to suppose that fish have no feelings," Westerners managed to convince themselves that Chinese people's physical sensation was "mercifully blunted" because they had been "schooled by aeons of suffering,"[73] their "absence of nerves" accounting for their indifference to comfort and convenience.[74]

Anticipated as early as 1867 by Zeng, who predicted that "millions of the common people of China when pushed to extremity would think of revolt and would regard [foreigners] as enemies,"[75] the emiseration of the

Chinese masses exploded in 1900 in xenophobic violence against Western-ers, particularly missionaries and their Chinese converts. Originating in Shandong Province, the Boxer Rebellion rapidly advanced upon Beijing, setting fire to churches and the British legation, and killing Christians and foreign diplomats. The Great Powers retaliated with an allied force that eventually suppressed the uprising. Beijing was sacked and a severely puni-tive settlement forced upon the Qing government. The Boxer Protocol of September 1901 demanded China's apology and expiation, banned the im-portation of arms and ammunition into China for five years, razed all forts from Beijing to the coast, and required that China pay an indemnity of 67 million pounds over a period of 39 years. The amortization of the indem-nity and its accrued interest came to 20 million pounds a year. Until the in-demnity was fully paid, the Powers would hold as collateral China's mar-itime and internal customs, together with the revenue generated from its salt tax. The Qing government sought recourse to usurious taxation, al-most quadrupling its revenue from 1901 to 1910. New taxes were piled on old under a variety of names, promoting corruption by provincial officials, who increased taxes at every level until they were ten or more times what the government itself had authorized.[76]

The Revolution of 1911 and Its Aftermath

Japan's defeat of China and the aborted Hundred Days' Reform made it clear to some of China's most enlightened intellectuals that unless drastic changes were undertaken, the very survival of their country was in peril. China's only hope lay in nothing less than the overthrow of the Qing dy-nasty and the thorough reform of the entire society.

Sun Yat-sen (1866–1925) was perhaps the most inspired of them. Born and raised in China, he had been educated, since the age of 13, in the West. In his childhood, Sun had witnessed his country's gradual disintegration under the pressure of Western imperialism. At the same time, however, he marveled at the West's science, appreciated the efficacy of its laws, and sought his country's salvation in the promise of economic growth and in-dustrial development. In 1894, Sun petitioned the Qing authorities for re-form, but was rebuffed. Losing all hope for peaceful change, he turned to revolution and established his first revolutionary organization, the Society to Revive China (Xingzhong hui), in Honolulu, with overseas Chinese ex-patriates his first supporters. Beginning in 1894, Sun's followers martyred themselves in a series of failed uprisings in China. In 1905, in Tokyo, Sun gathered Chinese students in Japan to form a successor organization, the Alliance Society (Tongmen hui).

Sun's followers' efforts eventually culminated in a revolution in 1911 that ended the rule of the Qing dynasty. A new government of the Republic of China was installed; an effort was made to introduce representative government. Beyond that, Sun enjoyed very little more in the way of success. He discovered that neither he nor the fledgling government commanded the authority and power to rule over the country. Without an army, the revolutionaries lacked the coercive means for credible power; lacking a national consensus on its ideological program, the new government could not wield effective authority. Instead, for at least a decade after 1915, China fragmented into warlordism, resembling less an integral country than an unruly assortment of local and regional units controlled by their respective strongmen.

Sun's death in 1925 precipitated the fracturing of his revolutionary Chinese Nationalist Party (Kuomintang or KMT), into contending factions. Chiang Kai-shek, the commander of the new KMT army, assigned himself the task begun by Sun of suppressing the warlords and unifying China. By 1928, through military defeat or political compromise, Chiang succeeded in uniting the warlords under the nominal leadership of the Nationalist regime. A year earlier, in 1927, his government managed to persuade the Great Powers to return the administration of maritime customs to the Chinese, thereby restoring some of China's lost sovereignty.

For a decade after 1928, the Nationalist government undertook the reconstruction and modernization of the Chinese economy. Efforts were made to stabilize and standardize the currency; a modern banking system was introduced; and the first efforts at the systematic promotion of industrialization were undertaken. Beginning in 1931 the agricultural system was reformed and succeeded in producing 182 million metric tons of principal food crops by 1937—a quantity not attained again until well after World War II. There were improvements in the varieties of rice, wheat, corn, and potatoes. Insecticides were made available to peasant farmers for the first time in Chinese history. In a number of provinces, experimental stations, demonstration farms, and educational extension systems were introduced. Agricultural machinery and parts were imported, and the total amount devoted to those acquisitions grew from about half a million Chinese dollars between 1932 to 1934 to over a million Chinese dollars in 1936.

At the same time, progress was made in the development of industries and the infrastructure. Between 1928 and 1936, the availability of roads and track doubled, with domestic capital underwriting the construction of 7,995 kilometers of railway. Between 1926 and 1936, China sustained a compounded industrial growth rate of 8.3 percent per annum—during a period when the major economies of the world languished in Depression, with the general indices of production in the United States, France, and Germany falling by about 50 percent. In the judgment of many experts, by 1936, the economy of Nationalist China was on the threshold of self-sustained "takeoff."[77]

Japan's Invasion of China

Japanese aggression ultimately thwarted the Nationalist regime's efforts at modernization and development. That aggression began in 1931 when the Japanese Kwantung Army occupied Manchuria, a move that was conceived to be the beginning of what was disingenuously referred to as a "Greater East Asia Co-Prosperity Sphere" that would ultimately encompass not just Japan, Korea, and Manchuria but all of China, Mongolia, Nepal, Vietnam, Thailand, Burma, the Philippines, Malaya, Indonesia, the Andaman Islands, India, New Zealand, and Australia.[78] To put a veneer of legitimacy over its occupation of Manchuria, Japan installed deposed Qing Emperor Puyi as the puppet ruler over the ostensibly independent kingdom of Manchukuo. In 1935, Japan occupied parts of Chahar and Hobei. Two years later, in 1937, a full-scale invasion of China began. In rapid succession, the vital regions of China from the industrialized northeast to the cities of Beijing, Tianjin, and Shanghai along the coast fell before the invading Japanese armies.

In December 1938, Japanese soldiers under the command of General Matsui Iwane took the Nationalist capital of Nanjing and began "an orgy of cruelty seldom if ever matched in world history." As recounted by Iris Chang in her pathbreaking book,[79]

> For months the streets of the city were heaped with corpses and reeked with the stench of rotting human flesh. . . . Tens of thousands of young men were . . . mowed down by machine guns, used for bayonet practice . . . and in decapitation contests, . . . or soaked with gasoline and burned alive. . . . An estimated 20,000–80,000 Chinese women were raped. Many soldiers went beyond rape to disembowel women, slice off their breasts, nail them alive to walls. Fathers were forced to rape their daughters, and sons their mothers. . . . Not only did live burials, castration, the carving of organs, and the roasting of

people become routine, but more diabolical tortures were practiced, such as hanging people by their tongues on iron hooks or burying people to their waists and watching them get torn apart by German shepherds.

By the time the mayhem was over, more than 260,000 Chinese civilians had been massacred. Some experts believe the figure to exceed 350,000, which would place the Rape of Nanjing in the ranks of the world's worst instances of barbarism. In a matter of a few weeks, the death toll in Nanjing exceeded the number of civilian casualties of some European countries for the entire duration of World War II. The figure in the case of Britain was 61,000; for France, 108,000; Belgium, 101,000; and the Netherlands, 242,000. More Chinese were killed in Nanjing than the Japanese death toll of 210,000 from America's atomic bombing of Hiroshima and Nagasaki.[80]

In all, in the eight years of China's War of Resistance (*Kangzhan*) against Japan from 1937 to 1945, Japanese war casualties (dead, missing, captured, and wounded) numbered some 400,000—one-fiftieth that of the Chinese.[81] By the time Japan surrendered to the Allies on August 10, 1945, more than 10 million Chinese civilians and soldiers had lost their lives—the equivalent of the entire population of Greece or Belgium. Forty million Chinese were rendered homeless.[82] Some estimates put the Chinese death toll at 20 million.[83]

More than the loss of lives, the War of Resistance also exacted incalculable economic costs. To begin with, the areas of Japanese occupation were precisely where China's modern industries were concentrated. Three provinces (Jiangsu, Zhejiang, and Anhui) and five cities (Shanghai, Wuhan, Wuxi, Guangzhou, and Tianjin) accounted for over 70 percent and 60 percent, respectively, of China's industrial plants. In 1937 in the city of Shanghai alone, some 2,270 factories were destroyed in three months of street battles between Chinese and Japanese forces, with losses totaling 800 million yuan.[84]

The economic costs incurred by China in the War of Resistance included the destruction of 300,000–400,000 kilometers of roads, 100,000 tons of ships, 52 percent of its farmland (600 *mou* out of a total arable acreage of 1.14 billion *mou*) and 34 percent of its oxen (8 million out of a national total of 23 million). The destruction of crops, draft animals, and farmland resulted in a precipitous decline in peasant income: Average farm income in Hobei province in 1941, for example, was only 44.7 percent of its prewar level. Altogether, the war affected 52 million peasant households and was responsible for farm losses totaling almost 6 billion yuan and industrial losses of more than 2 billion yuan. A study by the Military Affairs Academy of the People's Republic of China in 1985 put the total economic costs, including property losses and war expenditure, borne by China in its resistance against Japan at over U.S. $100 billion.[85]

There were other costs still. The War of Resistance also directly contributed to the demise and displacement of the Nationalist regime by the Chinese Communists. When the invading Japanese army took over Nanjing, the Nationalist government fled into the heartland to Chongqing to wage a sustained defensive war. Cut off from the coastal region that was its main source of revenue, the government continuously operated at a deficit. In 1937, its deficits were 37 percent of its expenses, increasing to 81 percent in 1941. To stay solvent, the government turned to its currency printing presses, the result of which was hyper-inflation that corroded public confidence and government legitimacy. By the time the war ended in 1945, the prices of goods had ballooned to 2,167 times the level in 1937. Government employees and others on fixed salary, such as school teachers, were especially affected, their real income in 1943 plummeting to only 20 percent that of 1937.[86]

In its remote wartime capital, Nationalist China sank into a black hole of insolvency and incompetence, corruption and delegitimacy, from which it was not to emerge. Even after World War II ended, instead of peace, the country disintegrated into civil war between the Nationalists and Communists. Abandoning elusive guerrilla tactics, the two sides took each other on in pitched battles. The Nationalist troops, already depleted by casualties totaling 3.12 million to the Japanese (compared to the Communist attrition of 15,000–45,000 dead and injured), were no match against the Red Army.[87] What did emerge from the cataclysm of civil war was a new China, the product of the revolutionary vision of Mao Zedong and the Chinese Communists.

In economist Cheng Chu-yuan's judgment, Japan's invasion of China was nothing less than a "holocaust" that retarded China's industrialization by at least half a century. Expressing the sentiments of many Chinese, Cheng vowed that although Japan "could be forgiven for its unspeakable crimes against China, that debt could never be forgotten." For if Japan had not invaded, and if Mao and his fellow Communists had not ascended to power, China's gross domestic product would have increased by 1.63 times between 1933 and 1953, so that its average annual per-capita income in 1985 would exceed U.S. $1,500—six times that of what the PRC attained.[88] Modern Chinese history would have been entirely different.

Notes

1. Mao Yuanyou, "Zhongguo bantu di xingcheng yu bianqian (Formation and Changes in the Map of China)," *Guofang (National Defense)*, Beijing, no. 3 (1994), p. 34.

2. Neil Smith and Anne Godlewska, "Introduction: Critical Histories of Geography," in Anne Godlewska and Neil Smith (eds.), *Geography and Empire* (Oxford: Blackwell, 1994), pp. 1, 7.

3. George H. Nadel and Perry Curtis, "Introduction," in Nadel and Curtis, *Imperialism and Colonialism* (New York: Macmillan, 1964), p. 1.

4. Thirty-five percent of the earth's surface (about 18 million square miles) was under the West's actual occupation and control. Grover Clark, *The Balance Sheet of Imperialism: Facts and Figures on Colonies* (New York: Columbia University Press, 1936), p. 5.

5. Ibid.

6. J. F. Horrabin, *An Atlas of Empire* (New York: Alfred A. Knopf, 1937).

7. Lesley B. Cormack, "The Fashioning of an Empire: Geography and the State in Elizabethan England," in Godlewska and Smith (eds.), *Geography and Empire*, p. 23.

8. Horrabin, *An Atlas of Empire*.

9. Tamar Y. Rothenberg, "Voyeurs of Imperialism: *The National Geographic Magazine* Before World War II," in Godlewska and Smith (eds.), *Geography and Empire*, p. 167.

10. James Shreeve, "Terms of Estrangement," *Discover* (November 1994), pp. 58, 60.

11. Stephen Jay Gould, "The Geometer of Race," *Discover* (November 1994), pp. 65–67.

12. David N. Livingstone, "Climate's Moral Economy: Science, Race and Place in Post-Darwinian British and American Geography," in Godlewska and Smith (eds.), *Geography and Empire*, p. 151.

13. John Brereton, *A Briefe and True Relation*, 1602, p. 15. As quoted in Cormack, "Fashioning of an Empire," p. 27.

14. Cormack, "Fashioning," p. 29.

15. As cited in Livingstone, "Climate's Moral Economy," p. 138.

16. George Gliddon, "The monogenists and the polygenists," 1857, p. 650, as quoted in ibid., p. 141.

17. V. G. Kiernan, *The Lords of Human Kind: Black Man, Yellow Man and White Man in An Age of Empire* (Boston: Little, Brown, 1969), p. 233.

18. Ellsworth Huntington, "The Adaptibility of the White Man," 1914, pp. 199, 211, as cited in Livingstone, "Climate's Moral Economy," p. 149.

19. Griffith Taylor, "Racial Geography," 1957, p. 454, as cited in Livingstone, "Climate's Moral Economy," p. 145.

20. James Bryce, "The migrations of the races," 1892, p. 420, as quoted in Livingstone, "Climate's Moral Economy," p. 140.

21. Kiernan, *Lords of Human Kind*, p. 10.

22. Albert Memmi, *The Colonizer and the Colonized* (New York: Orion, 1965), pp. 95, 96, 92.

23. See Chester J. Fontenot, Jr., *Frantz Fanon: Language as the God Gone Astray in the Flesh* (Lincoln, NE: University of Nebraska Press, 1979), p. 34.

24. Ibid., pp. 9, 35.

25. Memmi, *Colonizer and the Colonized*, p. 107.

26. Fontenot, *Frantz Fanon*, p. 47.

27. Memmi, *Colonizer and Colonized*, p. 107.

28. Fontenot, *Frantz Fanon*, p. 25.

29. Ibid.

30. Memmi, *Colonizer and Colonized*, p. 105.

31. Ibid., pp. 106, 97.

32. Ibid., p. 106.

33. W. E. B. Du Bois, *Souls of Black Folk* (New York: New American Library, 1969), p. 45.

34. Fontenot, *Frantz Fanon*, p. 19.

35. Memmi, *Colonizer and Colonized*, p. 120.

36. As late as 1987, blacks in the United States still suffered from the enduring effects of slavery and imperialism. Two studies showed that many black American children expressed a preference for white dolls, indicative of their lack of racial self-esteem. See Jamie Talan, "Studies Suggest Black Children Continue to Lack Self-Esteem," *The Seattle Times*, September 2, 1987, p. E5; and Itabari Njeri, "Shades of Black: Color-Consciousness Among Black Americans," *San Francisco Sunday Chronicle and Examiner*, May 8, 1988, p. 12 of "This World." For Asians, see the account by Xi Luo, "Buyishi zhongguoren weichi (Don't be ashamed for being Chinese)," *Guoji ribao (International Daily News)*, May 16, 1988, p. 19; and the interview with Asian American playwright David Henry Hwang in *U.S. News and World Report*, March 28, 1988, pp. 52–53.

37. Memmi, *Colonizer and Colonized*, pp. 112, 114.

38. Nadel and Curtis, *Imperialism and Colonialism*, p. 24.

39. Stewart C. Easton, *The Rise and Fall of Western Colonialism* (New York: Frederick A. Praeger, 1964), p. 11.

40. Cormack, "Fashioning of an Empire," p. 24.

41. Easton, *Rise and Fall of Western Colonialism*, p. 14.

42. Maurice Collis, *Foreign Mud: The Opium Imbroglio at Canton in the 1830's and the Anglo-Chinese War* (New York: W. W. Norton, 1968), pp. 178, 179.

43. W. H. G. Kingston, *The Three Midshipmen* (1873), chapter 28. As cited by Kiernan, *Lords of Human Kind*, p. 163.

44. Richard L. Walker (ed.), *China and the West: Cultural Collision Selected Documents* (New Haven: Yale University Far Eastern Publications, 1967), pp. 53, 54.

45. Arthur H. Smith, *Chinese Characteristics*, first published in Shanghai in 1890 (Edinburgh: Oliphant Anderson and Ferrier, 1900), pp. 5, 82–83, 88–89.

46. Walker, *China and the West,* p. 63.

47. Collis, *Foreign Mud*, pp. 225, 7.

48. Walker, *China and the West*, pp. 28–29.

49. Collis, *Foreign Mud*, p. 8.

50. American speculation in China's opium trade began in 1811. By 1817, American traders accounted for a tenth of that trade, increasing to a fifth of all opium entering Shanghai by 1858.

51. See Hsin-pao Chang, *Commissioner Lin and the Opium War* (New York: W. W. Norton, 1964), Appendix A: "Principal Opium Edicts, 1729–1839," pp. 219–221.

52. Each chest contained 40 opium balls, and each ball was "about the size of an apple dumpling." Jack Beeching, *The Chinese Opium Wars* (New York: Harcourt Brace Jovanovich, 1975), p. 26.

53. Ibid., p. 39.

54. N.A., *The Opium War* (Beijing: Foreign Languages Press, 1976), p. 17.

55. Walker, *China and the West*, p. 51.

56. Beeching, *The Chinese Opium Wars*, p. 164.

57. Ibid., p. 206.

58. Ibid., p. 209.

59. On October 8, 1856, Canton police arrested 12 Chinese sailors for piracy and smuggling; they were employees on *The Arrow*—a ship registered in Hong Kong, manned by a British captain and flying the British flag but owned by a Chinese. The British understood the arrest as China's noncompliance with its treaty agreements because it violated their right of extraterritoriality.

60. Among the treasures looted from the Summer Palace were three large enameled bowls that were presented to Queen Victoria, along with a Pekinese—a canine breed favored by Chinese royalty.

61. As a first sign of that equality, Lord Elgin was brought to the treaty-signing ceremony on a sedan chair borne by eight porters—hitherto, a privilege exclusive to Chinese emperors. Elgin's Chinese counterpart, Prince Kung, was carried by only six porters.

62. Beeching, *The Chinese Opium Wars*, pp. 330–331.

63. Ssu-yu Teng and John K. Fairbank, *China's Response to the West: A Documentary Survey 1839–1923* (New York: Atheneum, 1973), pp. 46, 23.

64. Walker, *China and the West*, p. 112.

65. Teng and Fairbank, *China's Response to the West*, pp. 85, 87.

66. The first unequal treaty was the Treaty of Kanagawa of 1854 between Japan and the United States, a result of Admiral Matthew Perry's gunboat diplomacy, which opened Shimoda and Hakodate to foreign commerce, provided for the posting of a U.S. consul in Shhimoda, and instituted the most-favored-nation principle. In 1854 and 1855, similar treaties were concluded with Britain, Russia, and Holland, followed by a Treaty of Commerce with the United States in 1858.

67. Li Kanghe (ed.), *Xuelei kangri wushinian (The 50-Year War of Resistance Against Japan With Blood and Tears)*, v. I (Taipei: Xiangcun, 1980), p. 41.

68. At the same time as the dynasty was contending with the Taiping Rebellion in the south, it was also troubled by the Nian rebellion of 1851–1868 in northern China.

69. The Treaty of Versailles in 1919 transferred German rights in China to Japan.

70. Teng and Fairbank, *China's Response to the West*, p. 127.

71. N.A., *The Revolution of 1911* (Beijing: Foreign Languages Press, 1976), pp. 2–3.

72. Teng and Fairbank, *China's Response to the West*, pp. 65–66.

73. Kiernan, *Lords of Human Kind*, pp. 162–163.

74. Smith, *Chinese Characteristics*, p. 5.

75. Teng and Fairbank, *China's Response to the West*, p. 66.

76. *The Revolution of 1911*, p. 4.

77. Cheng Chu-yuan, "Riben qinhua zhanzheng dui zhongguo jingji di yingxiang (The effects of Japan's war of invasion on China's economy)," in Hsu Cho-yun and Chiu Hungdah (eds.), *Kangzhan shengli di daijia (The Price of Victory in the War of Resistance)* (Taipei: Lianjing, 1986), p. 54.

78. Chiang Wei-kuo (ed.), *Kangri Yuwu (War of Resistance Against Japan)* (Taipei: Liming, 1978), p. 9; and account of a Japanese map of the Co-Prosperity Sphere from 1945, which was recently recovered in Jiangsu, China, in *Shijie ribao (World Journal)*, July 13, 1998, p. A9.

79. Iris Chang, *The Rape of Nanking: The Forgotten Holocaust of World War II* (New York: Basic Books, 1998), pp. 4, 6.

80. Ibid., pp. 4–6.

81. Hsu Cho-yun, "Daixu (Preface)," in Hsu and Chiu (eds.), *Price of Victory*, p. iv.

82. Dick Wilson, *When Tigers Fight: The Story of the Sino-Japanese War, 1937–1945* (New York: Penguin Books, 1982), p. 1.

83. Hsu Cho-yun, "Preface," p. v.

84. Cheng Chu-yuan, "Effects of Japan's War of Invasion," p. 55.

85. Ibid., pp. 56, 58–59.

86. Ibid., pp. 64–66.

87. Liu Yueyun, "Pinglun (Commentary)," in Hsu and Chiu (eds.), *Price of Victory*, pp. 18, 19.

88. Cheng Chu-yuan, "Effects of Japan's War of Invasion," pp. 51, 66–67.

5

The Early Nationalists

Japanese aggression, though incalculably destructive of Chinese lives and economy, would not be as devastating if it had not been preceded by a century of Western imperialism. For it was Western imperialism that tore apart the institutions and values of traditional China, "much as the earth's crust would be disrupted by a comet passing too near."[1] The West challenged, attacked, undermined, and overwhelmed every sphere of the old Chinese society. For China to survive at all, a civilization that had endured for some 5,000 years would have to be refashioned on a scale and at a tempo unprecedented in history.

Reactions to Imperialism

In their reaction to the Western challenge, the Chinese were not much different from other peoples who were scorched by their encounter with the West. Their responses to Western imperialism or colonialism spanned a broad range from a fawning xenophilia to rabid xenophobia.

An initial reaction of the subjugated non-Westerner might be a xenophilic search for assimilation. The non-Westerner apes every attribute of the Westerner—his language, clothing, food, music, and architecture—so as to transform himself to resemble the Westerner "to the point of disappearing in him."[2] In extreme cases, the mimicry is extended to the Westerner's physical appearance as when Africans bleach their skin to make it a little whiter, while East Asian women undergo cosmetic surgery to eliminate their epicanthic eyefolds.

But xenophilia carries a price, for the uncritical love of the Westerner implies a hatred for oneself and one's own culture. A mediocre gem from

Europe is preferred over the purest native jewel: Western manufactured products are accepted with confidence, while the exquisite artifacts of centuries-old native craftsmanship are left only to tourists to appreciate. But by devaluing his culture and people, of which the non-Westerner is inexorably a part, he concomitantly degrades himself. Even if the native were prepared to barter his soul for assimilation, he remains frustrated as he will never be fully accepted into the Westerner's rarefied world. For no matter how painstaking the mimicry, the Westerner could always detect in the native the telltale nuance of inauthenticity in speech or clothing. Having already renounced his own people and now been rejected by the Westerner, the native becomes a marginal man straddling two cultures, never finding the right pose.

Frustrated in her attempt at assimilation, the native may turn to revolt to deliver her personal and collective liberation—and the dignity that comes with independence. In that manner, the native might finally recover her selfhood. But rebelling against the West only opens the door to a new problem: the question of the nature of the self that is recovered. Western imperialism and colonialism, by disrupting the organic development of the native culture, distorted it into a reflection of the dominant Western culture. Who, then, is the newly independent native? What "self" should she recover if both she and her culture had become stunted in their unnatural growth? What should she be now that she has regained her right of self-determination?

One solution is to define oneself through xenophobia: the complete, *en bloc* rejection of the West. All Westerners are imperialists since they all had contributed—actively or passively, intentionally or unintentionally—to the perpetuation of imperialist oppression. In some cases, the belief in the West's collective guilt is accompanied by a conviction that every attribute and product of Western civilization is anathema and must be categorically renounced, even those that might be useful for development. But by demonizing the West, the native commits the very sin of racism of which she had accused her oppressor.

Another strategy pursued by some societies laboring under imperialism is archaism: the attempt to define oneself through a return to tradition. The ancient culture is "exhumed,"[3] in particular a putative "golden age" in the remote past. Examples include Mussolini's glorification of Imperial Rome and the medieval corporate state; Ataturk's exultation in the barbaric virtues of the Osmanli nomads; Meiji Japan's revival of an ancient mythology that deified the emperor; and Gandhi's exhortation that India return to the age of Rama Raj.[4]

As with the rejection of the West, the return to tradition can also lapse into extremism if the past is revived indiscriminately, regardless of its contemporary utility or relevance. In such cases, the native is restored to a moribund culture of frozen traditions and "a rusted tongue."[5] That atavism may work counter to the best interests of the aggrieved society. Like the xenophobic rejection of the West, archaism is also not a solution to the problem at hand, but an escape from it.

Yet another strategy resorted to by some non-Western communities is that of futurism, a utopian vision as the imagined elixir against imperialism, an example of which is Marxism. It has been observed that Marxism has particular appeal for uprooted peasants and those caught in transition between tradition and modernity. For them, Marxism offers the promise of an idealized future in which the coercive institutions of state and factory have both withered away.[6]

Whether the strategy adopted is xenophilia or xenophobia, archaism or futurism, the danger inherent in each is the creation of a counter-mythology. The new myth may glorify every single trait of the oppressed non-Westerner, warts and all; or it may insist on the total rejection of all foreign ideas. Alternately, the new myth may insist that everything transmitted from the past must be retained—even the anachronous, the immoral, the useless, or the mistaken; or it may take the form of a future utopia. Whatever the particular contents, by being as removed from reality as the West's racist myths concerning the peoples it subjugated, the counter-mythology may be as ersatz and detrimental to the well-being of the native. Most importantly, such a counter-fiction cannot deliver what the native most needs: the equanimity that can come only from genuine dignity and self-respect. As Albert Memmi observed:[7]

> From excessive submission to Europe . . . [the native] passes to such a violent return to self that it is noxious and esthetically illusory. . . . Uncertain of himself, he . . . demands endless approval. . . . He almost never succeeds in corresponding with himself.

Ideologies of Developmental Nationalism

Neither xenophilia nor xenophobia, archaism nor futurism, can ease the non-Westerner's sense of affliction since none of these strategies fully addresses the real reason why the West was able to impose its will on the less developed world in the first place. As one observer remarked, "Whether empires were agencies of civilization or of exploitation, they rested on power."[8] In the last analysis, it was the preeminent power of the West that made imperialism possible—a power that turned on the West's superior military capabilities facilitated by the Industrial Revolution. Given that, to regain their dignity, the non-Western peoples would have to industrialize, because only economic development can provide the modern armaments to defend their communities against the West's predation.

Among non-Westerners, it is the intellectual who best comprehends the meaning of the Western challenge and realizes what it demands of his people.[9] This is an individual with a modern, that is, Western education, whose profession is typically that of civil service, journalism, law, teaching, or medicine. Through his education, the intellectual attains a knowledge of the West, notably the source of its power and the threat it poses to his people. At the same time, that education also exposes him to a prolonged contact with modern culture, an exposure that makes the non-Western intellectual peculiarly vulnerable to the afflictions and disabilities that typify the colonial psychology.

The "assaulted"[10] intellectual is typically the first to experience the marginality of the subjugated and to experience it more acutely than the masses, as the latter's illiteracy provides a measure of insulation from imperialism's full psychological impact. Being unlettered, the populace "rechews scraps of oral culture,"[11] whereas the intellectual's bilingualism condemns him to live in cultural anguish. Being more exposed to the West, the intellectual is also more afflicted with ambivalence. He has an uneasy attitude toward himself and his own kind, often scorning his people (and by implication, himself) as pseudo or mongrel, being neither truly native nor truly Western. Toward the West he is equally ambivalent, embracing the polar extremes of xenophobia and xenophilia.[12]

But the intellectual is also the most outraged by imperialism. Appalled by the great discrepancies in standards of living and culture between his people and the West, he develops a special calling.[13] Convinced that something must be done to regain his people's collective dignity, he grows resolved that the masses must be mobilized to meet the challenge of the industrial West. Mass mobilization requires an animating and illuminating ideology that both accounts for the problems created by imperialism and proposes solutions to those problems, including especially a program for industrialization and modernization—all under a unifying framework of nationalism. The fashioning of such an ideology of developmental nationalism would have to be undertaken by intellectuals because only intellectuals devise ideologies.

Mary Matossian noted that a certain type of ideology seemed to prevail among the less developed nations. Seemingly disparate ideologies like Marxism-Leninism, Shintoism, Italian Fascism, Kemalism, Gandhism, the Indonesian Pantjasila, and Sun Yat-sen's Three Principles of the People all share an important "similarity of context." That contextual similarity is an industrially backward country that has been in contact with the West for at least 50 years, possessed of a native Western-educated intelligentsia.[14]

Irrespective of its particular contents, according to Matossian, if such an "ideology of delayed industrialization" were to meet the challenge of imperialism, it must eschew the extremes of xenophobia-xenophilia and archaism-futurism because they are counterproductive to the interests of less developed societies.[15] Selectively applied, however, each has its utility. A hatred of the West can galvanize and unite a people fragmented by feudal loyalties into a modern nation. Western science and technology are appropriate models for emulation as both are essential to industrialization. An appeal to ancient native traditions can impart a sense of collective pride and identity. The vision of a utopian future can be a potent source of hope and inspiration, spurring people to heroic efforts of sacrifice and economic construction.

Matossian suggested that the successful ideology of developmental nationalism must resolve at least three questions: (1) What is to be rejected of the West? (2) What is to be borrowed from the West? and (3) What elements from the past should be retained—specifically what characteristics, habits, and behaviors of the population are to be encouraged? To aid in answering those questions, some standard or criterion is needed. That standard should be pragmatism: whatever advances the national interest and strengthens the nation. Such a pragmatic criterion means that neither archaism, futurism, xenophobia, nor xenophilia should exist "as an axiomatic, self-justified good."[16] Whatever elements that are rejected or borrowed from the West, retained from the past, or envisioned for the future should be selected and deployed only as means toward the advancement of the greater national good. In the case of societies caught in the doldrums of underdevelopment, national good necessarily entails economic modernization in as rapid, humane, and dignified a fashion as possible.

Chinese Responses to Western Imperialism

In the case of the Chinese, their responses to Western imperialism traversed three phases. The first, from 1840 to 1860, constituted an adamant rejection of the West. From 1870 to 1885, that hostility evolved into a resentment accompanied with an admiration of the West. Beginning in 1895 until about 1925, Chinese turned inward, overcome with remorse and self-deprecation.[17] Each phase finds representation in a distinctive group of personalities. As examples, there were the Boxers, who lashed out in xenophobic violence, covertly supported by conservatives in the Qing court who insisted on an obdurate attachment to an antiquated tradition. In contrast, there were those who, reluctantly or willingly, saw emulation of the West as the solution to China's predicament. Among their ranks were the Confucian reformists of the Tongzhi Restoration, their more radical counterparts of the Hundred Days' Reform, the even more radical Sun Yat-sen and his fellow revolutionaries, and the utopian Marxists of the Chinese Communist Party.

Viewed as a group, however, Chinese who favored emulating the West repeatedly shifted their point of emphasis: from advocating the adoption of Western gunboats in the 1860s, to liberty and scholarship in the 1890s, to science and democracy in 1919, to Marxism after 1920. For some, the shift reflected a process of natural selection among ideas that gained currency through their applicability—real or illusory—to the needs of China's leaders.[18] For others, Chinese vacillation probably owed more to their beliefs' being shallow, rising "more out of environment than out of understanding."[19]

Whatever the reason for their shifting points of focus, it was not for lack of recognizing that only a finite range of options was available. As articulated by Hu Shi (1891–1962), the stark choices Chinese had vis-à-vis the West were the following:[20]

> China may refuse to recognize this new civilization and resist its invasion; she may accept the new culture whole-heartedly; or, she may adopt its desirable elements. . . . The first attitude is resistance; the second, wholesale acceptance; and the third, selective adoption.

What follows is an effort to reconstruct and summarize the thoughts and ideas of leading Chinese intellectuals on the Western problem and their proposed solutions. That reconstruction begins with their view of the world.

Worldview

If we consider the turbulence that overtook China beginning with the Opium War, it comes as no surprise that Chinese intellectuals perceived the world to be an arena of social Darwinian struggles where only the fittest of nations could survive. As an example, Yan Fu (1853–1921) maintained that a basic principle of nature for animals, plants, people, and nations was that "the weak become the prey of the strong." In the case of nations, "If . . . the people are slow, unenlightened, and selfish, the group cannot last and will be humiliated and annihilated when faced with stronger groups." This meant that Chinese were doomed unless "the basic causes of their inferiority" could be removed.[21]

Liang Qichao (1873–1929) similarly understood the world in Darwinian terms, convinced that conflicts among nations were as natural as struggles among men. Civilization advanced through national competition, and a nation's strength depended on the vitality of its people. The young martyr Zou Rong (1885–1905) went further. In his tract, *Revolutionary Army (Geming jun),* he postulated that without a revolution, the iron law of evolution would work in reverse to return China to a primeval condition in which the Chinese would sink deeper into slavery and devolve into "apes, wild pigs, oysters, and finally become extinct."[22]

The Importance of the Group

The Darwinian worldview of Chinese intellectuals reinforced their belief in the importance of the group for human survival. As Liang Qichao expressed it in 1901, "No man can exist apart from the group." Liang maintained that since time immemorial, human beings had developed in different groups, each with its own language, customs, and "spirit." Of all groups, the nation was "the most nearly perfect," for only through it could men defend themselves in wars and share their lives in peace. The nation, for Liang, was "the unit of self-love and the climax of human fraternity," without which man "would fare worse than the birds and beasts."[23]

Group Spirit and Nationalism

The primacy of the group in human survival dictated that morality be fundamentally collective in nature. As Liang insisted, the purpose of human morality, ultimately, was to benefit the group. For a group to survive and thrive, a vibrant group spirit was necessary. In the case of nations, their very existence was contingent on the willingness of each man to defend it to the last drop of his blood.[24] In Liang's words:[25]

> [A] nation which can endure in the world must have some peculiar characteristics on the part of its nationals [who must] . . . all share a kind of independent spirit which has been handed down from grandfather to father and inherited by their descendants. . . . This is really the fundamental source of nationalism.

Liang understood the concept of nation as a people who "regard each other as brothers," being of the same race, the same language, the same religion, and the same customs; who "work for independence and self-government" in order to organize "a more perfect government" for the public welfare and "oppose the infringement of other races."[26] In effect, Liang's conception of nationalism is nearly identical to that of John Stuart Mill[27] in its emphasis on a people's political self-determination. Where Liang's definition departed from Mill's was in the former's emphasis on biology and blood, as Liang believed that only Chinese had "the right to control Chinese affairs," a right that all non-Chinese lacked. The Manchus would be the very last foreign "race" that ruled China. Liang vowed that "if there should again be another race who wished to . . . be the masters of China again, that is something that would never happen till the seas dry up and stone rot."[28]

Patriotism

Not all Chinese intellectuals shared Liang's identification of group spirit with nationalism. For some, a country's group spirit should be simple patriotism. That conviction compelled them to give their political loyalty and affiliation to the Manchu state rather than the Han Chinese populace. Among the patriots was Zeng Guofan (1811–1872), leader of the Tongzhi Restoration, who was instrumental in the Manchu dynasty's successful suppression of the Taiping and Nian rebels. Despite his Han ethnicity, Zeng identified his interests with those of the Confucian monarchy and was unwavering in his fidelity to the albeit Manchu Son of Heaven.[29] Zhang Zhidong (1837–1909) was another patriot, who wrote in 1898 that Chinese and Manchus were of the same race, both being "descendants of the gods." This meant that the protection and preservation of the "Chinese race" required the preservation of the Manchus also, leading him to advocate "an ardent patriotism" to "conserve the country."[30]

Kang Youwei (1858–1927), Liang Qichao's teacher and co-reformer in the quixotic Hundred Days' Reform, also conceived patriotism to be "the foundation of national existence." For Kang, the group spirit of patriotism was an entirely natural human disposition. Membership in a national group of mutual assistance gave "pleasure to man's nature." As Kang explained,[31]

> Being that we are born into one country, have received [its] civilization . . . and . . . knowledge, then we have the responsibilities of a citizen. If we . . . abandon this country, this country will perish and its people will be annihilated, and then civilization will be destroyed.

Ethnic-racial Nationalism

In direct contrast to the patriotism of Zeng Guofan, Zhang Zhidong, and Kang Youwei was the ethnic and racial nationalism of other Chinese intellectuals. The earliest of the ethnic Chinese nationalists were intellectuals of the late Ming dynasty who nursed an abiding hatred and resentment of the Manchus for their conquest and rule over China. Among their ranks were Gu Yanwu (1613–1682), Zhu Zhiyou (1600–1682), and Wang Fuzhi (1619–1692), who bitterly opposed the alien rule of the Manchus or of any other non-Chinese group for that matter. The ideas of Wang on nationalism, in particular, merit some attention in that they anticipated those of Mill as well as Arthur Keith.[32]

According to Wang Fuzhi, "Self-preservation is a natural law." Every "species and race, all the way from insects to human beings, aims at its own preservation and organization." Like Keith, Wang maintained that "the forming of groups is inherent in human nature." Like Mill, Wang conceived of the nation as a group that seeks to govern itself, explaining that "Since . . . the establishment of a ruler is for the purpose of protecting the group, it is logical and necessary for the group to govern itself." But Wang went beyond both Keith and Mill in his espousal of a racial nationalism when he asserted that because "races" lived in different geographical zones and possessed "differences of culture," each race should "be controlled by its own ruler." All states should be self-governing national units—a principle that pertained to the Han Chinese and the assorted "barbarians" who historically resided on the borders of China with their own breeding places, "spirit, actions, and customs." China "should not allow barbarians to invade her territory and her culture." Better that a usurper should occupy the throne than that a foreign race, such as the Manchus, rule China.[33]

Not surprisingly, given their anti-Manchu ethnicism, the writings of the late-Ming intellectuals were suppressed by the Qing dynasty in a literary inquisition that began with the inception of the dynasty in 1644 and peaked during the eighteenth century under Emperor Qianlong, when more than 2,000 Chinese works were wholly or partly destroyed. Despite the suppression, some of the writings of the late Ming intellectuals were used two centuries later by Chinese intellectuals who sought an ideological basis for modern Chinese nationalism. As a direct result of the Qing dynasty's suppression, ethnic Chinese nationalism was driven underground after the late eighteenth century to survive in secret societies of various names and forms, which continued to agitate for the overthrow of the Manchus. Some of the societies contributed men and resources to the Taiping Rebellion and, later, to Sun Yat-sen's revolutionary movement.[34]

Many among Sun's followers were virulently anti-Manchu and saw the world in racial terms. They considered a common race, instead of language, culture, or geography, to be the most important factor linking the inhabitants of a country. Their conception of nationhood was intricately tied to race as they believed that nations were formed through racial struggles. The survival of a race required that it formed its own nation; if there were two races in a country, the unity between people and state would be destroyed because a racially divided country lacked internal strength and risked destruction.[35]

In the revolutionaries' view, Chinese and Manchus were fundamentally different peoples although the differences between them were less than those between both of them and the white race. As an example, Zou Rong maintained that the "yellow race" was divided into two main categories, Chinese and Siberian. The Manchus, being a Tungusic Mongol people, belonged to the Siberian sub-race. More than being a separate sub-race, the Manchus were inferior to the Chinese and compounded their illegitimate rule by being vicious in their conquest and exploitation of China. They discriminated against Chinese, and were subservient and cowardly toward the Western powers, ceding to them such Chinese territories as Hong Kong, Macao, Guangzhou Bay, and Kowloon. To maintain their power, the Manchu rulers deliberately weakened the Chinese people by suppressing their sense of nationalism, which accounted for the dearth of nationalism that Sun and other revolutionaries repeatedly lamented. Above all, the Manchus must be faulted for failing to protect China against Western predation. Being more concerned with preserving their rule, the Manchus opted for a policy of appeasement, placating the imperialists by bartering away China's national territory and interests in successive treaty concessions. At the same time, the Manchu government distrusted and regarded as enemies Chinese nationalists who urged that further imperialist encroachment be resisted by strengthening the country through systemic reform. This left the nationalists with little choice but to overthrow the Manchus, gain control of government, and rally the country to nationalism, so as to expel the Westerners.[36]

Reactive Nationalism

In effect, at the root of anti-Manchu Chinese nationalism was a reactive nationalism against the imperialist West. Despite their objections to the Manchus, both Sun's revolutionaries as well as the reformist Liang Qichao identified the West as China's principal foe, arguing that once the Manchus were removed from power, all the ethnic groups in China should unite in common cause against the imperialist West.[37] Resentment of the West was also a motivating impulse for the patriots Zeng Guofan and Kang Youwei. Kang, for one, was greatly perturbed by the Chinese's having allowed themselves to be ruled by "a different race" of Westerners who regarded "other races as enemies." Reactive nationalism also animated the conservatives in the Qing court. As an example, Woren (d. 1871), Grand Secretary of the Qing dynasty and tutor to the emperor, wrote in 1867 that the Western "barbarians" were "our enemies," whose "humiliation" of China stirred scholars and officials with "heart-burning rage."[38]

It was not just the elite who harbored resentment against the West, that resentment prompted the first stirrings of popular Chinese nationalism in Guangzhou in 1841. Western traders who ventured outside of Guangzhou into the countryside were stoned or beaten and, in some cases, killed. That popular Chinese nationalism first appeared in Guangzhou is no surprise since the city was where trade with Westerners first began. Guangzhou was also ground zero in the Opium War.[39]

Chinese popular nationalism expressed itself in placards posted in public places denouncing the presence and activities of foreigners. As an example, a poster by the "patriotic people" of Guangdong Province's Sanyuanli village referred to the British as "wolves" who came to China "merely to covet profit" like animals greedy for food, plundering and seizing things by force. The village had suffered economically from the Opium War and claimed to have repulsed the British troops. Ignorant of Chinese laws, institutions, and "right principles," the British had "no gratitude for the great favor" of trade extended to them by the emperor. In return for his signal favor, the British treated Chinese "like enemies" by using opium to hurt the common people and cheat them of silver and cash. Heaven, itself, was "angered" by the evil deeds of the "English barbarians" who killed and injured countless Chinese. Declaring that their hatred for the foreign barbarians was "at white heat," the villagers vowed that "If we do not completely exterminate you pigs and dogs, we will not be manly Chinese able to support the sky on our heads and stand firmly on the earth."[40]

Beyond their hatred of Westerners, the conservatives, the patriots, and ethnic nationalists shared little else in common. The three groups were especially divergent in their views on how to deal with the West.

Xenophobic Rejection of the West

To begin with, there were those who thought that the West could simply be ignored. In 1867, as an example, Woren asked why it was necessary to learn from the "barbarian" enemies. Confident that the Chinese Empire was "so great that one should not worry," he dismissed the methods of the barbarians as "techniques" and "trifling arts" that did not warrant emulation.[41]

The conservatives' dismissal of the West's methods stemmed from their ignorance of Western science and technology. As examples, Huang Renji so misunderstood mathematics that he equated it with "a moral principle"; Shen Chun thought that Chinese human labor and experience were superior and could achieve "better results than machines"; Zhu Yixin (1846–1894) feared that the use of machines by China would lead to massive unemployment and social unrest. Others, like Yu Yue (1821–1907), thought that industrial production would deplete the world's natural resources and the earth would become so barren that it would "no longer be able to maintain human life."[42]

The conservatives rationalized their rejection of the West by convincing themselves of China's inherent superiority. Westerners were "materialistic" seekers of profits who were slaves to the numerical system but neglected human relations. In contrast, Chinese were "spiritual" and "moral" seekers of "larger and higher purposes" who upheld righteousness and practiced benevolence. Other Chinese resisted Westernization for reasons that had less to do with false pride than a pessimistic fatalism. Despairing that Western material civilization was so far ahead that it would be absolutely impracticable for the Chinese to try to learn the Westerners' methods, they concluded that Westernization should be avoided and another method of self-preservation be sought. What that alternate method was, however, was not entirely clear. Yu Yue, for one, sought refuge in Daoism's vague and mystical notion of opposites when he proposed that China could achieve "an assured victory" over the West by overcoming the latter's "sharp knife" and "steel" with "dullness" and "softness" and counteracting its "cleverness" with "great stupidity."[43]

Critical Self-Examination

Notwithstanding those Chinese who contented themselves with delusions of their country's putative superiority, successive defeats in war and humiliating treaty concessions forced other intellectuals to begin the painful process of self-reflection. An example of the latter was Li Hongzhang (1823–1901), a leader of the Tongzhi Restoration, who in 1863 criticized his countrymen for not rewarding manual work and innovation. Instead, "Chinese scholars and officials have been indulging in . . . remembering stanzas and sentences and practicing fine model calligraphy, while our warriors and fighters are . . . rough, stupid, and careless." Similarly, officials in China's Zongli Yamen admitted in 1867 that whereas Westerners knew "completely" China's geography and its spoken and written languages, Chinese "do not know a thing" about the West. Instead, "We merely continue our empty talk about moral principles and righteousness, and confusedly argue without end." The next year, in 1877, the head of the Chinese legation to London Guo Songtao wrote a letter to Li Hongzhang in which he offered the following critique of his countrymen:[44]

> [T]here is something in the minds of the Chinese which is absolutely unintelligible. Among the injuries that Westerners do us there is nothing more serious than opium. . . . Yet Chinese scholars and officials are willing to indulge complacently in it, without any sense of remorse. . . . There have been foreign relations for thirty years, but the provincial authorities are entirely ignorant of them.

More than their ignorance, Yan Fu took Chinese to task for their profound selfishness, even during wartime. He noted that in the Sino-Japanese War of 1894–1895, "one province showed no concern for the defense of another; the service commanders were both corrupt and incompetent; the court officials . . . even took advantage of the crisis to make personal fortunes." Yan attributed that selfishness to the Chinese lack of education and freedom, being treated "like slaves" by their government. "As a result they felt no concern for public interest." Yan believed that "patriotism arose from a sense of possession, a concern for that which was one's own." The way to improve Chinese morals was through democratization, "making China the private possession of all."[45]

One of the most incisive critics of Chinese national character was Lu Xun (1891–1934). In his famous "Diary of a Madman," Lu revealed the hypocrisy and emptiness of the vaunted Chinese regard for human relations. He observed that accounts of Chinese history were filled with words such as "righteousness" and "moral virtues." But, in reality, those words masked a "man-eating" reality.[46]

Selective Learning from the West

The ability to be self-critical led some Chinese to the recognition that emulation of Western achievements was needed, beginning with the most visible symbol of Western power—its weaponry. With the passage of time, as they gained more understanding of the West, the advocates of reform broadened their appreciation of the West to include their ships, railways, and political and social institutions.

Champions of selective learning from the West included both reformers as well as revolutionaries, many of whom were natives of Guangdong Province experienced with Westerners. One of the earliest advocates of Western learning was none other than the erstwhile commissioner Lin Cexu who was exiled to Ili after China's defeat in the Opium War. There, in 1842, he admitted in a letter to a friend that China was militarily inferior to the West and must acquire modern weapons "to drive away the crocodile" and "get rid of the whales."[47] He proposed that China purchase and manufacture Western ships and guns, translate Western books, build shipyards and arsenals, hire foreign technical instructors, train Chinese personnel, and reform the antiquated civil service examinations. But he kept his suggestions private because of opposition from the Imperial Court. Had his plans for making modern weapons been carried out, China's modernization might have been advanced 20 years.

Lin was succeeded by the Tongzhi Restoration reformers, one of whom was Feng Guifen (1809–1874), who is credited with being the first to use the expression "self-strengthening" *(ziqiang)* and who coined the Restoration's motto of "Chinese learning as fundamental structure, Western learning for practical use." Lamenting the control of the largest country in the world by "small barbarians," Feng attributed China's "shameful humiliation" to its economic backwardness and unproductivity. He urged his countrymen to learn from the barbarians how to construct "solid ships and effective guns" because "only thus will we be able to . . . restore our original strength, and redeem ourselves from former humiliations."[48] Some of Feng's ideas were implemented by Zeng Guofan and Li Hongzhang, including the construction of China's first arsenals and its first steamship in 1869, albeit with an imported engine.

The Tongzhi reformers were followed by others who advocated more extensive Westernization. As an example, Hong Rengan (1822–1864), foreign minister and prime minister of the rebel Taiping government in Nanjing, was tutored in astronomy and other sciences by Western missionaries in Hong Kong. In his book of 1859, *A New Work for Aid in Administration (Zizheng xinpian),* he offered a program for China's economic modernization that included the construction of railroads, locomotives, and ships, and the creation of banks, patents, postal service, provincial newspapers, currency, grain storehouses, public welfare agencies, hospitals, and mines.[49]

Journalist Wang Tao (1828–1897) was even more experienced with the West, having traveled to the British Isles, Europe, and Japan. Wang urged his countrymen not to copy "the superficialities" of Western methods without acquiring "actual substance." Like Hong Rengan, Wang went beyond military reforms to advocate the construction of telegraph lines and railways, the modernization of the civil service exams, and the introduction of popular elections, constitutional government, and rule of law.[50] In proposing reforms that reached into the political sphere, Wang anticipated the aborted Hundred Days' Reform.

As Western reforms broadened in scope and increased in scale, some Chinese intellectuals became increasingly disquieted. Among them was Zhang Zhidong, who feared extensive Westernization would lead to a loss of Chinese identity, believing that the more profound one's knowledge of the West, "the more severe will be his contempt for China." To counteract those destructive effects, Zhang proposed that "As one who is recuperating must first get some energy from rice, and then be offered all sorts of delicacies,"[51] Western learning must first be preceded by the systematic study of Chinese classics, history, and philosophy so that "our ancestors will not be forgotten."[52]

Wholesale Acceptance of the West

In contrast to Zhang, who clung to tradition as a buoy in a stormy sea, were those intellectuals who saw little of China's tradition that was worth retaining. They were the advocates of thorough and total Westernization. One of the earliest was Tan Sitong (1865–1898), who favored the abandonment of tradition because, as he put it, "there is not a single one of the Chinese people's sentiments, customs, or political and legal institutions which can be favorably compared with those of the barbarians." Another was Wu Chihui, who wrote in 1923 that "the sum-total of Chinese morality is low and shallow" and urged Chinese to throw their "so-called" national heritage onto the garbage heap.[53]

The most notable advocate of complete Westernization was Hu Shi, who wondered whether there was anything in China's civilization of which Chinese could "really boast." Hu rued that whatever past glories China had enjoyed belonged to the past and could not provide a solution to contemporary problems of poverty, disease, ignorance, and corruption, which were all that remained of Chinese civilization. With a brutal bluntness, Hu remarked, "What else is there? Has the country produced during the last hundred years a painter, a sculptor, a great poet, a novelist, a musician, a dramatist, a thinker or a statesman?" As for the much-trumpeted "spirituality" of the Chinese, Hu found very little of it in a civilization that, "for a thousand years," could tolerate without protest a grotesque custom such as foot-binding. Instead, it was the West that was humane and spiritual because its science and democracy made the fullest possible use of human intelligence, relieved human suffering, multiplied human power, and reformed social and political institutions "for the greatest happiness of the greatest number." Hu concluded that the only possible attitude for China was to wholeheartedly embrace Western civilization, especially its science, technology, and democracy, because selective adoption was both "impossible" and "quite unnecessary." It was precisely the inability of Chinese leaders to completely accept Western civilization that caused the country to remain retarded.[54]

The advocacy of wholesale Westernization and the concomitant rejection of Chinese tradition reached a peak during the May Fourth Movement in 1919. The movement inspired the publication of more than 400 new magazines, including the influential *New Youth*. Chinese youth, in particular, welcomed the idea of abandoning the national heritage and revolted against all existing institutions, including the traditional family and its relations, some going so far as to change their family names. Presaging Mao's Cultural Revolution almost half a century later, the students of May Fourth went on strike and claimed the right to engage and dismiss teachers. They refused to take examinations, boycotted newly appointed school principals and university presidents, and demanded changes in the curriculum. Confucianism became so thoroughly discredited that "the mere name connoted musty obscurantism."[55]

Futurism

The repudiation of Chinese tradition, however, raised more problems than it settled. For some 2,000 years, Confucianism had served as China's comprehensive template of beliefs and values, the repudiation of which necessarily left a serious void. To fill that void, some Chinese intellectuals turned to the chimera of utopian futurism. As an example, Wang Tao thought that the future would herald the arrival of Confucius's *datong,* a united and pacific world given a modern interpretation. Wang predicted that new scientific inventions would conquer distance to unite the nations of the world in universal harmony.[56]

Probably the best-known portrait of *datong* was provided by Kang Youwei in his book *Datong Shu (The Book on the Great Unity)*. According to Kang, nations were the source of wars and evils, "selfishness and strife." As he put it, "[S]tates having been established, patriotisms are born. Everyone looks to the advantage of his own state, and aggresses against other states," resulting in the incalculable "poisoning of the human race." So long as there are nations and states, wishing to plan for disarmament is like "ordering tigers and wolves to be vegetarians." To save the human race, national and state boundaries must be abolished, along with other barriers of family, class, gender, and race that divide humanity and cause untold suffering. The removal of those barriers would result in a united world of peace and equality under the aegis of a single government. Universal harmony and unity are entirely possible because all men and women, being human instead of "furred or feathered, scaly or finny," share a basic affinity. Kang explained, "Being that I was born on the earth, then mankind in the ten thousand countries of the earth are all my brothers. . . . Being that I have knowledge of them, then I have love for them." Insisting that his dreams were not "empty imaginings," he had faith that his utopian vision would become "realities." In that halcyon future of *datong*, according to Kang, the world would be united in communism, children would be cared for and educated by the state, and there would be no class distinctions as all property would be publicly owned and operated. As described by Kang,[57]

> Life . . . is pleasant for all. Machines have done away with long hours of toil, and everyone has ample leisure time. . . .[T]he people live on a communal basis . . . [their] competitive drive . . . channeled into constructive action. . . . [A]ll human beings are entirely equal. . . . The races have become blended into one great race. . . . [Goodness] is extended even to the birds and beasts . . . [as the] eating of meat is no longer a human practice. . . .

Kang's successors in utopianism were the members of the Chinese Communist Party who eschewed nationalism for the salvific promise of Marxist internationalism. As Chen Duxiu (1880–1942), a founder of the Party, wrote in 1920: "I recognize the existence of only two nations, that of the capitalists and that of the workers." Chen and his colleagues found in Marxism-Leninism a seemingly perfect solution to their predicament. By adopting the Western ideology of Marxism-Leninism, they could claim they had rejected Confucianism while retaining some of the latter's essential characteristics. Marxism-Leninism was similar to Confucianism in that each constituted a single body of doctrines which extolled the group above the individual and laid claim to being comprehensive truths. As Richard Walker observed, "Marxism-Leninism was perfectly at home in China because it was sufficiently similar to Confucianism to satisfy the subconscious habits of the intellectuals and yet different enough from it to rouse new hopes."[58]

Conclusion

In their varying reactions to the Western challenge, Chinese intellectuals were similar to other non-Westerners who found themselves besieged by the West. Some reacted with xenophobic rejection or xenophilic embrace of the West, others championed a return to archaic traditions or consoled themselves with imaginings of a future utopia. In all cases, their posturings were psychological balm that mitigated and soothed their much-abused national ego but failed to deliver lasting relief because they neglected to address the real problem confronting China—its material poverty and underdevelopment.

Some Chinese intellectuals managed to escape ideological extremism. They neither rejected tradition nor indiscriminately adopted the Western model (democratic or Marxist) but instead chose pragmatism as the discriminating criterion. One of them was Xue Fucheng, who, in his 1879 essay "On Reform," maintained that modernization was universal and not specifically Western. With keen insight, Xue observed that "The way revealed is one that belongs to all the universe; it is not a monopoly of the Westerners."[59]

Liang Qichao similarly did not believe that human knowledge was delimited and confined by national borders. Rejecting the Western versus Chinese distinction, he maintained that all knowledge "belonged to the world" and should be pursued as an end in itself. The proper consideration was how to strengthen China with the most suitable means, regardless of whether those means were Western or Chinese. There was no need either to reject the past—to "give up entirely what is old in order to follow others"—or to become "intoxicated" with the West. Instead, China should "investigate extensively the methods followed by all other nations and races in becoming independent." For only through selecting and appropriating the superior attributes of others could Chinese compensate for their shortcomings and be regenerated as a "new people."[60]

Modern China's first ideology of developmental nationalism would arise out of precisely that pragmatic approach to the Western challenge. It was Sun Yat-sen who assembled select elements from the West and from Chinese tradition into a systematic program for the economic development and political modernization of China. That ideology is the subject of the next chapter.

Notes

1. Ssu-yu Teng and John K. Fairbank, *China's Response to the West: A Documentary Survey 1839–1923* (New York: Atheneum, 1973), pp. 1–2.

2. Albert Memmi, *The Colonizer and the Colonized* (New York: Orion, 1965), p. 120.

3. Edward Shils, "The Intellectuals in the Political Development of New States," in Jason L. Finkle and Richard W. Gable (eds.), *Political Development and Social Change* (New York: John Wiley and Sons, 1971), p. 260.

4. Mary Matossian, "Ideologies of Delayed Industrialization," in Finkle and Gable, *Political Development and Social Change,* p. 118.

5. Memmi, *Colonizer and Colonized,* pp. 137, 133.

6. Adam Ulam, "The Historical Role of Marxism and the Soviet System," *World Politics,* 8, pp. 20–45.

7. Memmi, *Colonizer and Colonized,* pp. 139–140.

8. V. G. Kiernan, *The Lords of Human Kind: Black Man, Yellow Man and White Man In An Age of Empire* (Boston: Little, Brown, 1969), p. 312.

9. Shils, "Intellectuals in the Political Development," pp. 251, 252.

10. Matossian, "Ideologies of Delayed Industrialization," p. 115.

11. Memmi, *Colonizer and Colonized,* p. 120.

12. Matossian, "Ideologies," p. 115.

13. Shils, "Intellectuals," p. 251.

14. Matossian, "Ideologies," p. 113.

15. Ibid., p. 118.

16. Ibid., pp. 122, 118, 120.

17. Y. C. Wang, *Chinese Intellectuals and the West 1872–1949* (Chapel Hill, NC: University of North Carolina Press, 1966), p. 234.

18. Teng and Fairbank, *China's Response to the West,* p. 275.

19. Wang, *Chinese Intellectuals and the West,* p. 316.

20. Richard L. Walker, *China and the West: Cultural Collision Selected Documents* (New Haven: Yale University Far Eastern Publications, 1967), p. 137.

21. Wang, *Chinese Intellectuals and the West,* pp. 196, 197, 201.

22. Ibid., pp. 214, 238; Mary Backus Rankin, *Early Chinese Revolutionaries: Radical Intellectuals in Shanghai and Chekiang, 1902–1911* (Cambridge, MA: Harvard University Press, 1974), p. 29.

23. Wang, *Chinese Intellectuals and the West,* pp. 434, 214.

24. Ibid., p. 214.

25. Teng and Fairbank, *China's Response to the West,* p. 222.

26. Ibid., p. 221.

27. For Mill's definition of nationalism, see Chapter 2 of this book, pp. 15–16.

28. Teng and Fairbank, *China's Response to the West,* pp. 272–273.

29. Ibid., p. 61.

30. Walker, *China and the West,* p. 113; Teng and Fairbank, *China's Response to the West,* p. 165.

31. K'ang Yu-wei, *Ta T'ung Shu (The One-World Philosophy of K'ang Yu-wei),* translated by Laurence G. Thompson (London: George Allen and Unwin, 1958), pp. 69, 93, 65.

32. For a discussion of Keith, see Chapter 2 of this book, pp. 19–22.

33. Teng and Fairbank, *China's Response to the West,* p. 10.

34. Ibid., pp. 7, 11–12.

35. Rankin, *Early Chinese Revolutionaries*, p. 26.

36. Ibid., pp. 251 (f. 37), 27, 32; Wang, *Chinese Intellectuals*, pp. 232, 216, 217; Teng and Fairbank, *China's Response*, p. 37.

37. Wang, *Chinese Intellectuals*, p. 221.

38. Teng and Fairbank, *China's Response*, pp. 76, 152–153.

39. Ibid., p. 35.

40. Ibid., p. 36.

41. Ibid., p. 76.

42. Ibid., pp. 183, 186–187.

43. Ibid., pp. 183, 185–186.

44. Ibid., pp. 185–186, 71, 70, 79, 100.

45. Wang, *Chinese Intellectuals*, pp. 197–200.

46. Ibid., pp. 308–309.

47. Teng and Fairbank, *China's Response*, p. 28.

48. Ibid., pp. 52–54.

49. Ibid., pp. 57–58.

50. Ibid., pp. 135–139.

51. Ibid., p. 169.

52. Walker, *China and the West*, p. 114.

53. Ibid., p. 139; Teng and Fairbank, *China's Response*, pp. 158, 160.

54. Wang, *Chinese Intellectuals*, pp. 141, 140, 138.

55. Walker, *China and the West*, pp. 309–311.

56. Teng and Fairbank, *China's Response*, p. 136.

57. K'ang Yu-wei, *Ta T'ung Shu*, pp. 82, 80, 81, 83, 67, 65, 84, 38, 40–41.

58. Walker, *China and the West*, pp. 316–318.

59. Teng and Fairbank, *China's Response*, p. 145.

60. From Liang's *Yin-ping-shih wen-chi* (Kunming, 1941), as quoted in Wang, *Chinese Intellectuals*, p. 220; Teng and Fairbank, *China's Response*, pp. 222, 223.

6

The Developmental Nationalist Ideology of Sun Yat-sen

Lasting an agonizing near-century, Western imperialism ravaged China, only to be followed by the even more devastating invasion by the troops of Imperial Japan. The response to foreign predation by Chinese political and intellectual elites spanned the extremes of xenophobia to xenophilia, archaism to futurism. But it remained for Sun Yat-sen to meet the challenge of imperialism by articulating modern China's first ideology of developmental nationalism.

Sun's ability to assemble such an ideology is partially explained by his biographical profile, for he was the quintessential "assaulted intellectual"[1] who straddled two worlds. Born in 1866 in China, he received a traditional education in the Confucian classics until age 13, when he left his native Guangdong Province to join an older brother in Hawaii. There, in Honolulu, he attended an American missionary school, followed by medical studies in the British colony of Hong Kong. Instead of practicing medicine, however, Sun devoted his life to the cause of revolution—a calling that consigned him to years of exile from China, with extensive sojourns in Europe and the United States. He was not to return to his homeland until after revolution broke out in 1911 and toppled the Qing dynasty. In effect, Sun had spent most of his life outside China.

The thought of any political thinker is often subject to conflicting evaluation. That observation is no less true in the case of Sun. Not only are there widely divergent opinions regarding the nature and content of his ideas,[2] judgments concerning the intrinsic merit of his thoughts are just as disparate. As an example, we are told that Sun was a "great thinker and scholar" and that the ideological system he bequeathed to China is comparable to that left by Karl Marx.[3] With equal assurance, however, we are told that Sun was not a great thinker[4] and that his political philosophy was "a sham," comprising theories and arguments "unworthy of a kindergarten pupil."[5] On the one hand, Sun is spoken of as a genius whose intellectual contributions were precise and consistent. On the other hand, we are told that he was "changeable, superficial and vague,"[6] his thought "a wilderness of mental abstraction" and "a hotchpotch" of Western and ancient Chinese borrowings devoid of originality and relevance.[7] More than that, he failed to improve upon the ideas he borrowed because he lacked "real understanding."[8] One observer concluded that Sun was "remarkably sterile in original thought"[9] altogether.

Contrary to the above assertions, a case instead can be made that Sun's thoughts on nationalism, economic development, and political democratization were surprisingly sophisticated in that they anticipated, by half a century, some of the most significant ideas of contemporary Western social science. Sun's ideology also bore the hallmark of rationality, a characteristic that Mary Matossian maintained was essential to effective ideologies of delayed industrialization. According to Matossian, such an ideology should eschew axiomatic or self-justified ends, especially the extremes of xenophobia-xenophilia and archaism-futurism. It should employ pragmatism in determining which elements are to be borrowed from the West and those to be retained from tradition. The reigning criterion for the selection of ideological contents should be whatever promotes national interest and well-being.[10]

Sun's ideology of developmental nationalism, conventionally referred to as the Three Principles of the People *(sanmin zhuyi)*, displays all of Matossian's requisite traits. To regenerate China, Sun conceived a formula that began with the revolutionary overthrow of the Qing dynasty, followed by a program of economic and political modernization. Throughout, the defining characteristic of his thought is one of pragmatic rationality: the employment of reason and judgment to the resolution of problems, and the selection of the most appropriate means to achieve identified ends. What follows is an effort to reconstruct the developmental nationalist ideology of Sun Yat-sen, beginning with his view of the world.

Worldview

In his worldview, Sun eschewed Marxist class analysis as well as the Western liberal tradition's emphasis on the individual. Instead, he regarded *minzu (ethnos,* people, or nation) as the basic units in the world—an arena in which nations were caught in a "violent" Darwinian struggle for survival where only the strong nations would prosper and prevail. Communities that were weak and divided were consigned to certain extinction—the fate of countless peoples in the wake of Western Europe's global expansion. China, being "the poorest and weakest state in the world," was no exception to the Darwinian law. It was "the fish and the meat" before "the carving knife and the serving dish" of the Great Powers. Sun warned his countrymen that, unless something was done to rescue China from its "extremely perilous" circumstances, they were doomed to "political extinction" and "the destruction of our race."[11]

In a Darwinian world, it was Sun's contention that all self-sustaining and self-regarding communities were necessarily concerned with collective defense and sustenance,[12] tasks that required and depended on the maintenance of group cohesion, unity, and commitment—which could only be discharged by the nation-state in the modern world. It was imperative for all peoples to construct strong nations on which their very survival and continuity depended. The construction of a strong nation, in turn, required that it be industrialized because only industrialization could provide the collective capability to defend and resist predators. A strong nation also required that its people be animated by the vigorous group "spirit" *(jingsheng)* of "nationalism" *(minzu zhuyi)*. They must identify with each other and be cohesive and united, ready to subsume and sacrifice individual interests for communal well-being. Just as "the pen is the tool of livelihood for a scholar, nationalism is the tool for the survival of the race *(zhongzu)*."[13] As Sun explained,[14]

> In today's world . . . nations without military power are destroyed. Amidst this violent competition, we must establish patriotism and the maintenance of our race as our central concerns. . . . The extinction of a nation cannot solely be due to its [material] weaknesses. . . . What ensures a nation's survival is the undaunted spirit of independence of its people. . . . If the people are undaunted . . . then even the nation that has perished can be regenerated. . . .

In effect, for the survival of the group as well as the individuals within it, each nation-state must pursue its own objectives, dictated by its own interests. Relations between nation-states, as a consequence, should be founded on a basis of "enduring" mutual interests, instead of "universal laws" *(gongli)*, "humane principles" *(rendao)*, and ephemeral sentiments that "arise and fade with the vicissitudes of time." As Sun put it,[15]

> By what universal law did England snatch *[duo]* Hong Kong and Burma from us. . . , France swallow *[tun]* our Annam, and Russia usurp our Manchuria and divest us of Outer Mongolia? . . . By what moral principle were we forced

to smoke opium and carve out pieces of our national territory to others?. . . . [U]niversal laws and humane principles . . . only function as verbiage by war-mongers to disguise their true national interests. . . .

Only when the nations of the world achieved parity in power, according to Sun, could they set aside their separate interests to embrace a more inclusive and expansive "globalism" *(shijie zhuyi)*. Only then would human evolution reach the epoch of international peace—the Great Harmony *(datong)* that Confucius anticipated.[16] Until that halcyon day, it would be foolish for weaker states to champion the cause of international brotherhood because cosmopolitanism only serves the interests of powerful imperialist countries "so as to maintain their privileged status as the masters of the world."[17]

This was Sun Yat-sen's philosophical perspective on the world and the individual's place in that world. That philosophy was the foundation for his ideological prescriptions of the Three People's Principles: those of nationalism *(minzu)*, people's livelihood *(minsheng),* and democracy *(minquan)*. Each principle reflected an eclectic but pragmatic collection comprising Western ideas as well as select elements from Chinese tradition. With clarity and logic, Sun unfailingly explained his reasons for including each idea in his program for the regeneration of China, regarding none as an axiomatic, self-justified good. Instead, his ideas were selected and justified entirely because of their instrumental value toward the construction of a strong and powerful Chinese nation-state.

Minzu: The Principle of State-Nationalism

Definition of Minzu

Given the centrality of *minzu* in Sun's ideology, its meaning as the concept was employed by Sun requires some explication, beginning with *minzu*'s suffix. The Chinese word *zu* refers to an organic—as opposed to a consciously organized—collectivity or group. The specific nature of the group is dependent on the word that precedes and qualifies *zu*. Thus, *jiazu* refers to the family group, *zongzu* the clan group, *buzu* the tribe group, *minzu* the people group, *guozu* the state group, and *zhongzu* the race group. These various groups, according to Sun, were expressions of human beings' natural and instinctive disposition to enter into association. The most powerful of human groups were those based on consanguinity: organic affinity groups whose members were bound together by commonalities of blood, language, mode of production, religion, tradition, custom, and habits.[18]

The literal translation of *minzu* as "people group" still leaves its meaning somewhat opaque. Further clarification may be found in Sun's conception of the "first level" in the classification of humanity. According to Sun, the largest organic groups were the five "human races" *(renzhong)* of "white, black, red, yellow, brown," with each race subdivided into various *minzu*. In Asia, the "yellow race" was comprised of Mongolian, Malay, Japanese, Manchu, and Han *minzu*.[19] In effect, Sun conceived *minzu* to be sub-races, peoples, ethnicities, or in the parlance of contemporary social science, "ethnic nations."

Both races and sub-races, according to Sun, were the products of five "natural forces" *(tianran li)* of human evolution, the first and greatest of which was "common blood." As Sun explained, "The blood of ancestors is transmitted by heredity down through the race, making blood kinship a powerful force." Chinese, according to him, belonged to the "blood stock" *(xuetong)* of the "yellow race." The second "great force" that formed human races was common "livelihood," "the means used to obtain a living." A third force was language. As Sun explained, "If foreign races learn our language, they are more easily assimilated by us and in time become absorbed into our race." Religion constituted the fourth force in that "[p]eople who worship the same gods or the same ancestors tend to form one race." Customs and habits were the fifth force, so that people with "markedly similar customs and habits" would, "in time, cohere and form one race."[20]

Being sub-races, *minzu* were also organic groups formed by the same natural forces of common blood, livelihood, language, religion, customs, and habits. A "state" *(guo)*, in contrast, was an intentional and self-conscious creation by dint of "military force" *(wuli)*—a sovereign entity with the power and authority to "execute orders and regulate public conduct."[21] According to Sun,[22]

> States originated when people united to invade others or to prevent others from invading. In either case, war is involved. But war cannot be undertaken by one person, which led to the formation of groups. Groups require organization, and organization needs leadership. . . . All of which resulted in the permanent consolidation of the group into a state.

In effect, Sun clearly differentiated between the organic national group and the consciously created state, a distinction that is embodied in the German concepts of *Gemeinschaften* and *Gesellschaften*, which Max Weber employed to distinguish between nation and state. Sun recognized that nation and state were not necessarily one and the same, and that the two could exist separately. Just as there could be a nation without its own state, there were also multinational states that united a variety of nations or peoples under a sovereign authority to form politically cohesive but ethnically heterogeneous communities. For Sun, however, the ideal condition was found when a natural affinity group had its own sovereign state so that nation and state were conjoined to form a single nation-state (*guojia:* state-family).[23]

It was that distinction between nation and state that led Sun to insist that, in the case of China, his first principle of *minzu* should not be understood as "nationalism" *(minzu zhuyi)* but more properly as "statism" *(guozu zhuyi)*. As Sun explained,[24]

> The English word for *minzu* is "nation," but that word has two meanings: one is *minzu*, the other is state. . . . In China, nation *(minzu)* and state *(guozu)* are identical . . . because China has been a state comprised of one people since the Qin and Han dynasties. . . . This makes nationalism the same as statism in China. . . . That is not so for other countries, where the same people *(minzu)* may inhabit several states . . . as, for example, the Anglo-Saxons in Britain and America . . . and the same state may contain several peoples within its borders . . . as in the case of England, where a core nationality of white people have united with browns and blacks to make the Great British Empire. . . .

Although Sun admitted that China had been an empire in its past, he nevertheless insisted that China constituted a single nation. His reasoning was that, despite the Mongolian, Manchu, and Turkish ethnic minorities, Hans made up the "vast majority" of China's 400 million population who shared common blood, livelihood, language, religious beliefs, traditions, and customs that made them into "one single people." More than that, Sun maintained that because China's estimated total of about 400 clans were all interrelated *(liandai)*, this meant that all "the people of China" (*zhongguo ren* or Chinese), including the ethnic minorities, were connected to each other by blood.[25] All of which led Sun to conclude that China was a single nation where nation and state, nationalism and statism were one and the same, inextricably bound together.

In effect, instead of the conventional English translation of Sun's *minzu zhuyi* as "the principle of nationalism," the more appropriate rendering should be "the principle of state-nationalism" because Sun conceived *both* nationalism and statism to be equally important. To ensure China's survival in a hostile world, Sun composed his principle of state-nationalism in which he identified foreign imperialism, Manchu rule, and Marx's dictum concerning class struggle to be the bane of China.

Foreign Imperialism

It was Sun's contention that nations became extinct either due to the "forces" *(li)* of "natural selection" *(tianran taotai)* or "man-made" *(renwei)* reasons. Of the latter, politics and economics were two especially powerful man-made forces, both of which were wielded by foreign "imperialism" *(diguo zhuyi)* against China.[26]

For nearly a hundred years, Sun maintained, China had been subjected to the "political oppression" *(zhengzhi yabo)* of foreign imperialist powers. As a result of defeats in war and the unequal treaties with the imperialist powers, China lost countless pieces of its "national territory" *(lingtu)*. China lost to Russia "the fertile land along the shores of Heilongjiang," Burma and Hong Kong to Britain, Annam to France, and Taiwan to Japan. China leased Kowloon and Weihaiwei to Britain, Guangzhou Bay to France, Luxun and Dalian to Russia (which were later transferred to Japan). China acceded to the creation of foreign "spheres of influence" *(shili fanwei)* on Chinese soil, which included the following: a British sphere comprised of Tibet, Sichuan, and the Yangzi River, totaling 28 percent of China's national territory; a Russian sphere that included Outer Mongolia, Xinjiang, and Northern Manchuria, totaling 42 percent of China; and a Japanese sphere comprised of Southern Manchuria, eastern Inner Mongolia, Shandong, and Fujian, totaling more than 5 percent of China's territory. Altogether, China's lost territories included Weihaiwei, Luxun, Dalian, Qingdao, Kowloon, Guangzhou Bay, Korea, Taiwan, Penghu, Burma, Annam (Vietnam), Heilongjiang or the Ussuri, Ili, Hohhot, the Riukius, Siam (Thailand), *Puluni, Sulu,* Java, *Xinan,* Nepal, and Bhutan.[27]

After the ineffectual Qing dynasty was overthrown in the 1911 Revolution, the imperialist powers turned to economic means to "subjugate" *(zhengfu)* China. By wresting control of China's tariffs, the powers prevented the government from developing and nurturing native industries through import substitution and protectionist policies. As a result, the flood of foreign imports not only destroyed China's textile industry, but engendered ever-rising trade deficits. All of which added to the ruination of a Chinese economy that was already burdened with war indemnities, the installation of foreign banks, the circulation of foreign currencies, and the profits accumulated by foreign businesses within China. Altogether, Sun estimated that the Powers' economic imperialism exacted an annual 1.2 billion yuan from China.[28]

The Manchus

What made China so vulnerable to the imperialists' predation and exploitation was its ineffectual government and its people's dearth of national sentiment—both of which Sun blamed on the Manchus. Sun's abiding lament was that Chinese lacked the group spirit of nationalism, resembling more "a tray of loose sand." That deficiency was a result of a systematic policy on the part of the Manchus to "stamp out the patriotic spirit of the Chinese" so as to secure and maintain their own rule.[29]

In their rule, the Manchus regularly placed their ethnic interests above and before those of China. They delayed reforms that could have modernized and strengthened the country. They repeatedly succumbed to the West's imperialist importunings with treaty concessions, and bartered away Chinese territories and other interests so that they could maintain their own rule. Whatever reforms the Manchus eventually undertook in the Tongzhi Restoration were ineffectual, based as they were on a flawed understanding of the Western challenge and what was required to meet that challenge.

An example of the Manchu government's failure to undertake effective reform was its unreceptiveness to Sun's petition in 1893 to Li Hongzhang, a leader of the Tongzhi Restoration and the imperial grand secretary of Zhili Province, in which he offered a schematic plan for the economic development of China.[30] But his memorandum fell on deaf ears. After that, Sun more and more despaired at the prospect for peaceful change. When the quixotic Hundred Days' Reform was aborted by Dowager Empress Ci Xi's palace coup, he became convinced that the Manchus must be dislodged by revolution if China's future were to be secured. Through their selfishness and failure to discharge critical state functions, the Manchus had forfeited their right to rule.

In order to mobilize the Chinese people in revolution, their anti-Manchu sentiments would have to be provoked by emphasizing and magnifying the ethnic differences between Hans and Manchus, as well as the mistreatment of Hans by their alien rulers. Although some of Sun's followers, such as Zou Rong, thought the Manchus to be racially inferior, Sun himself refrained from such characterizations. He took issue with the Manchus not for their ethnicity but because they were incompetent in their stewardship of China. He maintained that a reconciliation between Hans and Manchus could be effected if the latter surrendered their political privileges and their control over government. If the Manchus were removed from power, he was fully prepared to welcome them back into the fold as equals in a unified Chinese state.

Class Struggle

The logic that governed Sun's opposition to the Manchus also accounted for his rejection of Marxist class struggle. Sun harbored no intrinsic objection against either the Manchus or Marxism. Instead, he took issue with both for an entirely practical reason—because he believed them to be inimical to Chinese nationalism and to the well-being of the national community.

Mindful that the lack of nationalism among Chinese could not solely be due to its suppression by the Manchus, Sun attributed the dearth also to the Chinese traditional attachments to family, clan, and geographical region. To unite them into a nation, it was imperative that they redirect their parochial affiliations toward the greater nation-state.[31] Given the already extant disposition of Chinese to be fragmented like particles of sand, the introduction of class struggle into China, like adding oil to fire, could only add to already dysfunctional divisions.

More than that, Sun took theoretical issue with Marx, maintaining that Marx was fundamentally mistaken in his conception of class struggle as the driving force of social progress. Instead, Sun believed that "Society progresses through the adjustment of major economic interests rather than through the clash of interests." Far from being the cause of social progress, class war was "a disease" due to poverty.[32] Like tribal warfare or the competition between city-states, class struggle was an episode in the evolution of humankind that surfaced when a community could not produce adequately for all its members or maldistributed whatever it did produce. Class struggle, according to Sun, was a symptom of, and not a solution to, a society's material poverty. A society that engaged in class strife would only exacerbate its material poverty by fomenting conflict and impairing collective viability.

In Sun's conception, an economic class, unlike a nation, was not an organic community capable of surviving in and of itself in a competitive world. A class was an association of limited interests, necessarily and intimately connected with other classes by its very nature. Given that, it would be suicidal and "pathological" for an imperiled people to identify with their separate classes instead of with the nation.[33] By precipitating the disaggregation of the national community, internecine class war endangered the viability of the entire society, along with its constituent classes. For China to engage in class struggle would endanger its survival in a fiercely competitive world inhabited by powerful and expansionist nation-states. At a time when the entire nation was in peril, Chinese of all classes should unite against their common external enemy rather than descend into internal strife that would expose China to further predation and eventual partition by the advanced powers. What was needed was social unity to undertake economic development that could ensure and improve the livelihood of all classes in society. How China might undertake a successful program of economic development was addressed in Sun's second principle of the people: that of *minsheng* or "people's livelihood."

Minsheng: Principle of People's Livelihood

Sun's program for economic development began with his insistence that certain conditions must be in place before China could embark on industrialization. According to him, "The survival of a country mainly depends on people, land, and sovereignty *(zhuquan).*"[34] Of those three requisites, China was rich in land and people; what was missing was a sovereign, independent, powerful, and uncorrupt Chinese state. Such a government was needed for both external and internal reasons: externally to resist the exploitation of foreign powers, and internally to enforce unpopular but necessary economic policies on the populace. More than being sovereign and powerful, the developmental state must also be informed and insightful, able to formulate an overarching plan of economic development. Such a plan would enable Chinese to industrialize and achieve autonomy and power, so that in the future China could "make use of others rather than be used by others."[35]

With a strong government to protect and ensure China's national interests against external predators and domestic opponents, the program for economic development could commence. Mindful that industrialization required surplus capital,[36] Sun identified several potential sources. One would be domestic savings that would accrue from the elimination of government waste and corruption. Another source of capital would be the increased state revenue generated from taxation on unearned increments in land value.[37] Yet another source of capital would come from increases in farm yield as a result of a program of agricultural development.

Agricultural Development

Because China's economy was agrarian, any domestic surplus capital necessarily would have to be generated from China's farmlands through increased yield. To achieve that objective, Sun proposed a number of ideas.

The first was the application of Western science and technology to agriculture to improve and enhance production. Farm yield could also be increased through a program of "land to the tillers."[38] Believing that human beings worked harder when they directly benefited from their labor, Sun proposed that land be redistributed to the peasants, the actual tillers. Ownership of land meant that peasants could directly profit from their labor, which would spur them to harder work and greater productivity. That, in turn, would lead to increased yields and a corresponding rise in farm income that would be accrued as savings in banks. The banks, in turn, would use the savings to extend loans to budding entrepreneurs to invest in start-up businesses and industries. In this manner, land reform would create the surplus investment capital for the industrialization of China.

Industrial Development

The industrialization of China would proceed through a mixed economy of state capitalism, as suggested by the term *minsheng,* which Sun explicitly defined to be "nation-state socialism" *(guojia shehui zhuyi).*

According to Sun, the state would have to assume a vital role in industrialization for at least two reasons. The first was that China's poverty made it unlikely that private individuals would possess the large sums of surplus capital needed for certain kinds of undertakings. Those projects included the development of an industrial infrastructure and heavy industries, both of which are capital- and technology-intensive. Infrastructural development included mining, energy supply, and the construction of a national transportation system of railways and roads to bring the raw materials to industrial plants, as well as finished products to markets. An industrial infrastructure also included the development of human resources through a mass education and healthcare system so as to create a literate and healthy workforce for the new economy.

There was a second reason for a state sector. Sun maintained that having the state assume a major role in industrial development would better serve the interests of the greater national community because whatever profits that accrued would benefit all the people of China, instead of a few "big capitalists" *(da zibenjia).* In effect, state-owned enterprises would ensure that China would not only become industrialized, it would also be an equitable society without the gross income inequalities that foment and fuel class conflict.[39] In this manner, a developed and prosperous China would also be a stable and peaceful society.

Aside from those state-owned enterprises, Sun insisted that the rest of the economy should be private. China's private sector would be comprised of the light or consumer industries, from which would grow a burgeoning middle class of property-owning entrepreneurs.

For both the state and private sectors, foreign capital, technology, and expertise would have a role. Foreign loans and investments would constitute a final source of investment capital for China.[40] Rather than succumb to a xenophobic hatred of the West, Sun rejected the Leninist notion that relations between a less developed society and the industrially advanced West necessarily would devolve into a zero-sum game that only benefited the West. Instead, he was convinced that so long as the government of the less developed society properly managed its economic transactions with the West, a positive-sum relationship could be achieved in which both parties could benefit.[41]

In effect, Sun eschewed a dependency-theory conception of international economics. Rather than view economic relations with more developed countries as intrinsically and unavoidably exploitative, he instead proposed that China undertake an "open-door policy"[42] to attract foreign investments and loans. But in proposing such a policy, he was not a naïf; he was fully cognizant that foreigners came "only to profit from China."[43] Despite that, he maintained that the Chinese government could intervene to ensure that economic relations with foreigners would not damage Chinese national interests. To ensure that any economic relationship between China and foreign capital would be a win-win game, Sun offered the following instructions and guidelines:

- Domestic capital and production were preferable to foreign loans and investments.[44]

- Joint Chinese–foreign production was preferable to outright foreign loans.[45]

- Even outright foreign loans were not harmful to Chinese national interest provided they were employed for productive purpose.[46]

- Although in the beginning, the lack of native skilled labor would require Chinese enterprises to employ foreigners, their employment must be contingent on their agreeing to train eventual Chinese replacements.[47]

- Foreign-owned enterprises must be nationalized after a specified period of time.[48]

- China should export manufactured goods rather than unprocessed raw materials.[49]

- The government should nurture infant Chinese industries through a policy of import substitution.[50]

In effect, these guidelines precisely addressed the complex of problems that dependency theorists have identified for less developed countries. Those problems include a dependence on foreign debt, unproductive foreign investments that do not develop backward and forward linkages in the native economy, and an export economy of un- or semi-processed raw materials. More than that, Sun's program also anticipated the economic policies of Asia's newly industrialized countries of South Korea, Hong Kong, Singapore, and Taiwan.[51] What Western economists now identify as "the East Asian pattern of development"—made up of land reform, state capitalism, import substitution, "outward oriented" economic policies, the promotion of education, and a premium placed on political stability[52]—turns out to be the very formula Sun Yat-sen had proposed almost a century ago.

Minquan: Principle of Democracy

Of all of Sun's ideas, possibly the most misunderstood by sinologists are his thoughts on democracy. The misunderstanding begins with the conception of Sun as being insincere in his advocacy—or simply confused in his understanding—of democracy. R. R. Palmer, as an example, asserted that Sun's principle of democracy "easily shaded off into a theory of . . . dictatorship."[53] In that, Palmer could not be more mistaken. Not only was Sun persuaded of the intrinsic and instrumental merits of democracy, he possessed a sophisticated understanding of what was required for successful democratization. More than that, his *minquan* principle anticipated much of contemporary Western social science's thinking on the preconditions for successful democratization.

To begin with, Sun was normatively committed to democracy as the ideal form of government for China, convinced as he was that representative government was "in accord with the global trend" and "the highest form of nation in the world."[54] He shared the philosophy that underlies democratic government—one that conceives human beings as equals, endowed with sovereignty and other inalienable rights. Like the philosophers of the Enlightenment, Sun believed that "all men are alike, being of the same species," each "endowed by nature with human rights *(renquan),*" including "the original rights of the people" of equality and liberty.[55] The fundamental equality of all human beings meant that a just government must be one based on popular sovereignty, where "the monarch cannot enslave the people" and where the people are "the rulers of the nation," because it is only from the people that the right to govern is derived.[56]

Nor was Sun confused in his understanding of democracy. He was unequivocal in stating that *"minquan* means popular sovereignty," which he explicitly defined as "government of the people, by the people, for the people." According to Sun, "only with such a government are the people really the masters of a nation" and its leaders and officials their "servants."[57] In another essay, Sun provided an operational and institutional definition of democracy when he stipulated that *minquan* meant the political system of Switzerland, which he described as "a true republic" where the people had "the four great rights . . . of legislation, referendum, and the election and recall of officials."[58]

In addition to those "four great rights," Sun understood democracy to include other civil rights and liberties, especially the right of "assembly" *(jihui),* which he conceived to be "the first step in the development of *minquan.*"[59] Another "imperative" right was the freedom of religion and worship, the provision of which, in his judgment, would help unify China by eradicating "the clashes and conflicts over religion . . . under Manchu rule."[60]

Not only did Sun value individual rights and liberties, he also recognized the importance of other democratic principles—those pertaining to the separation of powers, checks and balances, opposition parties, and the rotation of parties in power. To begin with, Sun maintained that the separation of governmental powers into separate executive, legislative, and juridical organs would "ensure their proper behavior" and prevent government from degenerating into "despotism."[61] The separation of powers was nothing other than the very "foundation" of democratic constitutions. Of the three powers, Sun thought the legislature to be the most important, describing it as "the foremost" governmental power, having "no power over and above itself."[62] It was precisely his recognition of the importance of separating governmental powers that led him to propose the addition of two traditional Chinese institutions (inspection and examination) to the West's three branches of government to form "five powers in total."[63]

As for political parties, Sun fully realized the importance of multiple and competing parties. He insisted to an audience in 1924 that "Today ... more than ever we need political parties" because they were the bulwark that prevented politics from becoming "increasingly retrograde" and the republic from devolving into despotism. As he explained,[64]

> The purpose of political parties is to assist political development. The two parties ebb and flow. . . . When one party governs, it cannot be perfect in everything. Of necessity, an opposition party is needed to . . . supervise the government's every move. . . . When the people find the policies of the ruling party to be of no benefit to the country . . . they will give the opposition party their approval and trust . . . and make it the governing party.

Sun's advocacy of democracy was more than idealistic; it was also prompted by utilitarian considerations. He thought that political democracy would be instrumental toward unifying the Chinese nation. According to him, in China's millennial history, Chinese of "talent and ambition" had fought wars over who would be the next emperor, causing "endless misery for the people." If China became a republic, Chinese would no longer fight each other to be emperor because the people would be king. In this manner, "internecine strife" could be avoided and "the incidence of warfare" reduced.[65]

While advocating republican government for China, Sun realized that the establishment of democratic government was a long and arduous undertaking. He cited the example of England: how its democracy evolved over hundreds of years with periods of devolution, most notably the revival of the monarchy under Charles II after the Cromwell interregnum. France's quest for democracy, according to Sun, had also been tortuous. Instead of democratic government, the hopes and elation of the French Revolution ended in bloodbath, chaos, and the installation of the Napoleonic monarchy. Democracy would not make its appearance in France for another 80 years.[66]

Mindful of the certain difficulties in transforming autocratic China into a republic, Sun proposed that democratization be realized in three stages, beginning with "military rule" *(junzheng),* followed by "tutelary rule" *(xunzheng),* and culminating in "constitutional government" *(xianzheng).*[67] In fact, he attributed the unsuccessful attempt to create a republican government after the 1911 Revolution to precisely his countrymen's failure to "sequentially construct" democracy.[68]

Junzheng

Sun conceived the first stage in the construction of a democratic China to be one of martial rule, a period of "destruction," in which the revolutionary army would "obliterate the despotic system of the Manchus, sweep away bureaucratic corruption, and reform pernicious cultural habits."[69] A major task in this first period was the suppression of the warlords so as to secure territorial integration. "Only by so doing," Sun explained, "could a secure economic foundation be erected, on the basis of which the entire nation would be unified in an effort to achieve a genuine democracy. . . ."[70]

In effect, the first stage of *junzheng* would accomplish many of the elements of political development identified by Western social scientists: those of territorial integration, the dismantling of the old order, the securing of political authority, and the assurance of order and stability. All of which would ensure a firm foundation upon which a new social order could be constructed.

Xunzheng

Only when the military government had succeeded in imposing and securing its authority over all of China would the second stage in democratization begin: that of "tutelary rule" *(xunzheng)* by the revolutionary party. The military regime would be dismantled and society demilitarized to prevent the permanent entrenchment of martial power. As Sun explained, "when the military flourishes for too long a time, soldiers are nourished only to become a plague on society."[71]

Following "the conversion of soldiers into workers," the revolutionary party would install itself in authoritarian rule over China—but the authoritarianism was for an expressly instrumental purpose to tutor the people "to become masters of the republic."[72] Contrary to some writers' opinion that Sun's notion of tutelary rule amounted to "a theory of dictatorship,"[73] he clearly intended one-party tutelage to be "a transitional stage."[74] A single party would rule so that it could put in place the preconditions for a stable and viable democracy. Those conditions included an enhancement of national income and wealth through a program of economic development, and the creation of a civic culture by fostering appropriate attitudes, values, and behaviors among the populace.

The first of the democratic preconditions was the creation of national and individual wealth via a program of economic development. Although Sun accorded the state a significant role in the economy, he did insist that there be a substantial private sector, including the private ownership of land and privately owned and operated businesses and industries. That private economy, in turn, would create a property-owning middle class in Chinese society, a class to which social science imparts much significance.

In his program of economic development, Sun was particularly emphatic about the importance of education, going so far as to say that "national regeneration is entirely dependent on the development of the Chinese people's formal learning."[75] As he explained,[76]

> A nation's strength or weakness is determined by the level of education of its students. . . . Although the masters of the republic may be immature, with every passing day . . . the number of enlightened people will multiply . . . ideas of freedom and equality will flourish, eventually leading to the full realization of democracy. . . .

Aside from economic development, authoritarian rule by the tutelary party was also intended as a means to transform Chinese culture into one that would be congruent with democratic government. Explaining the importance of culture for the effective functioning of democracy, Sun observed that "If the people are apathetic and unconcerned about politics, government will devolve into rule by the politicians"[77] instead of government by the people.

Acutely aware of the lack of fit between democracy and China's traditional culture, Sun attributed the failure of the 1911 republic (and the success of Yuan Shikai's "counterrevolution") to "the persistence of feudal thinking" that infected even "those who call themselves revolutionaries."[78] The "poison" from centuries of despotic rule had "deeply infected the hearts" of the Chinese people and "fettered" their "body and spirit," causing them to "regard democracy as their enemy."[79] In particular, Sun lamented the inability of Chinese to unite and form effective associations, which he attributed to their having been "forbidden to associate" for hundreds of years by successive dynasties. As a result, Chinese "lost their natural instinct for uniting into a group" and became "deficient in the principles, methods, habits, and experience of assemblage," resembling instead "a disorderly mob."[80]

But Sun refused to join those who despaired that the anarchic Chinese could only be governed by an autocrat. Instead, he argued that "a nation is like a human being." Just as a newly born infant could not walk, a new nation could not "suddenly take flight." Just as an infant must learn to walk by being taught by a nanny, "the same applies to a nation."[81] In the case of China, given its long despotic tradition, the tutelary state would have to be the nanny to instruct Chinese in self-government. In that task, the state would be assisted by Sun's *Primer on Democracy,* which would "teach the people how to take the first step in democracy." All groups and associations—be they "[f]amilies, social groups, schools, farmers' associations, labor unions, business associations and corporations, the National Assembly, provincial assemblies, local assemblies, national affairs committees, military affairs committees"—must use the *Primer* "as their guide" until its teachings became "common knowledge." It was precisely by learning through practice that Westerners acquired facility in self-government. As Sun explained, "Westerners are trained in parliamentary conduct since childhood, so that when they are in secondary school, it already is second nature to them. This is why their ability to unite in groups often surpasses that of the Chinese."[82]

Western democratic theorists have often emphasized the importance of due process. Harry Eckstein, as an example, noted that in democracies, procedures "are not merely procedures, but sacred rituals." This is because democracies "invest with very high affect the procedural aspects of their government and with very low affect its substantive aspects; they behave like ideologists in regard to rules and like pragmatists in regard to policies."[83] It is in this context that Sun's *Primer on Democracy* assumes special significance, for the *Primer* is none other than a collection of painstakingly detailed instructions on due process: on rules of order and the proper conduct of meetings.

The *Primer* begins with a recognition of the importance of voluntary "autonomous" *(duli)* associations, whose purpose, according to Sun, was to "assist in the reform and improvement of government, guide social progress, and unite with like-minded individuals in common purpose. . . ."[84] More than voluntary associations, the *Primer* also addresses a number of other issues that are critical to the functioning of democracy, including the following: the need for the regular rotation of officers; the proper conduct of elected officers; the rights of the minority; potential conflicts of interest of officers, especially the chairman; how to elect officers; the rights and duties of membership; when and how elected officers can be dismissed; when and how to have special emergency sessions; how to propose, second, and approve a motion; the importance of allowing for ample discussion of a motion before a vote is taken; the need to keep discussion impersonal, friendly, and respectful; amendments; and, lastly, "rules of order" *(chixu).*[85]

Sun proposed that the *xian* (county or district) would be the basic political and economic unit for the government's tutelage in democracy.[86] It is in the *xian* that the Chinese people would learn about and practice self-government so that "popular sovereignty . . . [would] be more than empty verbiage." Sun instructed that, on the day that military rule ended,[87]

> Each *xian* would immediately promulgate a provisional local constitution *(yuefa)* establishing the rights and duties of the people and the powers of the revolutionary government. A popular election for local officials will be held after a period of, at most, three years. But if the local authorities succeed in eradicating pernicious traditional practices . . . or if over half of the population of the *xian* have understood the Three Principles of the People, the election may be held in less than three years.

In this learning process, China's elite had a special role. Although Sun believed in equality of rights, he nevertheless recognized that "China's four hundred million people are not equal in intelligence" and that "not everyone has the intellectual capability to participate in government." Despite that, Sun did not propose an oligarchy for China, arguing instead that those who are specially gifted have special responsibilities. He insisted that those with "a surplus of intelligence and ability" *(xianzi xianjue)* must assist "those who are less adequate" by serving as "workers in government and servants of society" so that their knowledge and intellect could be used "to enhance the happiness of the common people and strengthen and enrich the nation."[88] As servants of the people, the elite "must sacrifice their personal freedom" for the public interest. In particular, they must strictly observe organizational discipline—which should be "firm and clear"—in the interest of building strong and effective institutions. According to Sun,[89]

> Discipline *[jilu]* must be strictly observed in the institutions of government, with everyone attending to his own affairs. . . . If government officials, military or civilian, defy rules and regulations . . . organizations will not be cohesive . . . and officials will lack designated functions, becoming like a tray of loose sand. Under such circumstances, how can they work for the people? It is therefore imperative that bureaucratic functionaries subscribe to organizational discipline, so that the entire institution is like a machine, with its many wheels working flawlessly in perfect coordination.

Xianzheng

When the Chinese people had proven their ability to govern themselves at the local level—"when every *xian* is totally self governing"—China's transition to democracy would proceed to its third and final stage of "constitutional rule" *(xianzheng)*. Having proven themselves to be their own masters at the local level, the Chinese people could now participate fully in national government. After a process of national deliberation and consultation, a democratic constitution would be promulgated, according to which popular elections would be held to form a representative government. As Sun described,[90]

> [E]ach *xian* will elect one representative to the National Assembly that will decide on and enact a five-power national constitution. . . . [A] government composed of five branches will be formed. . . . The people of each *xian* will vote in a national election for the state president and the representatives to the Legislative *Yuan*. With the legislature's approval, the president will compose the Executive *Yuan* and appoint the leaders of the remaining three branches. All five branches of government are responsible to the National Assembly. . . . At this time, the revolutionary [interim] government turns over its power to the popularly elected president, and the period of tutelage comes to an end. . . . [With that] the revolution will have finally achieved its objectives, and the task of national reconstruction completed.

Through the three stages of democratic transition—from martial rule to tutelary single-party rule to constitutional rule—China would finally become a republic where government would be checked and balanced by a free press,[91] where political power was separated into five branches,[92] and where good government would be assured through a two-party system and their regular rotation in power.[93]

More than that, what Sun aspired to was not simply a carbon copy of Western democracies. Instead, he urged that Chinese "should not mimic Europe and America in advocating popular sovereignty." It was his belief that although the West was superior in science and technology, it was flawed in governance, "the management of people." Sun was particularly critical of certain attributes of Western culture that "emasculated" government, in particular, the insistence on absolute freedom and equality, and the adversarial nature of relations between government and the governed.[94] Instead of Western-style democracy, Sun wanted a democracy with Chinese characteristics, tailored to the special needs and circumstances of China. It would be a democracy that valued public interest over private ends, where individual liberty was not conceived as absolute, where government was powerful and effective "to work for the good of the people."[95] As in the West, good government would be assured through a competitive party system and the regular rotation of power.[96] But political power in a democratic China would be separated into five branches, instead of three. Citizens would have responsibilities as well as rights.[97] Government would be checked and balanced by a free press that exercised self-restraint.[98]

For, in the last analysis, democracy was not simply an end in itself but also an instrumental good to Sun Yat-sen. He valued democracy not merely as an axiomatic, self-justified good, but for its utilitarian value toward his abiding objective of a strong and cohesive Chinese nation.

Sun Yat-sen and Modern Social Science

Sun's conception of nation and nationalism is strikingly similar to the formulations of contemporary scholars of nationalism. By offering less developed countries a formula to achieve a win-win relationship with foreign capital, Sun's program of economic development effectively refutes the fatalistic convictions of contemporary dependency theorists. And by recognizing that democracy should be sequentially constructed, Sun anticipated the now common understanding in Western social sciences that stable and viable transitions to democracy demand certain prerequisites if the resulting polity were to be more than mere ephemera. Those prerequisites include economic, cultural, political-institutional conditions, and historical timing.

Democratic Preconditions

As far back as the ancient Greeks, Western conceptions of democracy included notions of the optimum conditions for a democratic order. None other than Aristotle wrote of two such contingent conditions that bear striking similarities to Sun's ideas. The first condition for democracy, according to Aristotle, pertained to economics, specifically a middle class. According to Aristotle, "the best political community is formed by citizens of the middle class," those with "a moderate and sufficient property," because they have "a greater share in government." In contrast, a society that is bifurcated between the haves and have-nots—those who "possess much" and those who have nothing—risks devolving into "an extreme democracy," an oligarchy, or a tyranny. As Aristotle put it, "when there is no middle class, and the poor greatly exceed in number, troubles arise, and the state soon comes to an end."[99]

Aristotle's second democratic precondition was a culture that valued and respected law and justice. He observed that "where the laws are not supreme, there demagogues spring up." Only in a society of laws could man rise to become "the best of animals"; separated from law and justice, man would devolve into the worst of all creatures.[100]

Centuries after Aristotle, beginning in the 1950s, Western social scientists developed similar ideas, conceiving self-government as neither simple nor easy. Instead, the conviction grew that democracy necessitated certain prior conditions if it was to be authentic and lasting.[101] Those prerequisites include Aristotle's economics and culture, as well as political institutionalization and the appropriate historical timing.

Economic Conditions

Among the social scientists who have written on the economic conditions for democracy is Seymour Martin Lipset. In his *Political Man,* first published in 1959, Lipset characterized the relationship between economics and democracy with this simple statement: "The more well-to-do a nation, the greater the chances that it will sustain democracy."[102] His thesis that "the level of a country's economic development independently affects the orientations conducive to democracy of its citizens" was subsequently confirmed by, among others, Robert Dahl, Larry Diamond, and Alex Inkeles.[103]

In the twentieth century, the source of national wealth was economic development. Employing four indices of economic development—those of wealth, industrialization, urbanization, and education—Lipset correlated them with countries classified on an ordinal scale from more to less democratic. He concluded that, "In each case, the average wealth, degree of industrialization and urbanization, and level of education is much higher for the more democratic countries. . . ."[104]

More than being correlated, Lipset maintained that economics and democracy were functionally related. He gave particular attention to the relationship between democracy and two indices of economic development—those of wealth and education. With regards to the first index, Lipset asserted that a poor society is more disposed toward political extremism and, therefore, less supportive of democracy because the poor, having little to lose, are more susceptible to anti-democratic extremist appeals. A country of high average per-capita income, on the other hand, tends to have greater socio-economic equity, a competent civil service, a large middle class, and a proliferation of autonomous voluntary associations—all of which are supportive of democracy. At the level of the individual, wealth is also correlated with personal characteristics conducive to successful self-government: those of self-esteem and receptivity to democratic norms.[105]

With regards to the second index of education, Lipset went so far as to assert that, "If we cannot say that a 'high' level of education is a *sufficient* condition for democracy, the available evidence suggests that it comes close to being a *necessary* one." This was because education broadens people's outlook, enables them to understand the need for norms of tolerance, restrains them from adhering to extremist doctrines, and increases their capacity to make rational electoral choices.[106]

Cultural Conditions

Quite apart from economic conditions, the stability of democratic government is also contingent on the society's possession of a democratic or civic culture. Gabriel Almond and Sidney Verba defined civic culture as "a pattern of political attitudes that fosters democratic stability, that in some way 'fits' the democratic political system." Those attitudinal attributes include, among others, the individual's possession of a sense of political efficacy and of interpersonal trust and cooperation.[107]

Although Almond and Verba identified the importance of a civic culture for democracy, they did not specify *how* that culture comes into being beyond stating that the civic culture is transmitted by "a complex process" that includes training in many social institutions and in the political system.[108] The illumination of the complex process by which civic culture is transmitted was provided by Harry Eckstein.

In "A Theory of Stable Democracy," Eckstein focused on one aspect of social life he took to be "most obviously and immediately relevant to political behavior on the governmental level"—that of "authority patterns" in social relationships. "Authority relationships" are relationships of "superordination and subordination among individuals in social formations"[109]—in families, schools, churches, social clubs, business organizations, trade unions, interest groups, political parties, and so on.

According to Eckstein, a government will tend to be stable if its authority pattern is congruent with the other authority patterns of the society of which it is a part. Authority patterns are "congruent" if they are identical or closely resemble each other, or at least "dovetail with, or support" the governmental pattern. As Eckstein explained,[110]

[I]t stands to reason that if any aspect of social life can directly affect government it is the experiences with authority that men have in other spheres of life, especially those that mold their personalities and those to which they normally devote most of their lives.

In other words, the success and stability of democratic government are contingent on there being reasonably democratic authority relationships throughout society, particularly in groups that are more closely related to government, such as political parties and interest groups. By the same token, governments will be unstable if the governmental authority pattern is "isolated," that is, substantially different from those of other social segments. *Simply put, the stability, authenticity, and viability of democratic government depends on there being a democratic culture in the larger society.*

Given this, for self-government to be successful, much would depend on a society's child-rearing practices, religion(s), and voluntary associations. The formative impact of early childhood experiences on adult political attitudes is well documented by social scientists such as Edward Banfield.[111] Likewise, the relationship between religion and political culture.[112] Together, the two institutions of family and church exert perhaps the most powerful influences on an individual's attitudes toward authority.

The role that voluntary associations play toward fostering self-government was noted as early as Alexis de Tocqueville. According to de Tocqueville and others, societal organizations independent of the state perform a vital role in fostering democracy by inhibiting the state, formulating opinions, communicating ideas (including opposition ideas), and most importantly, providing the training ground for the practice of democratic and other political skills.[113]

Political-Institutional Conditions

A third condition favorable to a democratic order is that of political institutionalization, "the process by which organizations and procedures acquire value and stability." The level of institutionalization of a political system is determined by its adaptability, complexity, autonomy, and coherence.[114]

Samuel Huntington's works on this subject exemplify the thesis that for a society to negotiate a successful transition from authoritarianism to pluralism, it is better that democratization be preceded by political institutionalization. Democratization or the broadening of political participation, in the absence of strong stable governmental institutions, is a recipe for political instability.[115] As Huntington put it,[116]

Men . . . cannot have liberty without order. Authority has to exist before it can be limited. . . . A government with a low level of institutionalization is not just a weak government; it is also a bad government. The function of government is to govern. . . . [E]ffective political institutions are necessary for stable and eventually democratic government. . . .

According to Huntington, political institutionalization can be achieved in a number of ways, one of which is to decelerate or limit political mobilization and participation. Another method is to build a single political party rather than proceed prematurely to a multiparty system. In Huntington's words,[117]

> Where traditional political institutions are weak or non-existent, the prerequisite of stability is at least one highly institutionalized political party. States with one such party are markedly more stable than states which lack such a party. States with no parties or many weak parties are the least stable.

Historical Timing

Western social sciences have suggested a fourth condition for the democratic order—that of "historical sequence" or timing, as exemplified in Robert Dahl's *Polyarchy*. In that work, Dahl sought to determine whether some sequences are more likely than others to facilitate the shift toward a more democratic regime.[118] Employing the concepts of "liberalization" and "inclusiveness" as his criteria, Dahl discerned three possible paths to democracy or polyarchy. By "liberalization," he meant a situation wherein an authoritarian regime (or "closed hegemony") makes available increased opportunities for opposition to the regime (or "public contestation"). "Inclusiveness," for its part, refers to the granting of the right to participate in the political system to a large proportion of citizens.[119]

According to Dahl, the first path to polyarchy is one where liberalization precedes inclusiveness: a situation where an authoritarian regime increases the opportunity for public contestation to a few in society, becoming thereby a "competitive oligarchy." In time, the competitive oligarchy expands political participation to include the masses, and eventually becomes a polyarchy. The second path to democratic government is one where inclusiveness precedes liberalization. The third and last path is that of the "shortcut," where an authoritarian regime is abruptly transformed into a democracy by the simultaneous lifting of prohibition against both public contestation and mass inclusiveness.[120]

It is Dahl's contention that the optimum path to democracy is the first sequence, whereby political competition among an elite precedes mass participation in politics. In so doing, the rules, practices, and culture of competitive politics could first be developed among a small segment of society. Later, as additional social strata are admitted into the political process, each successive group is socialized into the norms and practices of competitive politics with which the elite is already familiar. As a consequence, neither the newer strata nor the incumbents who were threatened with displacement would feel that the costs of toleration are so high as to outweigh the costs of repression.[121]

The other two paths, in contrast, were thought by Dahl to be "more dangerous." As he explained,[122]

> [T]o arrive at a viable system of mutual security is a difficult matter at best; the greater the number of people and the variety and disparity of interests involved, the more difficult the task and the greater the time required. Tolerance and mutual security are more likely to develop among a small elite sharing similar perspectives than among a large and heterogeneous collection of leaders. . . . This is why the first path is more likely than the other two to produce stable transformations . . . toward polyarchy.

In effect, Sun's proposal for a sequential construction of democracy addresses many of the democratic preconditions conceived by contemporary social scientists. His period of tutelary rule, wherein the state would undertake economic development with a substantial private sector of small and medium-sized entrepreneurs and landowners, amply provides for Lipset's economic preconditions of industrialization—particularly those of a large middle class and mass education. At the same time, Sun's authoritarian state would also tutor the people in democracy through their participation in local self-government and voluntary associations, resulting in the civic culture that Eckstein, Almond, and Verba emphasized. Sun's prescription that local self-government must precede mass participation at the national level addresses the central rationale in Dahl's thesis on historical timing. Finally, Sun also met Huntington's political institutionalization precondition by insisting that the installation of democratic government must be preceded by the periods of military and tutelary rule in order that the revolutionary government could secure order and stability.

Conclusion

The strategies that non-Western peoples employ in their attempt to ameliorate the effects of Western imperialism have included one form of extremism or another. Whether the strategy is xenophilia or xenophobia, archaism or futurism, such posturings are at best psychological anodyne that mitigates and soothes the much-abused ego of those who suffer from imperialism. None of those strategies, however, can deliver lasting relief since they fail to address the real problem—that of endemic poverty and economic underdevelopment.

In contrast to those extremist postures, the developmental nationalist ideology of Sun Yat-sen offers a constructive and pragmatic solution to China's predicament. In assembling his ideology, Sun rejected no idea outright, nor did he subscribe entirely to any particular thought—be it Western or Chinese. He refrained from an indiscriminate embrace of Western liberalism and capitalism; nor was he an uncritical disciple of Karl Marx, rejecting the latter's central tenet of class struggle. He eschewed the despairing perspective of dependency theory, believing instead that China could benefit from an open-door policy toward foreign capital and technology. He was neither enamored with the West nor unduly attached to Chinese tradition. Instead, he selected those ideas that were most useful for the construction of a strong Chinese nation-state, some of which were traditional Confucian virtues, modified and adapted to modern conditions.[123] Contrary to the opinion that his thought was superficial and confused, Sun was profound and complex. More than that, his ideas predated and anticipated many of the conceptions of contemporary social science concerning nationalism, economic development, and political democratization. As such, they not only have withstood the test of time but might well serve as a model for the developing countries of the world in their continuing quest for economic viability and popular sovereignty.

Notes

1. Mary Matossian, "Ideologies of Delayed Development," in John Hutchinson and Anthony D. Smith (eds.), *Nationalism* (Oxford and New York: Oxford University Press, 1994), p. 218.

2. As an example, M. Zolotow and M. William believed that Sun was a "thoroughgoing Marxist." See M. Zolotow, *Maurice William and Sun Yat-sen* (London: Hale, 1948), p. 9; and the "Author's Introduction" to M. William, *Sun Yat-sen versus Communism* (Baltimore: Williams and Wilkins, 1932), pp. xv–xx. Others, however, have insisted that "we cannot say that Sun Yat-sen was ever a 'Marxist,' for he never accepted the main tenets of Marxism. . . ." Tsui Shu-chin, "The Influence of the Canton-Moscow Entente Upon Sun Yat-sen's Political Philosophy," *The Chinese Social and Political Science Review*, 18:3 (October 1934), p. 346.

3. Li Ti-tsun, "The Life of Sun Yat-sen," *Chinese Students Monthly*, 24:1 (November 1928), p. 28.

4. Harold Z. Schiffrin, *Sun Yat-sen and the Origins of the Chinese Revolution* (Berkeley: University of California Press, 1968), p. 2.

5. Sagittarius, *The Strange Apotheosis of Sun Yat-sen* (London: Heath Cranton, 1938), p. 10.

6. Tai Tschi-tao, *Die geistigen Grundlagen des Sun Yat-senismus* (Berlin: Wuerfel, 1931), pp. 14F; Lucien Bianco, *Origins of the Chinese Revolution 1915–1949* (Stanford: Stanford University Press, 1971), p. 12.

7. Sagittarius, *Strange Apotheosis of Sun Yat-sen*, p. 188; M. N. Roy, *Revolution and Counter-Revolution in China* (Calcutta: Renaissance, 1946), p. 254.

8. Y. C. Wang, *Chinese Intellectuals and the West 1872–1949* (Chapel Hill: University of North Carolina Press, 1966), p. 335.

9. Roy, *Revolution and Counter-Revolution in China*, pp. 256, 257.

10. Matossian, "Ideologies of Delayed Development," pp. 222–223, 225.

11. Sun Yat-sen, *San Min Chu I* (Taipei: China Publishing, n.d.), pp. 3ff, 17, 5.

12. Ibid., p. 52.

13. Sun, "Minzu zhuyi (Principle of Nationalism)," *Guofu quanshu (The Complete Writings of Sun Yat-sen)* (Taipei: China Academy, 1974), p. 199.

14. Sun, "Zaocheng gonghe yinguo ji guomin zeren (The cause and effect of the creation of the Republic and the duties of the citizen)," speech of October 26, 1912 to the military academy at Nanjing, *Guofu quanji (The Complete Works of Sun Yat-sen)*, II (Taipei: Kuomintang Party History Committee, 1973), p. 316; and Sun, "Zhongguo cunwang wenti," p. 745.

15. Sun, "Zhongguo cunwang wenti (The Question of China's Survival)," written in 1917, *Guofu quanshu*, pp. 742, 723.

16. Sun, "Zaocheng gonghe yinguo," p. 316.

17. Sun, "Minzu zhuyi," p. 199.

18. Sun, *San Min Chu I*, pp. 3ff.

19. Sun, "Minzu zhuyi," p. 187.

20. Ibid.

21. Ibid., p. 186.

22. Sun, "Zhongguo cunwang wenti," p. 722.

23. Sun, *San Min Chu I*, pp. 51–54.

24. Sun, "Minzu zhuyi," p. 186.

25. Ibid., pp. 192, 187, 208.

26. Ibid., p. 191.

27. Sun, "Zhongguo cunwang wenti," p. 724; and "Minzu zhuyi," pp. 191–192. Sun clearly considered Vietnam, Burma, and Nepal to be integral parts of the Chinese Empire, writing that "Annam and Burma originally were Chinese territories *(lingtu)*", and that "Nepal had been a tributary state [of China] until 1912."

28. Sun, "Minzu zhuyi," pp. 193–195.

29. Sun, "The True Solution of the Chinese Question," *Guofu quanji*, V, pp. 115, 116.

30. Sun, "Shang Li Hungzhang tongchen jiuguo daji shu (A memorial to Li Hongzhang on the plan to save the nation)," *Guofu quanshu*, pp. 352–357.

31. Sun, *San Min Chu I*, p. 39; cf. pp. 31–35.

32. Ibid., pp. 157, 160, 161; see also Sun, "Minsheng zhuyi (Principle of People's Livelihood)," *Guofu quanshu,* p. 261.

33. Sun, *San Min Chu I,* p. 161.

34. Sun, "Zhongguo cunwang wenti," p. 723.

35. Sun, "Zhongguo shiye dang ruhe fazhan (How should China's industries be developed)," *Guofu quanji,* II, p. 168.

36. Sun, "Zhongguo cunwang wenti," p. 726.

37. Sun, "Minsheng zhuyi zhi shishi (The enactment of the principle of social-ism)," speech of May 4, 1912, and "Dijia choushui wenti (The problem of taxation on land value)," *Guofu quanji,* II, pp. 231–233 and 241–242.

38. Sun, "Gengzhe yaoyou qitian (Those who till should have land)," speech of August 23, 1924, *Guofu quanshu,* pp. 1004–1006.

39. Sun, "Minsheng zhuyi," p. 271.

40. Ibid.; Sun, "Zhongguo cunwang wenti," p. 726.

41. For a more detailed discussion of this, see A. James Gregor and Maria Hsia Chang, "Marxism, Sun Yat-sen and the Concept of 'Imperialism'," *Pacific Affairs,* 55:1 (Spring 1982), pp. 54–79.

42. "If we want to solve our difficulties . . . our only recourse is to welcome for-eign capital, to change our hitherto closed door policy into an open door policy." Sun, "Yu jiejue waijiao wenti xuqu menhu kaifang zhuyi (The problem in foreign relations requires the adoption of an open door policy)," speech of September 5, 1912, *Guofu quanji,* II, p. 264.

43. Sun, "Difang zizhi wei shehui jinbu zhi jichu (Local self-government is the foundation for social progress)," speech of August 25, 1916, *Guofu quanji,* II, p. 369.

44. Sun, "Difang zizhi kaishi shixingfa (How to begin local self government)," *Guofu quanji,* II, p. 173.

45. Sun, "Yu jiejue waijiao," p. 264.

46. Sun, "Minsheng zhuyi yu shehui geming (The principle of socialism and so-cial revolution)," speech of April 1, 1912, *Guofu quanji,* II, p. 217.

47. Sun, "Shiye jianshe (Material reconstruction)," *Guofu quanji,* I, p. 517.

48. Sun, "Yu jiejue waijiao," p. 264.

49. Sun, "Daolu wei jianshe zhuoshou zhi diyiduan (Roads are the starting point for reconstruction)," speech of August 9, 1916, *Guofu quanji,* II, p. 361.

50. Sun, "Jianshe yi xiuzhi daolu wei diyi yaozhuo (The first task of reconstruc-tion is railway construction)," speech of August 16, 1916, and "Gemingjun bukexi-ang shengguan facai (The revolutionary army must not seek wealth through official-dom)," *Guofu quanji,* II, pp. 363, 682.

51. For a discussion of how Sun's conception of economic development accords with Taiwan's industrialization, see A. James Gregor, Maria Hsia Chang, and Andrew Zimmerman, *Ideology and Development: Sun Yat-sen and the Economic History of Taiwan* (Berkeley: University of California, Institute of East Asian Studies, 1981).

52. See chapter 1 of Dwight H. Perkins, *China: Asia's Next Economic Giant?* (Seattle: University of Washington Press, 1986).

53. R. R. Palmer, *A History of the Modern World* (New York: Knopf, 1952), p. 772.

54. Sun, "Minquan zhuyi (The principle of popular sovereignty)," *Guofu quanshu,* p. 220; "Minquan chubu (The Primer of Democracy)," in "Jianguo fanglue (The strategy for national reconstruction)," *Guofu quanji,* I, p. 669.

55. Sun Yat-sen, "Sanmin zhuyi (The Three Principles of the People)," essay of 1919; "Sanmin zhuyi yu zhongguo minzu zhi qiantu (The Three Principles of the People and the future of the Chinese people)," speech of December 2, 1906; and "Yu kaizao xin guojia dang shixing sanmin zhuyi (To build a new nation requires the realization of the Three Principles of the People)," speech of January 4, 1922, *Guofu quanji,* II, pp. 157, 205, 508.

56. Sun, "Minquan chubu," p. 668.

57. Sun, "Sanmin zhuyi," pp. 156–157.

58. Sun, "Minquan chubu," p. 667.

59. Ibid., p. 668.

60. Sun, "Zongjiao yu zhengzhi (Religion and politics)," speech of 1923, *Guofu quanji,* II, p. 321.

61. Sun, "Xiugai zhangcheng zhi shuoming (Explaining the amending of the party constitution)," speech of November 4, 1920; and "Zhonghua minguo jianshe zhi jichu (The foundation for the construction of the Republic of China)," essay of 1922, *Guofu quanji,* II, pp. 395, 179.

62. Sun, "Xianfa zhi jichu (The foundation of the constitution)," speech of July 20, 1916; and "Guohui zhuquan lun (On the sovereignty of Parliament)," speech of March 22, 1913, *Guofu quanji,* II, pp. 359, 348.

63. Sun, "Zhonghua minguo jianshe zhi jichu," pp. 179–180. Implicit in this statement is Sun's advocacy of an independent judiciary.

64. Sun, "Zhengdang zhi yaoyi zaiwei guojia zao xingfu wei renmin mou luoli (The essential meaning of political parties is to create happiness for the nation and wellbeing for the people)," speech of March 1, 1924, *Guofu quanji,* II, p. 334.

65. Sun, "Minquan zhuyi," pp. 221, 220.

66. Ibid., pp. 218–220.

67. Sun, "Zhongguo gemingshi (The history of the Chinese revolution)," essay of 1922, *Guofu quanji,* II, p. 184.

68. Sun, "Zhonghua minguo jianshe zhi jichu," p. 180.

69. Sun, "Zhongguo gemingshi," p. 184.

70. Sun, "Zhongguo guomindang beifa xuanyan (The Northern Expedition Statement of the Chinese Nationalist Party)," September 18, 1924, *Guofu quanshu,* p. 767.

71. Sun, "Zhongguo gemingshi," p. 191.

72. Sun, "Sanmin zhuyi," p. 158.

73. Palmer, *History of the Modern World,* p. 772.

74. Sun, "Sanmin zhuyi," p. 158.

75. Sun, "Xuesheng ying zhuzhang shehui daode (Students should advocate social morality)," speech of August 1911 in Beijing, *Guofu quanshu*, p. 531.

76. Sun, "Fei xuewen wuyi jianshe (There can be no construction without learning)," speech of May 7, 1911 to students in Guangzhou, *Guofu quanshu*, p. 491; and "Sanmin zhuyi," p. 158.

77. Sun, "Zhonghua minguo jianshe zhi jichu," p. 179.

78. Sun, "Zhongguo gemingdang beifa xuanyan," p. 766.

79. Sun, "Zhongguo gemingshi," pp. 183, 190.

80. Sun, "Minquan chubu (The Primer of Democracy)," *Guofu quanshu*, p. 118.

81. Ibid.

82. Ibid.

83. Harry Eckstein, "Appendix B: A Theory of Stable Democracy," *Division and Cohesion in Democracy: A Study of Norway* (Princeton: Princeton University Press, 1966), p. 265.

84. Sun, "Minquan chubu," *Guofu quanshu*, pp. 120, 121.

85. Ibid., pp. 122, 123, 124, 125, 127, 128, 129, 130, 149–152.

86. In fact, Sun had a modern "political economy" notion of government and society. In arguing for the combining of political and economic functions in the *xian* government, Sun wrote that "Today, the governments of civilized nations have gradually combined political functions with economic responsibilities." Sun, "Difang zizhi kaishi shixingfa (The way to begin the implementation of local self-government)," *Guofu quanji*, II, pp. 169, 174.

87. Sun, "Zhongguo gemingshi," pp. 188, 183.

88. Sun, "Minguo jiaoyujia zhi renwu (The responsibility of the republic's educators)," speech of August 30, 1911, in Beijing, *Guofu quanshu*, p. 530; and "Xuesheng ying zhuzhang shehui daode," p. 531.

89. Sun, *Guofu quanji*, II, pp. 221–222.

90. Sun, "Zhongguo gemingshi," p. 184.

91. Sun, "Gebao yanlun xuqiu yizhi (Newspapers' commentaries should seek unanimity)," speech of April 27, 1912, *Guofu quanshu*, pp. 488–489.

92. Sun, "Caiyong wuquan fenli yijiu sanquan dingli zhibi (Adopting the system of five powers to amend the defects of the separation of powers into three branches)," speech of August 20, 1916, *Guofu quanshu*, pp. 709–710.

93. Sun, "Zhengdang yizhong danggang dangde (Political parties should heed their constitutions and morals)," speech of January 19, 1913, *Guofu quanshu*, pp. 556–557.

94. Sun, "Minquan zhuyi," pp. 241, 225–226.

95. Ibid., pp. 225–226, 228, 242, 245.

96. Sun, "Zhengdang yizhong danggang dangde (Political parties should heed their constitutions and morals)," speech of January 19, 1913, *Guofu quanshu*, pp. 556–557.

97. Sun specified that with the exception of the young, the old, the handicapped, and pregnant women, "all others enjoy their rights only if they serve their duties; those who do not meet their responsibilities will cease to have all rights of citizenship." Sun, "Difang zizhi kaishi shixingfa," p. 170.

98. Sun, "Gebao yanlun xuqiu yizhi (Newspaper commentaries should seek unanimity)," speech of April 27, 1912, *Guofu quanshu*, pp. 488–489.

99. Citations from "Politica" translated by Benjamin Jowett in Richard McKeon (ed.), *The Basic Works of Aristotle* (New York: Random House, 1941), pp. 1221–1222.

100. Ibid., pp. 1212, 1130.

101. Eckstein defined "stable democracy" as "persistence of pattern, decisional effectiveness, and authenticity." Eckstein, "A Theory of Stable Democracy," p. 229.

102. Seymour Martin Lipset, *Political Man: The Social Bases of Politics* (Baltimore, Maryland: Johns Hopkins University Press, 1981), p. 31.

103. Ibid., p. 473.

104. Ibid., pp. 33–38.

105. Ibid., 47–53.

106. Ibid., pp. 40, 39.

107. Gabriel Almond and Sidney Verba, *The Civic Culture* (Boston: Little, Brown, 1965), pp. 337–338 and chapter XIII. See also, Sidney Verba and Lucian Pye (eds.), *Political Culture and Political Development* (Princeton: Princeton University Press, 1965).

108. Almond and Verba, *Civic Culture*, pp. 366–367.

109. Eckstein, "A Theory of Stable Democracy," pp. 225, 233.

110. Ibid., pp. 234, 238, 239–241, 225.

111. See Edward C. Banfield, *The Moral Basis of a Backward Society* (Glencoe, Illinois: The Free Press, 1958).

112. See Gunnar Myrdal, *Asian Drama: An Inquiry into the Poverty of Nations* (New York: Pantheon, 1968); Max Weber, *The Protestant Ethic and the Spirit of Capitalism* (New York: Charles Scribner's Sons, 1950); *The Religion of China* (New York: Macmillan, 1951); and *The Religion of India* (Glencoe, Illinois: The Free Press, 1958).

113. Lipset, *Political Man*, p. 52.

114. Samuel P. Huntington, *Political Order in Changing Societies* (New Haven: Yale University Press, 1968), p. 12.

115. Ibid., p. 55.

116. Ibid., pp. 8, 28; Huntington, "Strategies of Institutional Development," in Jason L. Finkle and Richard W. Gable (eds.), *Political Development and Social Change* (New York: John Wiley & Sons, 1971), p. 478.

117. Huntington, "Strategies of Institutional Development," p. 483.

118. Robert A. Dahl, *Polyarchy: Participation and Opposition* (New Haven: Yale University Press, 1971), p. 33.

119. Ibid., p. 4.

120. Ibid., p. 34.
121. Ibid., p. 36.
122. Ibid., pp. 3637.
123. The virtues of loyalty, filial piety, benevolence, love, integrity, righteousness, peace, and equitableness. According to Sun, "loyalty to the nation should replace loyalty to a throne that no longer existed. The solution therefore lay in preserving and strengthening these virtues and not in discarding them. . . ." Y. C. Wang, *Chinese Intellectuals and the West*, pp. 322–323.

7

From Mao Zedong to
Deng Xiaoping

Despite having devised modern China's first ideology of developmental nationalism, neither Sun Yat-sen nor the party he founded would see his ideology realized on the Chinese mainland. The Revolution of 1911 managed to convince the last Manchu emperor to step down, bringing the long years of dynastic rule to a close, but it failed to install a stable new government, much less a republican one. Upon assuming the presidency of the nominal Republic of China, Yuan Shikai promptly declared Sun's Chinese Nationalist Party (Kuomintang) to be illegal, forcing Sun and his followers to flee to southern China. There, preparations began for a "second revolution": A military academy was established in Whampoa to create an army for the revolution, with Chiang Kai-shek at its helm.

When Yuan died in 1916, he took with him whatever semblance of national unity there was; China fragmented into regions ruled by warlords. In 1925, before Sun could initiate the Northern Expedition to reunify China, he succumbed to stomach cancer. His death precipitated a prolonged struggle for succession among Chiang, Wang Ching-wei, and Hu Han-min, which eventually was resolved in Chiang's favor at the end of World War II.[1]

Japan's defeat in 1945 only freed the Nationalists and the Chinese Communist Party to confront each other in civil war. In 1948–1949, the defeated Nationalists retreated to the island redoubt of Taiwan, where they would eventually realize two of Sun's principles.[2] Through a program of land reform and industrial development, the Republic of China (ROC) on Taiwan became newly industrialized in the 1970s. Beginning in 1987 in the last year of Chiang Ching-kuo's presidency, political reforms transformed the island so that it became fully democratized by the mid-1990s.

Meanwhile, on the mainland the victorious Communists installed a new government of the People's Republic of China on October 1, 1950. After a century of foreign predation and internal turmoil, mainland China was finally unified under a strong government and the charismatic leadership of Mao Zedong. It seemed that China was on the threshold of a promising new beginning. That promise would, however, be systematically undermined by the radical vision of Mao.

The New China of Mao Zedong

Born to a landowning peasant family in 1893, Mao was one of the founders of the Chinese Communist Party (CCP). In 1935, after a disastrous series of battles with the Nationalist forces, the Communists fled to Yan'an to seek refuge in the barren hills of northwestern China. There, the party rebuilt itself by appealing to Sun Yat-sen's ideology and a populist anti-Japanese nationalism.[3] By that time, Mao had emerged as his party's undisputed leader.

Through the 1930s and 1940s Mao and the CCP seemed to be genuinely animated by Sun's ideas. In September 1937, for instance, the party's central committee "solemnly declared" that "Dr. Sun Yat-sen's Three People's Principles [are] what China needs today" and that "our Party is ready to fight for their complete realization." In October 1943, Mao maintained that the Communists' activities in the war (against the Japanese) zones were completely compatible with the principles of Sun.[4] Again, in 1945, Mao insisted that CCP policies gave expression to and had been inspired by "Dr. Sun's principles."[5]

All of which seemed to indicate that, to the extent that they were sincere in their espousal of Sun's ideology, Mao and his party were developmental nationalists at least in the interwar years. Like Sun, Mao yearned for a renewed China capable of resisting the impostures of foreigners and in command of the human and material resources to protect its sovereign integrity. Once the Communists acceded to power, however, instead of rebuilding China in accordance with Sun's pragmatic program, Mao turned to the utopian futurism of Karl Marx, V. I. Lenin, and Josef Stalin. That Mao should choose that body of thought for the modernization of China is somewhat curious.

Simply put, classical Marxism is an ideology of *post*-industrial revolution. Marx and Friedrich Engels anticipated that a workers' revolution would occur in a highly developed capitalist society, after which a socialist state would be installed whose primary function (the economy being already well industrialized) would be the equalization of wealth rather than the resolution of the problem of production. The irony of the twentieth century turns on the fact that, instead of taking place in the industrialized capitalist states, self-identified Marxist revolutions succeeded only in economically less developed societies.

The anomaly began with the Bolshevik revolution in primarily agrarian Russia. Not surprisingly, the victorious Bolsheviks found scant guidance in classical Marxism for what was to be done in the economically retrograde Soviet Union they founded. To compound the problem, Lenin died before he could formulate an alternate post-revolutionary strategy, the reforms of his New Economic Policy notwithstanding. It was left to Stalin to put together a developmental strategy.

The result was the doleful system that survives in historical memory: one of forced capital accumulation through the systematic exploitation of the agrarian masses to provide for intersectoral resource transfers into heavy and military industrial production. The capital employed for industrialization would come from within the Soviet Union because Stalin accepted Lenin's thesis that the principal enemy of socialism was the international imperialism of the advanced capitalist countries. Less developed communities could achieve economic modernization only independent of the predatory capitalist powers. All of which meant that the Soviet Union would modernize and industrialize without major foreign assistance.

Mao Zedong considered all this in the context of China. Because he was essentially ignorant of the doctrines of Marx and Engels, whatever knowledge of Marxism he had was that given currency by Lenin and Stalin. From Lenin he inherited a perspective of Marxist class struggle generalized to include entire countries. The world was divided into two adversarial camps: On one side were the "progressive" socialist states led by the Soviet Union; on the other were the "decadent" capitalist-imperialist countries with the United States at the fore. In the global struggle that was to culminate in the inevitable collapse of capitalism, China must "lean to one side" by joining the socialist camp with the Soviet Union as its mentor. From Stalin, Mao adopted the model of the command economy. The state would determine production, control costs, fix wages, and set prices; capital assets would be autarkically generated through forced savings by the Chinese people. The preponderance of those assets would be funneled into heavy industrial development rather than agriculture or consumer industries.

To these ideas of Lenin and Stalin Mao appended his own notions concerning the persistence of class struggle and the imperative for a "continuous revolution" in which all must participate. Both turned on his inversion of Marx's conceptualization of the relationship between the base and the superstructure.

Instead of the classic Marxist dictum that the economic base determines the superstructure, Mao was convinced that superstructural elements of willpower and mass enthusiasm could transform the Chinese economy. Detached from the base, the elements of the superstructure became infinitely malleable, so that "class" became redefined by Mao as a state of mind—a decided departure from its original Marxian meaning. An individual could become a "capitalist" simply because s/he entertained "capitalist" thoughts (whatever that meant), despite neither owning the means of production nor exploiting the labor of others. Given his new definition of class and class membership, Mao could argue that the installation of a socialist state in China with the attendant abolition of private property had failed to eliminate all noxious class elements. On the contrary, so long as capitalism remained in the world, its pernicious influence could seep into socialist China to contaminate the masses, resulting in "antagonistic contradictions" between the unpolluted "people" and the infected "enemies of the people." Toward those enemies, the ranks of whom could include even leading members of the vanguard Communist Party, the state could employ "dictatorial" means for their eradication. Society and the state therefore must be constantly vigilant since corruption of the self and of others was a perpetual possibility. There would have to be regular and periodic campaigns to purify and instruct the masses. All of which meant that the revolution that brought the CCP to power in 1949 would have to be continuous and unceasing.[6]

Indeed, for as long as Mao was in power, China would lurch from one political campaign to another. In the 1950s there were the Land Reform, Three- and Five-Anti, Hundred Flowers, Anti-Rightist, and the Great Leap Forward campaigns. The 1960s were caught in the convulsion of the Cultural Revolution, followed in the 1970s by a bewildering succession of campaigns that included the Anti-Confucian and Water Margin campaigns. Punctuating all these were the periodic "rectification" *(zhengfeng)* campaigns within the Communist Party to purge itself of impure elements.

The first years of the People's Republic began with the "socialist transformation" of the Chinese economy, in which feudal remnants and rudimentary capitalism were eradicated to make way for socialism. In 1950–1952, land was confiscated from its owners and distributed to the heretofore landless peasants, in the course of which 1 to 15 million landlords were executed. In the cities, a process of deprivatization and demarketization began, aided by Soviet technicians and planners. Around a core of 130 industrial plants supplied by the Soviet Union, a Stalinist economy was constructed: The state rationed raw materials, maintained a monopoly of traded items, supplied producer goods, and established output quotas. By 1956, all of China's industries had come under state control, accounting for 93 percent of total national output and 97 percent of all retail sales.

The early years of socialist transformation coincided with China's involvement in the Korean War. Convinced that their national sovereignty and security were imperiled by the activities of the United Nations forces in the Korean peninsula, millions of Chinese "volunteers" went into battle to aid the North Koreans. The ill-equipped Chinese divisions were thrown into a mismatched conflict that exacted a devastating toll. By the time the war ended with an armistice in 1953, China had sustained about a million battlefield casualties.

The Korean conflagration further convinced Mao that socialist China was in a virtual state of war with international imperialism, which meant that the People's Republic must be mobilized into a war economy. Major commitments were made to the creation of heavy industries; resources were provided to specialized military research and development. What resulted was the creation of the People's Liberation Army (PLA) as the world's largest army and third largest air force and navy. At its peak, the PLA had 4.7 million people in main-force and local-force divisions and 200 million civilians in "people's militia" units—all of whom would have to be sustained by the Chinese economy.

By the late 1950s, bolstered by the results of the socialist transformation of China, Mao thought that the transition to communism was imminent. Between 1953 and 1957, the Chinese economy registered an annual real rate of growth of 6.2 percent, the gross value of industrial output increased by 128 percent and agriculture by 24.8 percent. Mao was convinced that what was needed was a concerted effort to mobilize China's human resources to accelerate the pace of economic development, so that production could be doubled in a single five-year period. With that, China would leapfrog over the Soviet Union by making "a great leap forward" from socialism into utopian communism.

That leap would be effected through the sheer will and enthusiasm of the masses. Notwithstanding its unskilled populace and backward technology, Mao believed that China could conquer its poverty if only the people had sufficient faith and commitment. Industrial development would not be confined to the urban centers; instead, the peasants could produce steel in backyard furnaces. Impassioned by his vision, millions of Chinese were mobilized to undertake massive programs of excavation, construction, reforestation, and water control—a modern analogue of the corvée labor enterprises of dynastic China. To free men and women for this heroic purpose, peasant families were merged into gargantuan communes, each comprised of thousands of households. In anticipation of the imminent arrival of communism, private property ownership was totally abjured, including farm tools and draught animals.

Rather than the realization of utopia, the Great Leap Forward ended in signal disaster. The "steel" produced in backyard furnaces turned out to be entirely useless. To curry favor with Mao, commune cadres exaggerated their farm production figures, on the basis of which Beijing exacted its quota of grain harvest to feed China's urban populace, leaving little for the peasants. The result was a famine that ended the 1950s in which at least 15 million starved to death—a direct consequence of misguided policies and wasted resources.

In the cost accounting that followed, Mao relinquished his post as head of state to Liu Shaoqi (while retaining his chairmanship of the party) and retreated from active governing. Liu, with Deng Xiaoping as his assistant, took over the affairs of governance. The new leadership eschewed the more radical features of Maoism. Instead of ideological appeals, the party turned to capitalist measures to revive the economy: Peasants could own small private plots, and material incentives of differential wages were used to spur production.

Meanwhile, in his political hiatus Mao became increasingly troubled by the direction of the new leadership, convinced that the party under Liu had betrayed the revolution by conceding to selfish capitalist appetites and corroding the egalitarian ideal. Most alarmingly, Mao discerned in the *apparatchik* of the rapidly mushrooming government bureaucracies nothing less than the formation of a new ruling class. To stem the erosion, Mao emerged out of his sabbatical. When he failed to correct his errant colleagues through the customary method of a rectification campaign within the party, he resolved that the apparatchiks would have to be dislodged. In the gathering storm of what became the Great Proletarian Cultural Revolution (1966–1969), he brought together his lieutenants: a small coterie composed of his wife, Jiang Qing, and Defense Minister Lin Biao. To dislodge the apparatchiks, Mao used his charismatic authority to mobilize the masses with the Red Guards, the naïve and impressionable youth of China, at the fore.

In the hysteria that ensued, entire provinces were engulfed in a frenzy of recrimination and destruction. Bands of Red Guards roamed the country, laying waste to life and property. Schools and universities were closed and productivity declined in critical sectors of the economy. "Enemies of the people" were subjected to public vilification and abuse: In some areas, the vengeful masses took to cannibalism against their presumed class enemies.[7] Finally, even Mao thought the chaos and mayhem had exceeded all limits. The military was brought in to rein in the revolution. The Red Guards, for their part, who had only sought to do their revered Chairman's bidding, were banished in permanent exile to the remote countryside.

Costly though the Cultural Revolution was, Mao achieved his objective of removing his opponents in the party. Countless numbers of them, including "capitalist roader number one" Liu Shaoqi, perished from the abuse. Others, like Deng Xiaoping, survived but were removed from public office. Once again ensconced in power, Mao seemed to lose active interest in politics. The affairs of state devolved to Jiang Qing and her cronies—collectively known as the Gang of Four—who went about reinstituting the substance of Maoist socialism. The Chairman himself sank into increasing senescence. The lone moderate in government was Zhou Enlai, veteran survivor of political campaigns and longtime premier of the State Council. He struggled to introduce some modicum of rationality into policy deliberations, particularly in the arena of foreign relations where the impact of Mao's radicalism had been as disastrous as in the domestic arena.

Maoist foreign policy was predicated on the assumption that history ordained the certain triumph of the "proletarian" less developed countries over the capitalist industrialized states. To foster this historical inevitability, China would aid and support revolutionary communist movements in the Third World—in Asia, Africa, and the Middle East. But that effort met with little success. In one case in particular, China's complicity in the subversive activities of the Indonesian Communist Party resulted in a major policy debacle. Only in Vietnam, where China had contributed to the defeat of the United States, could Beijing claim some success.

More ominously, along the long Sino-Soviet border in the north, there were developments that threatened the very survival of China. Since the death of Stalin in 1953, relations between Beijing and Moscow had become increasingly strained. From the perspective of the Chinese, Nikita Khrushchev's denunciation of Stalin reflected badly on the cult of Mao. For their part, the Soviet leaders harbored increasing reservations regarding the direction of Mao's foreign policy. At a time when Moscow began to entertain the possibilities of a peaceful coexistence with the preeminent capitalist power, the United States, Mao agitated instead for the active promotion of the "proletarian" world revolution. He expected that nuclear war between the two superpowers was inevitable and that China, with its massive population, would survive the devastation and emerge the victor. While Moscow was ill-disposed toward adventurism, Mao sought every opportunity to provoke foreign confrontations. In 1958, the PLA fired at the ROC's offshore islands of Quemoy and Matsu in the Taiwan Strait, inciting a crisis that almost engaged the United States. In 1961, border disputes between China and India erupted into open conflagration. Not surprisingly, Beijing received scant support from Moscow in both incidents. More than that, the Soviet Union so distrusted China that it decided it would not share nuclear weapons technology with its socialist brother.

The already strained friendship between Moscow and Beijing was further attenuated during the Cultural Revolution when a band of Red Guards, armed with the "mighty atom bomb" of Mao Zedong thought, challenged Soviet troops along a contested sector of the border. In March 1969 a new phase of the simmering dispute erupted when Chinese irregulars ambushed a Soviet border patrol in Zhenbao Island and killed a number of Soviet troops. Two weeks after, Moscow responded by savaging Chinese border troops with massive artillery and rocket attacks that destroyed Chinese emplacements miles within PRC territory.

As the 1970s began, China seemed beset by external and internal crises. Domestic politics took a bizarre turn in 1971 when it was revealed that Mao's designated heir, Lin Biao, had perished in a plane crash in Outer Mongolia after twice attempting to assassinate the Chairman himself. At the same time, the Soviet Union was threatening to use its most "modern and devastating weapons" of tactical and target specific nuclear strikes against China. Mao's foreign policies had created a threat environment that jeopardized the very continuity of the People's Republic. Clearly, China's foreign posture required reassessment.

That reassessment was undertaken under the direction of Zhou Enlai. The Manichaean notion that the world was divided into a capitalist and a socialist camp gave way to a conviction that reality was complex, where socialist China could be threatened by socialist Russia in league with socialist Vietnam. Suggestions began to be bruited that appeals be made to the capitalist powers for capital, technology transfers, and security assistance. Finally, Beijing announced that it no longer considered the United States to be China's "number one enemy." With that, China's rapprochement with the West began—a process that spanned Mao's remaining years, culminating in the normalization of relations between the United States and the People's Republic of China on January 1, 1979.

The Post-Mao Assessment

The year 1976 had all the signs of the end of an epoch. It began in January with the death of Premier Zhou; July saw the death of another communist titan, Marshal Zhu De, followed by a calamitous earthquake in Tangshan that took a quarter of a million lives. On September 9, Mao himself died. Less than a month later, his successor Hua Guofeng had the Gang of Four arrested. With that, the pages were closed on a turbulent chapter in China's millennial history.

This was the legacy Mao left his people. Since the Communists' accession to power, China enjoyed a territorial unity and integrity it had not had since the Opium War. Sovereign pride and dignity were restored to a people who for a century had suffered from the indignities and humiliation inflicted by the imperialist powers. However great the cost, by successfully fighting to a standstill the vastly superior U.N. forces on the Korean peninsula, China communicated to the world that it was no longer an inert prize to be plundered.

These political achievements, however considerable, must be balanced against the costs. If nationalism means a people's sentiments of love and fellowship for each other, then Mao's "continuous revolution" of unceasing class struggle was the very antithesis of nationalism. In human lives alone, his 27-year reign exacted a toll of 45 to 72 million Chinese lives. According to the 848-page tome *The Black Book of Communism*, they included the following: 6 to 10 million who were killed by the CCP before it came to power in 1949, not counting the civil war with the KMT; 20 to 43 million who died between 1951 and 1961 from land reform and the Great Leap; 1 to 3 million who lost their lives in the madness of the Cultural Revolution of 1966–1976; perhaps 20 million "counterrevolutionaries" who died in prisons and camps; as well as 10 to 20 percent of the inhabitants of Tibet who were killed by the PLA in the uprising of 1959.[8] Together with the millions who languished in "labor reform" camps, were tortured and abused by Red Guards, or "sent down" to the countryside to learn from the peasants, the population of China probably suffered more death, privation, and politically engineered devastation than at any other time in its history.

The economic balance sheet of Maoism was equally mixed. Admittedly, Mao supervised a substantial expansion and deepening of the Chinese economy, the products of which probably were more equitably distributed than at any time in Chinese history. China's industries produced relatively advanced, if unoriginal, aircraft and seaworthy vessels. Housing, education, elementary medical service, farm equipment, and energy supplies were provided to almost one billion human beings. At the same time, however, the rate of economic growth was irregular and fitful. Mao's voluntarism and adventurism, not to mention the relentless campaigns, created institutional instabilities that resulted in a variability in economic growth three times as violent as that of India or Japan and four times as violent as that of the Philippines or the Republic of China on Taiwan. More than that, Mao's policy of population enhancement effectively canceled out the benefits of economic growth. Since 1952, the results have been an absolute decline of 3.2 percent in the per-capita availability of food grains, a 33.3 percent decline in the per-capita availability of edible oils, and a 2 percent overall per-capita decline in the availability of cotton cloth.

Despite the economic achievements, Mao bequeathed China an average per-capita GNP of $253 in 1978, comparable to that of Haiti or the Central African Republic, making the People's Republic one of the poorest countries in the world.[9] In contrast, China's neighbors in Asia—Japan, Taiwan, South Korea, Singapore, Hong Kong—rebuilt their economies from the devastation of World War II and increased the per-capita income of their people ten times over. However equitably distributed its poverty, the People's Republic failed to significantly improve the life circumstances of its people. Whereas Taiwan's average per-capita income rose by 753 percent from $149 in 1957 to $1,122 in 1976, Communist China's increased from $58 to only $139 during the same period.[10] For all its claims of having conquered hunger, Beijing admitted in 1979 that as much as 27 percent of its population lived at marginal subsistence.

The balance sheet on foreign policy was equally dismal. Not only had China failed to capture the leadership of revolutionary movements in the Third World, the prospect for a proletarian world revolution itself seemed to recede further and further into the future. Apart from that, there were more immediate and urgent problems. While China frittered away its time and resources, the Soviet Union had assiduously mounted a formidable military expansion. By the late 1970s, one third of all Soviet nuclear delivery capabilities and almost 50 mechanized and armored Soviet divisions were deployed along the Sino-Soviet border, threatening China's Xinjiang, Inner Mongolia, and the northeastern provinces, where 30 percent of Chinese industrial capabilities were concentrated. Worse still, all of China was exposed to Soviet rocket and ground-launched cruise missile attack.

As if China needed further demonstration of its vulnerability, in February 1979, Beijing chose to undertake a "punitive war" against its onetime ally, the Socialist Republic of Vietnam. Rather than achieving victory, the war became instead an object lesson in the PLA's incompetence and inferiority. If the purpose of the Chinese Communist revolution had been the revitalization of China through the construction of a unified nation, economic development, and a strong military, the Maoist era must be considered a failure.

Two years after Mao's death, like a phoenix rising from its ashes, the thrice-purged[11] Deng Xiaoping returned to political life to assume command of China. Under his direction, the Communist Party began the painful process of review and reassessment. A consensus was reached regarding the problems confronting the country and the solution that would be required. In December 1978, the decision was made to undertake economic reform that would leave its mark on every sector of society. That the party embarked on major reform of an economic system identified by its own economists as "irrational"[12] is a testament to the gravity of the situation. In their judgment, the "chaos" of Mao's Cultural Revolution had pushed the economy to "the brink of collapse."[13]

Deng Xiaoping's Return to Developmental Nationalism

To legitimate the reforms, an ideological justification would have to be provided. In a system devoid of any meaningful popular participation, political legitimacy must derive from some other source. What was needed was a new theoretical rationale to justify the departure from Maoism while, at the same time, credibly claim to be still faithful to Marxism. It was Deng Xiaoping who provided that ideological rationale. In putting together his ideas, Deng used as his springboard classical Marxism's emphasis on the productive forces.

The Primacy of the Productive Forces

Classical Marxism (the ideas of Marx and Engels) conceived society's economic base as composed of the forces of production (means of production) that determine the relations of production (the nature of economic classes and their relations—who gets what, when, and how). The economic base, in turn, determines the epiphenomenal superstructure composed of such elements as law, philosophy, religion, and ideology. The relations of production were subordinate to and contingent upon the productive forces—as productive forces change, social relations change; as social relations change, all of life changes.

Marx was unequivocal on the determinant role of the forces of production. In the 1859 Preface to his *Critique of Political Economy*, he wrote that "in the social production of their life, men enter into definite relations that are indispensable and independent of their will," relations that "correspond to a definite state of development of their material productive forces."[14] "[T]he multitude of productive forces accessible to men determines the nature of society"[15] as well as the "forms of intercourse" between human beings. Even the "phantoms formed in the human brain"—religious convictions, ethics, and law—were "sublimates" of the more fundamental processes of production.[16] In the final analysis, the "productive forces . . . are the basis of all . . . history."[17]

It follows that socialism could only be a product of a fully developed economy. As early as the *German Ideology* of 1845, Marx had insisted that socialist revolution could come only to advanced industrial systems because only those systems would inherit the productive potential to fully satisfy human needs without having recourse to invidious class distinctions and oppressive political rule. If an attempt were made to introduce socialism into an economically underdeveloped environment, Engels foresaw the consequence to be a "slide back . . . to [the] narrow limits" of the old system. True socialist liberation was a function of "the level of development of the material means of existence." To attempt to build communism on a primitive economic base could only be a "chiliastic dream fantasy."[18]

Mao never seemed to fully grasp the problem of the disjuncture between China's primitive productive forces and the socialist productive relations he and his party imposed upon the country. Instead of productive forces, he conceived productive relations and the superstructure to be primary in the process of socioeconomic change. He believed that superstructural elements like revolutionary commitment, political enthusiasm, personal sacrifice, and selfless dedication would shape reality to his utopian vision.[19] In effect, Mao seized on the power of his convictions "to change the world arbitrarily,"[20] in his quest to create socialism out of thin air.

In contrast, like the first Marxists, Deng believed that the forces of production—not productive relations or superstructural elements—constituted the engine of history. Given that, China's poverty was a direct consequence of its immature industrial and technological base. It follows then that no amount of faith or enthusiasm could create the mature industrial economy of socialism; instead, the dream of socialism required the resources of a fully developed industrial system.

As early as 1975, Deng already was critical of Mao's conception of the role of the superstructure in revolution, social change, and economic development.[21] After the Chairman's death, Deng was no longer constrained. He identified the fundamental task that faced the People's Republic to be that of economic development and proceeded to formulate a strategy—one that employed the forces of production as the theoretical justification for reform. Deng's appeal to the Marxist dictum on productive forces served dual purposes. It enabled Deng to claim that he was a truer Marxist than Mao, lending doctrinal legitimacy to the much-needed reforms. More than that, by emphasizing the determinant role of productive forces, Deng managed to transmute Marxism into something it never fully was—an ideology of developmental nationalism.

That Deng's reformist ideology is developmental is attested to by his insistence that "the first thing" or original purpose of the Chinese Communist revolution was economic development, which he understood to be the elimination of poverty through "the emancipation of the productive forces."[22] In so saying, Deng effectively returned to the theme of economic modernization as the historic mission of all twentieth-century Chinese revolutions, including that of the Communists.

Born in 1904, Deng belonged to the generation of Chinese intellectuals who chafed under imperialism and were convinced of the urgent need for industrialization and modernization. They held in common the objective of China's renascence; what differentiated them were the means proposed to achieve that objective. However much of a Marxist, Deng had always been a nationalist committed to the restoration of China's power, integrity, and prestige. In that quest, his dream was identical to those of the reformers and revolutionaries who preceded him, from Zeng Guofan to Sun Yat-sen. Through the long years of the Chinese Communists' struggle to power, Deng consistently argued against the "leftism" and "ultraleftism" of party enthusiasts.[23] Like a true nationalist, he understood that the imperative of modernization on which "salvation for the nation" depended required the mobilization and cooperation of "all social forces" and "all strata of the population."[24] Instead of class struggle, Deng urged that consideration be given "to the interests of workers and peasants" as well as "those of the landlords and capitalists."[25] Toward the landlords, he proposed an end to the practice of "settling very old accounts" and the return of any property that was seized. Instead of persecution, landlords should be allowed to "make a living and enjoy a certain economic status" and to have "their legitimate right of property [be] safeguarded."[26]

Regrettably, in Deng's judgment, rather than adopting a conciliatory approach, the party under Mao detoured into ruinous class warfare and made "a lot of mistakes."[27] From 1957 until Mao's death, China was "plagued" by the ideas and policies of the "Left," which hindered economic development. The result was a "sluggish" economy with a very low standard of living and a per-capita GNP in 1978 of less than $250. As Deng explained,[28]

> Many strange things happened in those days. . . . [P]eople were told that they should be content with poverty and backwardness and that it was better to be poor under socialism and communism than to be rich under capitalism. That was the sort of rubbish peddled by the Gang of Four. There is no such thing as socialism and communism with poverty. . . . According to Marxism, communist society is a society in which there is overwhelming material abundance. Socialism is the first stage of communism; it means expanding the productive forces. . . .

The Primary Stage of Socialism

The disagreement between Deng and the Maoists on the primacy of the productive forces centered on a more basic issue of whether China, after 1949, had successfully and securely entered into the period of socialism. The answer to that question would determine the identity of the principal contradiction in the post-revolutionary People's Republic.

After the collapse of the Great Leap and as the Sino-Soviet dispute intensified, Mao began to harbor doubts as to whether a socialist system really had been installed in China. By 1962, he decided that the construction of socialism was a sustained and arduous process in which the abolition of private property was merely a necessary first step. During that long process, socialism would be continuously imperiled by the constant reproduction of "new bourgeois elements." This meant that despite the party's abolition of private ownership and socialization of the means of production, there would still be "classes" in nominally socialist China, as well as class struggles between the "proletariat" and the "bourgeoisie," and between the "people" and its "enemies." All of which meant that class struggle was the primary contradiction in socialist China, a struggle that Mao expected to be "a protracted, complex, sometimes even violent affair." These were the ideas that underlay Mao's theory of "continuing the revolution," which was adopted as official CCP ideology in 1969 and reaffirmed in 1973.[29]

In direct contrast to Mao, Deng had always thought otherwise. As early as his 1956 Report on the Revision of the Constitution of the Communist Party of China, Deng was convinced that socialism had taken secure roots in China. Believing that "material conditions" rather than superstructural elements constituted "the foundation" of socialism,[30] Deng maintained that the abolition of private ownership and the socialization of the means of production had brought about "a fundamental change" in class relations. Classes no longer existed in the People's Republic because the bourgeoisie was "on its way to extinction" and the working class had become "the leading class." Deng further elaborated that[31]

> Casual labourers and farm labourers have disappeared. Poor and middle peasants have all become members of agricultural producers' co-operatives, and before long the distinction between them will become merely a thing of historical interest. . . . The vast majority of our intellectuals have now come over politically to the side of the working class. . . . The conditions in which the urban poor and the professional people used to exist as independent social strata are virtually no longer present. . . . What is the point, then, of classifying these social strata into two different categories? And even if we were to try and devise a classification, how could we make it neat and clear-cut?

All of which meant that, for Deng, class warfare was no longer a matter of great concern in the People's Republic. Instead, the principal contradiction in society was the "very low" level of China's productive forces, the enhancement of which should be the party's "central task" and focus.[32]

But the socialism that China had entered into, Deng argued, nevertheless was only a "primary" or "underdeveloped" stage of socialism.[33] Given the situation he inherited, the concept of a primary stage of socialism was, at once, an ingenious and expedient device that enabled Deng to explain away mistakes of the past and present while, at the same time, justifying the economic reforms that would follow. On the one hand, it is argued, China had become socialist—which meant that the Communist Party would continue to rule as the vanguard of the "dictatorship of the proletariat." On the other hand, it was understandable that, being only in socialism's initial stage, China would still have superstructural detritus from its recent feudal past, which included Mao's one-man rule and his "patriarchal" cult of personality, as well as the bureaucratism and political sinecure of the party and government.[34] Being in the primary stage of socialism could also explain China's poverty and justify the need for market reforms to develop the economy.

Deng further maintained that the retardation of the Chinese economy had been exacerbated by Mao's misguided policies that caused the country to have "wasted 20 years" while the world developed rapidly.[35] With Mao dead and the Gang of Four imprisoned, China would make up for lost time. Through the Four Modernizations (of agriculture, industry, national defense, and science and technology), China would "find a way" to develop as quickly as possible into "a modern and powerful socialist state"[36] because, as Deng put it, "Pauperism is not socialism, still less communism."[37]

Darwinian Worldview

The urgency of modernization was informed by Deng's conviction that the world was dominated by advanced industrial "hegemonist" and "imperialist" powers who "bully" less developed countries and attempt to "interfere" in their economic development and political independence.[38] Even more than in the past, the contemporary world was inhospitable to poor countries, whose environment had become more difficult, requiring that they "struggle even harder."[39]

In China's case, not only was it poor, Deng warned that "there are many people in the world who . . . are out to get us"—especially the capitalist industrialized countries that aimed "to defeat socialists in the long run" either through military force or the "peaceful evolution" of China away from socialism. China's situation was exacerbated by the fall of communism in the Soviet Union and Eastern Europe, which left the People's Republic one of the last bastions of socialism in the world. Worse still, China was surrounded by newly industrialized neighbors in Asia which could "move ahead" by capturing China's export markets. Given such a hazardous and threatening global environment, if China were to remain underdeveloped, it "would have no future."[40]

Reactive Nationalism

In a difficult and hostile world, nation-states remain the basic units that could ensure the collective well-being of peoples. Like any other country, China must "look after [its] own" and safeguard its own interests, sovereignty, and territorial integrity[41]—particularly in view of its past century of humiliation. Stating that "I am a Chinese, and I am familiar with the history of foreign aggression against China,"[42] Deng recounted how Chinese were "looked down upon"[43] and abused by the imperialist powers for over a century since the Opium War. It was only with the founding of the People's Republic that Chinese finally "achieved status," "stood up,"[44] and "changed China's image." Having felt inferior for more than a century,

Chinese finally attained confidence in themselves and would no longer be intimidated.[45]

Under the leadership of the Communist Party, China became a proud and independent nation-state that would no longer be the "vassal" of others or submit to anything deleterious to its interests.[46] All that achievement, however, would be lost if the people forsook socialism and the leadership of the Communist Party, as "[o]nly socialism can save China, and only socialism can develop China." Without the continuing leadership of the party, China would once again be subjected to "the will of the Americans, or of people in other developed countries."[47]

Deng clearly saw the Chinese nation as being larger than the People's Republic, encompassing all ethnic Chinese in the world. He maintained that "no matter what clothes they wear or what political stand they take," all Chinese had a sense of pride and identification with the Chinese nation and would want the PRC to become strong and prosperous. Appealing to what he believed to be their innate sense of nationalism, Deng called on the "tens of millions" of ethnic Chinese across the world to "love our country and help to develop it." For in the last analysis, "The image of China depends on the mainland, and the prospects for China's development also depend on the mainland."[48]

Economic Development

To ensure that China would "stand firm forever" in the world,[49] it must acquire advanced military capabilities that only an advanced industrial economy could provide. As a consequence, the "overriding" task "for a considerable time to come" must be that of working "single-mindedly" for economic modernization. Nothing less than the "destiny for generations to come" hinged on the success or failure of that endeavor.[50]

That process was conceived by Deng to take three stages. The goal of the first stage in China's economic modernization was the doubling of its per-capita GNP from $250 in 1980 to $500 by 1990, so as to "ensure that the people have adequate food and clothing." Happily, in 1988 the first goal was accomplished "ahead of time" by two years. Stage two's objective was another doubling of the per-capita GNP to $1,000 by the year 2000, at which time Deng expected China to have "shaken off poverty and achieved comparative prosperity." By then, China could afford a military budget of at least $10 billion—1 percent of a $1 trillion GNP—with which "a great deal" could be done. It would enable China to become "quite powerful," placing it "in the front ranks of countries." That GNP of $1 trillion, in turn, would be "a new starting point" for the last stage in China's economic modernization, which would conclude by the year 2030 or 2050. By that time, China would be fully industrialized, on a par with moderately developed countries.[51]

Reform of the Command Economy

For all that to happen, certain reforms would have to be undertaken, beginning with the dysfunctional command economy. Deng was convinced that the Communist Party's adoption of the Soviet command model in the early 1950s was a mistake, because the political bureaucracy that managed it was "utterly incompatible with large-scale production," being overstaffed, burdened with overlapping organizations, complicated procedures, "extremely low" efficiency, and a misplaced emphasis on quantity instead of quality. The result was that the entire Chinese economy became "hampered."[52]

Another problem with the command model was its irrational pricing system wherein the state determined all prices, "contrary to the law of value," which led the state to assume the "heavy burden" of providing subsidies in "tens of billions of yuan" a year to make up for the disparity between purchasing and selling prices. Those subsidies diverted precious resources away from investment in education, science, and culture—all to the detriment of economic development.[53]

In the interest of modernization, market mechanisms must be introduced to improve productivity and efficiency. The pricing system would have to be rationalized; state subsidies would have to be reduced, if not eliminated altogether. The economy would have to be freed by devolving power to local governments and the managers of state-owned enterprises. Private businesses would have to be sanctioned. To justify the introduction of market features into China's socialist economy, Deng argued that socialism was not synonymous with a planned economy. What distinguished socialism from capitalism was not "a market economy as opposed to a planned economy" because even "socialism has regulation by market forces, and capitalism has control through planning." Unless the Chinese people were to "reconcile" themselves "to lagging behind," they would have to adopt some of the features of capitalism.[54] For in the last analysis, whatever economic features that China adopted should be determined by the pragmatic criterion of whether they were conducive to the development of the productive forces.

Open-Door Policy

In the interest of pragmatism, Deng advocated an open-door policy to trade, investment, and other contacts with the world, especially the advanced industrial democracies in the West and Japan. Deng attributed China's backwardness to its isolation during centuries of dynastic rule, which was continued into the twentieth century by Mao's autarkic policies. By closing itself off from interaction with the rest of the world, China acted "only to its own disadvantage." For China to develop, it must "persist in opening to the outside world" and refrain from "blind opposition" to anything that is foreign. There must be a long-term policy of learning from the advanced industrial countries to "catch up with and surpass them." More than that, even after China had become developed, it must continue to learn from other countries "in areas where they are particularly strong."[55]

Under Deng's plan, China would trade with other countries and import their capital, skills, and technology. Special Economic Zones and open cities would be created, offering favorable terms and conditions to attract foreign investment in joint and foreign-owned enterprises. International academic exchanges and scientific cooperation would be expanded. All of which was justified by Deng's reasoning that not "everything developed in capitalist countries is of a capitalist nature." He reminded his colleagues that "Marx said that science and technology are part of the productive forces." Not only is there "no class character" to science, technology, and advanced management techniques, they constitute "primary" productive forces on which the rapid development of the entire economy depends. As such, they are useful to any society, capitalist or socialist.[56]

Speaking very much like a technological determinist, Deng exulted that "science is a great thing" and urged that "its importance" be recognized through the allocation of more "money and effort." Scientific research and training should be enhanced; education must be expanded, "even if it means slowing down in other fields." As Deng put it, "We have already wasted 20 years. . . . If we paid no attention to education, science and technology, we would waste another twenty years, and the consequences would be dreadful to contemplate."[57]

Deng was convinced that China would be the ultimate beneficiary of its policy of openness, provided that its national interests were protected by ensuring that foreign imports serve, instead of threaten, the integrity of "socialist production." Nor would China's sovereignty and integrity be compromised if it interacted with other countries "on the basis of equality and mutual benefit."[58] All of this marked another of Deng's radical departures from Maoism. Not only had Mao instituted economic autarky, he was convinced that the world was divided into two hostile and irreconcilable camps, from which China could not be neutral. Instead, the People's Republic must "lean to one side" with its socialist compatriots across the world.

Deng's open-door policy was predicated on an entirely different perspective. According to Deng, the world had become more "pluralistic" *(duoji hua)* and varied, no longer bifurcated into rival camps of socialist versus capitalist countries. The end of the Cold War had also ushered in a more peaceful era in which "for a long time to come," there would be less likelihood for large-scale world wars. Although wars between states would still erupt, they would be limited in scope. All of which meant that China should eschew a simplistic division of the world into friends versus foes. Instead, China should seize the opportunity afforded by this period of relative global peace to concentrate its resources and attention on economic development. In its foreign relations, China should insist on five basic principles of mutual respect for national sovereignty and territorial integrity, non-interference in internal affairs, equality, and peaceful coexistence.[59]

Intellectuals

The promotion of science and technology required attendant changes in the superstructure—specifically the treatment of intellectuals. Here, Deng's views once again departed significantly from those of Mao. The latter was suspicious of, and antipathetic to, intellectuals whom he regarded as members of the "black" capitalist class, being more "expert" than "red." The very traits that made them intellectuals—their professional knowledge, training, and expertise—made them politically suspect. As a consequence, in the Maoist years intellectuals were often singled out for special abuse.

Deng could not take a more different position on this matter. He derided the Maoists for their celebration of ignorance, a particularly vivid example of which was their elevation of "an ignorant reactionary clown" who handed in a blank examination paper as a model for mass emulation. In direct contrast to Mao, Deng refused to regard intellectuals as members of the bourgeoisie, believing instead that "Everyone who works, whether with his hands or with his brain, is part of the working people in a socialist society." Unlike their counterparts in capitalist societies, intellectuals in socialist China were not "exploitative" because they had been trained by and were in service to the "working class." The intellectuals differed from other workers "only insofar as they perform different roles in the social division of labour." Deng also dismissed the Maoist dichotomy of "red" versus "expert" by redefining "red" to mean anyone who "loves our socialist motherland and is serving socialism." In effect, according to Deng, an "expert" could also be "red" provided that he or she contributed to the motherland and refrained from taking "a reactionary political stand" against the Communist Party. As Deng explained, "So long as they keep to the socialist political stand . . . their devoted work is a concrete manifestation of their socialist consciousness."[60]

Under Deng, intellectuals would no longer be vilified simply because they were intellectuals. On the contrary, Deng urged that they be raised "to first place," accorded more respect, and rewarded with higher salaries. Knowledge must be valued and teachers must be better remunerated, no matter "how many difficulties we have." Everything must be done to encourage the return of the thousands who left China to study abroad, "regardless of their previous political attitudes." To encourage their return, Deng proposed that a comprehensive scientific research center be created to increase employment opportunities. "Otherwise," he warned, "these people will not come back, and it will be a great loss to the country."[61]

Material Incentives

Intellectuals were not the only people who would be provided material incentives. Deng apparently believed that human beings in general would work harder and better if they could benefit directly from their labor. It would be "idealism" to ask that people toil in selfless sacrifice, because "revolution takes place on the basis of the need for material benefit." Ever the pragmatist, Deng cautioned that expecting people to be selfless was a strategy that simply "won't work in the long run." In particular, special treatment should be accorded the high achievers and the talented, including promotion "without hesitation," pay raises of "more than one step at a time," and "free rein" in their work.[62]

In advocating the principle of "more pay for more work," Deng was not unaware that it could lead to differential income and wealth but thought it "only fair that people who work hard should prosper." Convinced that egalitarianism would not work, Deng regarded the rich as performing a potentially useful function by becoming "an impressive example" who would motivate others to excel, thereby causing the whole economy to "advance wave upon wave."[63]

To avoid a permanent "polarization" between the rich and poor, Deng imagined that when the time was "right," the government would enforce a redistribution of wealth—through taxes and voluntary contributions—from the rich to the poor, and from the prosperous coastal to the economically backward inland regions. But Deng was rather vague as to when that time would be, cautioning against "overhastiness" that would "only cause damage to economic development." He urged the party to "study when to raise this question and how to settle it" and suggested the year 2000 as "the right time." By that time, he expected that the Chinese people would be living "a fairly comfortable life" with a per-capita GNP of $1,000 and could thus afford to share their wealth.[64]

Order and Stability

Until that time, Deng argued, China must maintain an orderly and stable environment for economic development to proceed, which only the Communist Party could provide. Deng cautioned that if China were to descend into "turmoil," the situation would be far worse than during the Cultural Revolution because the country no longer had "prestigious leaders" like Mao and Zhou Enlai to hold it together. China would deteriorate into civil war, with each region dominated by a faction and "blood flowing like water." The economic and transportation systems would be devastated, and "hundreds of millions" of refugees would flee into neighboring countries, resulting in a "disaster on a world scale."[65]

China's "overriding interest" therefore must be stability. Given that, anything that could help maintain that stability was "good." For Deng, the "democratic dictatorship" of the Chinese Communist Party was one of those "good" things. Despite his admission that the party had made many mistakes, he still insisted that it was "the center" that could ensure political stability and unity.[66]

To perform that critical function, the party must maintain internal cohesion and not degenerate into factional rivalries. Deng was particularly wary of the "Leftists" who opposed his reforms and "would like nothing better than nationwide confusion." He feared their resurgence and warned darkly, "Don't think that there can be no more chaos in China. . . ." Much depended on the ability of party leaders to stay united on major policy goals and directives. As long as they "remain stable and firm," Deng was convinced that "nobody will be able to do anything against China."[67]

Party unity, in turn, was contingent on the ideological solidarity of its members on "Marxism-Leninism and Mao Zedong Thought." For that reason, Deng refrained from completely denouncing Mao, although he held Mao and his policies to be responsible for untold human suffering and economic devastation. He implored his party not to be "too critical of the mistakes Mao made in his later years." After all, Mao was the founding father and charismatic leader *nonpareil* of Chinese Communism. If the Communist Party were to repudiate him, there would be "ideological confusion and political instability" because its own legitimacy would be jeopardized. As Deng put it, "To negate the contributions of such a great historical figure would mean to deny all our achievements during an important period of the country's history."[68]

The Rejection of Democracy

More than party unity, political and social stability also demanded a continuous effort to combat "bourgeois liberalization"—an "evil trend" that if left unchecked "would plunge the country into turmoil once more." By bourgeois liberalization Deng meant the rejection of socialism and Communist Party rule, and the "wholesale Westernization of China." The exponents of bourgeois liberalization were those who "worship" Western notions of "democracy," "human rights," and "freedom"—all of which Deng equated with the anarchic "mass democracy" of the Cultural Revolution.[69]

Deng expected that the party would have to continue to combat bourgeois liberalization for 50 to 70 years until China became fully developed. But in resisting bourgeois liberalization, Deng proposed that the party employ "education and persuasion" instead of the Maoist method of "launching political movements," because Deng was mindful that Maoist mass mobilization had been destructive of both the economy as well as the Communist Party itself.[70]

The priority Deng placed on stability also accounted for his rejection of Western democracy, although he did not seem to object to it in principle, maintaining that "We have no objection to the Western countries doing it that way." Deng simply thought that Western democracy's emphasis on the individual over the group was unsuitable for China. He also found the Western system of governing to be wasteful and inefficient. According to Deng, instead of three branches of government, the U.S. separation of political power into three branches had devolved into "three governments," each pulling the country "in different directions." To Deng, Western democracy was nothing other than unbridled individualism and, in effect, anarchy.[71]

Such a system would be totally unsuited to China because it "would only make a mess of everything." If China were to become a Western-style democracy, it would achieve neither economic development nor any of the "substance" of democracy, and would instead descend into chaos and disorder. As Deng put it, "China has a huge population; if some people demonstrated today and others tomorrow, there would be a demonstration 365 days a year. . . . [W]e would have no time to develop our economy."[72]

Rather than mimic the West, China should have its own brand of "socialist democracy." Although Deng was never clear in defining "socialist democracy," he seemed to mean a society in which the interests of the individual, "the part," and the short term were subordinated to those of the collective, the whole, and the long term.[73] It would be a political system where power was monopolized by a single party—the Communist—that would determine what constituted society's overriding collective and long-term interests.

That having been said, Deng's conceptualization of party dictatorship differed significantly from the totalitarianism of Mao Zedong. For one, there is more personal space in Deng's "socialist democracy"—by virtue of his eschewal of Mao's utopian insistence on transforming and perfecting the consciousness of each and every individual. Deng seemed to have greater confidence in the judgment of the common man and woman. For him, the devolution of authority to the lower levels, down to the peasants, was "the height of democracy." He urged his party to have "faith that the overwhelming majority of the people are able to use their own judgment," even conceding that "[t]he masses should have the full right and opportunity to express responsible criticisms to their leaders and to make constructive suggestions."[74] While all of this is extremely vague, Deng seemed to draw a clear distinction between thought and behavior, which Mao never did. Deng appeared ready to allow individuals the privacy of their opinions, provided that they refrain from directly challenging and attacking the power and rule of the Communist Party. As he put it, "You can reserve your opinions, so long as you don't take part in activities against the Party or socialism."[75]

More intriguing still, Deng seemed to conceive "socialist democracy" to be a work-in-progress rather than a finalized reality. According to Deng, "Democracy is our goal" to be developed "only gradually" and not "in haste" because the country must be kept stable. He seemed to regard democracy as contingent on educational achievement, and held out the possibility that the people might be accorded a greater measure of political participation once their educational level had increased.[76] If this analysis is correct, it could be that Deng envisioned a future when the Communist Party could tolerate the expansion of popular participation in government—as China became increasingly modernized and its people acquired higher levels of income, education, and capacity for rational thought and decisionmaking.

Conclusion

One of the abiding curiosities of the twentieth century must be the phenomenon of Marxist revolutions in societies where Marx and Engels would never expect a workers' revolution to occur. In complete contradiction to the precepts of classical Marxism, "proletarian" revolutions succeeded in underdeveloped societies instead of mature industrial economies. After the revolutionaries acceded to power, they were confronted everywhere with the vexation of creating socialism in a primitive economy. On this matter, neither classical Marxism nor Leninism could provide guidance or illumination. It was left to each socialist state to improvise a way out of the dilemma.

In the case of China, the Communist Party under Mao attempted to create socialism with sheer willpower. Instead of being the reflection of the economic base, the superstructure would be the engine of socioeconomic change. Mao was convinced that ideological fervor and mass enthusiasm could transform individual consciousness and create an advanced industrial economy. Not only did his strategy fail in industrializing China, the ceaseless campaigns against class enemies, real or imagined, took the lives of at least 45 million, almost destroyed the Communist Party, and brought China to the precipice.

Unlike Mao, Deng understood the problem of constructing communism in a retrograde economy. He admitted that neither Marx nor Lenin could be expected "to provide ready answers" to questions that arose years after their deaths. This meant that each country must build socialism according to its own conditions as "[t]here are not and cannot be fixed models."[77] By returning to classical Marxism's emphasis on the productive forces, Deng managed to transform Marxism into a developmental nationalist ideology. Whatever his Marxist persuasion, Deng's ideology, for the most part, is informed by an overriding pragmatism. In order to develop China's retarded economic base, he proposed a number of instrumentalities that included privately owned businesses, differential wages, an increasingly unequal income distribution, as well as the importation of foreign capital and technology—all of which is anathema to the Maoist true believer.

If Deng's ideology is reminiscent of Sun Yat-sen's developmental nationalism, it is no happenstance. As early as 1942, Deng had urged his party colleagues to always "act in conformity with [Sun's] Three People's Principles,"[78] which could explain the many similarities of approach, philosophy, and economic program between the two. Like Sun's, Deng's basic approach to problems was one of pragmatism. Like Sun, Deng recognized that class struggle would be destructive for national construction. Like Sun, Deng eschewed ideological doctrinairism, preferring instead to borrow whatever elements—even if they were capitalist—that could promote economic development. Like Sun, Deng refused to conceive of relations between underdeveloped China and the advanced industrial countries as inevitably zero-sum. Instead, just like Sun, Deng believed that China could benefit from Western capital and technology, provided that China's national interests were protected by a strong and vigilant government. Like Sun, Deng regarded no instrumentality as an axiomatic, self-justified good, including the dictatorial rule of the Communist Party itself—which he justified on the basis that only a one-party system could best provide the requisite orderly and stable environment for economic modernization.

To the question of why that one party should be communist and the political system socialist, Deng had ready answers. To begin with, according to Marxist precepts, socialism was the necessary prelude to communism. Despite all the devastation wrought by Mao, and despite having endured three purges himself, communism remained Deng's inspiration and guiding star: "We believe in communism, and our ideal is to bring it into being." Communism remained the "ultimate goal" and dream that sustained him and his party even in their "darkest days," for which "countless . . . people laid down their lives."[79]

There were other reasons for Deng's insistence on socialism. He seemed convinced that socialism would lead to a faster development of the productive forces than capitalism and, in so doing, better provide the material basis for the transition into communism. More than that, Deng maintained that only socialism could eliminate the greed, corruption, and injustice "inherent in capitalism and other systems of exploitation." As long as "the basic means of production" remained publicly owned, Deng was confident that "no new bourgeoisie" would emerge. He was prepared to admit that if his economic reforms should lead to a polarization between rich and poor, the reforms would have to be considered "a failure."[80]

As for why that one party that rules China would necessarily be communist, Deng reinvoked the notion of the vanguard. The Communist Party deserved to rule because its members were supposedly uniquely possessed of special moral virtues, wisdom, and competence. They were selfless beings who only worked "for the good of the people" and did not "exploit the labor of others." Nor did they "lord it over" or impose their will "by decree" on the people but kept in close contact with the masses, representing their will and interests and inspiring their enthusiasm. They dared "to speak the truth and oppose falsehood," always making "a clear distinction" between public and private interests. They did not seek personal favors "at the expense of principle" and appointed people on their merits. They practiced criticism and self-criticism, exposed and corrected shortcomings and mistakes, and always strove for excellence. They were truthful and honest, efficient and quick, producing quality results instead of "empty talk."[81]

More than their moral virtues, Deng demanded that members of the Communist Party be technocrats who could supervise the reformed economy of market socialism, as well as undertake the forward planning of society. They must provide for the training of workers and professionals to meet the country's immediate and future needs by studying "the objective laws" of science and technology and lead the people in "conquering the heights of world science." At the same time, while exercising leadership, CCP members must be careful not to "intervene in too many matters."[82]

In effect, Deng's entire program of economic development was dependent on the Chinese Communist Party members' actually having the moral virtues and professional competence he demanded. It is the possession of those qualities that would ensure the party's continuous rule "for a hundred years" as well as the country's long-term peace and stability.[83] What Deng was reluctant to address was whether the Communist Party should relinquish its power if reality proved either its incompetence or fall from virtue or both. It is here that one finds the greatest difference between Deng and Sun.

Although Sun favored the authoritarian rule of the revolutionary party, he conceived of it strictly in instrumental and transitional terms. One-party rule, for Sun, was expressly for the purpose of tutelage and stewardship: to teach the norms and behaviors of self-government to the people and to ensure that the economic preconditions for democracy would be in place through the achievement of industrialization. In contrast, whatever vague suggestions Deng had regarding the expansion of democratic participation to the masses when China had become fully industrialized, his concept of a "socialist democracy" precluded Communist Party rule as strictly an interim and transitional device toward eventual democratization. Although Sun, like Deng, was critical of Western democracy, Sun was unequivocably in favor of democracy and democratic institutions and principles such as opposition parties and competitive elections. Unlike Deng, Sun proposed to redress Western democracy's flaws by being more, not less, democratic—proposing five, instead of three, branches of government so as to better check and balance governmental power. Deng, in contrast, had no use for institutionalized checks and balances to limit political power.

All of which meant that when Deng averred that "[i]f any problem arises in China, it will arise from inside the Communist Party,"[84] he could offer little in the way of solution, other than the CCP's shop-worn formula of an internal rectification campaign. For all his ingenuity in crafting a program for economic development out of a moribund Marxist-Maoist ideology, Deng's failure to provide for his country's political development would continue to cloud China's future.

Notes

1. Chiang's victory was made possible, in large part, because of the death of Hu and the discrediting of Wang because he headed a puppet regime in Nanjing for the Japanese during the war.

2. In retrospect, the KMT clearly failed at achieving Sun's first principle of Chinese nationalism on Taiwan, in view of the party's historic loss in the presidential election of March 18, 2000, to opposition party candidate Chen Shui-bian. Chen's Democratic Progressive Party favors independence for Taiwan, its membership being composed of ethnic "native Taiwanese"—descendants of immigrants from China's Fujian Province who migrated to Taiwan some 300 years ago.

3. In late 1939 and early 1940, the chief of staff of the Japanese Imperial Army occupying northeastern China reported that Chinese Communist recruitment successes were accomplished under the "plagiarized slogans of [Sun's] Three Principles of the People." See Chalmers A. Johnson, *Peasant Nationalism and Communist Power: The Emergence of Revolutionary China 1937–1945* (Stanford: Stanford University Press, 1962), p. 41.

4. Mao Zedong, "A Comment on the Sessions of the Kuomintang Central Executive Committee and the People's Political Council," *Selected Works* (Beijing: Foreign Languages Press, 1965), v. 3, p. 147.

5. Mao, "On Coalition Government," in Mao, *Selected Works*, p. 281.

6. For a more extensive treatment of Mao's thought and its impact on China's economic development, see chapters 2 and 3 in Maria Hsia Chang, *The Labors of*

Sisyphus: The Economic Development of Communist China (New Brunswick, NJ: Transaction, 1998).

7. See the account by Zheng Yi in *Scarlet Memorial* (Boulder: Westview, 1996).

8. See Jean-Louis Margolin's account in Stephane Courtois et al., *The Black Book of Communism: Crimes, Terror, Repression* (Cambridge, MA: Harvard University Press, 1999), pp. 463–546.

9. Jan S. Prybyla, "China's New Economic Strategy," *Backgrounder* (Washington, DC: The Heritage Foundation, 1985), p. 3.

10. Alvin Rabushka, *The New China: Comparative Economic Development in Mainland China, Taiwan, and Hong Kong* (Boulder: Westview, 1987), pp. 217, 206.

11. Deng was first purged in 1933 for supporting Mao's then-unorthodox strategy of guerrilla warfare and peasant mobilization against the CCP center's policy of inciting a revolution among urban workers. He was rehabilitated in 1934. In 1966 during the Cultural Revolution, Deng was purged again, dispatched to perform manual labor in Jiangxi province and remained purged until 1973. In 1976, Deng was purged by the Gang of Four for being a "capitalist revisionist" but was reinstated in July 1977.

12. Zhou Shulian, "Changing the Pattern of China's Economy," in Lin Wei and Arnold Chao (eds.), *China's Economic Reforms* (Philadelphia: University of Pennsylvania Press, 1982), p. 57.

13. Wang Zhenshi and Wang Yongzhi, "Epilogue: Prices in China," in ibid., p. 225.

14. Karl Marx, "Preface to *Critique of Political Economy*," in *Selected Works* (Moscow: Foreign Languages, 1955), *1*, pp. 362–363.

15. Karl Marx and Friedrich Engels, *The German Ideology* (Moscow: Progress, 1964), p. 41.

16. Ibid., pp. 37–38.

17. Marx, Letter to Annenkov, 28 December 1846, in *Selected Works, 2*, p. 442.

18. Friedrich Engels, "The Peasant War in Germany," *Collected Works, 10* (New York: International, 1976), pp. 469–471.

19. Mao Zedong, *A Critique of Soviet Economics* (New York: Monthly Review Press, 1977), p. 51.

20. Stuart R. Schram, "Deng Xiaoping's Quest for 'Modernization with Chinese Characteristics' and the Future of Marxism-Leninism," in Michael Kau and Susan Marsh (eds.), *China in the Era of Deng Xiapoing: A Decade of Reforms* (Armonk, NY: M. E. Sharpe, 1993), p. 410.

21. A good treatment of the Maoist versus Dengist conceptions of productive forces and relations is Michael Sullivan, "The Ideology of the Chinese Communist Party Since the Third Plenum," in Bill Brugger (ed.), *Chinese Marxism in Flux 1978–84: Essays on Epistemology, Ideology and Political Economy* (Armonk, NY: M. E. Sharpe, 1985), pp. 67–97.

22. Deng Xiaoping, "Excerpts from Talks Given in Wuchang, Shenzhen, Zhuhai and Shanghai" and "We Are Undertaking an Entirely New Endeavour," *Selected*

Works of Deng Xiaoping (1982–1992), III (Beijing: Foreign Languages Press, 1994), pp. 358, 250.

23. Deng, "The Party and the Anti-Japanese Democratic Government (1941)," p. 17; "A General Account of the Struggle Against the Enemy Over the Past Five Years," p. 42; "The Establishment of Base Areas and the Mass Movement (1943)," p. 76; "The Situation Following Our Triumphant Advance to the Central Plains and Our Future Policies and Strategy (1948)," p. 107; "Carry out the Party Central Committee's Directive on the Work of Land Reform and of Party Consolidation (1948)," pp. 111, 113, 114, 115, 116, 118, 123; and "Some Suggestions Concerning Our Entry into New Areas in the Future (1948)," p. 131, *Selected Works, I* (Beijing: Foreign Languages Press, 1984).

24. Deng, "Carry out the Party Central Committee's Directive," p. 119; and "The Situation Following Our Triumphant Advance," pp. 105–109.

25. Deng, "The Establishment of Base Areas and the Mass Movement (1943)," *Selected Works, I,* pp. 75, 76.

26. Deng, "Carry Out the Party Central Committee's Directive," pp. 119–123.

27. Deng, "We Shall Draw on Historical Experience and Guard Against Wrong Tendencies," *Selected Works, III,* p. 225.

28. Deng, "We Shall Expand Political Democracy and Carry Out Economic Reform," *Selected Works, III,* p. 121.

29. Michael Sullivan, "Ideology of the Chinese Communist Party," pp. 71–72.

30. Deng, "Speech at the Third Plenary Session of the Central Advisory Commission of the Communist Party of China," *Selected Works, III,* p. 95.

31. Deng, "Report on the Revision of the Constitution of the Communist Party of China," *Deng Xiaoping: Speeches and Writings* (New York: Pergamon, 1984), pp. 2, 29–30.

32. Deng, "Uphold the Four Cardinal Principles," *Selected Works, III,* p. 190; and "Speech at the Opening Ceremony of the National Conference on Science," *Speeches and Writings,* p. 41.

33. Deng, "Excerpts from Talks Given in Wuchang," p. 367; and "In Everything We Do We Must Proceed from the Realities of the Primary Stage of Socialism," *Selected Works, III,* p. 248.

34. Deng, "On the Reform of the System of Party and State Leadership," *Selected Works, III,* pp. 317–318.

35. Deng, "We Should Draw on the Experience of Other Countries," June 3, 1988, *Selected Works, III,* p. 261.

36. Deng, "Speech at the National Conference on Science," p. 40; and "We Are Undertaking an Entirely New Endeavour," October 13, 1987, *Selected Works, III,* p. 250.

37. Deng, "Building a Socialism with a Specifically Chinese Character," June 30, 1984, *Selected Works, III,* p. 73.

38. Deng, "Maintain the Tradition of Hard Struggle," *Selected Works, III,* p. 283.

39. Deng, "We Must Adhere to Socialism and Prevent Peaceful Evolution Towards Capitalism," *Selected Works, III*, p. 333.

40. Deng, "Review Your Experience and Use Professionally Trained People," "With Stable Policies of Reform and Opening to the Outside World, China can have Great Hopes for the Future," and "We Are Confident That We can Handle China's Affairs Well," *Selected Works, III*, pp. 357, 309, 316, 310.

41. Deng, "We Are Confident" and "No One can Shake Socialist China," *Selected Works, III*, pp. 316, 318.

42. Deng, "We Are Working to Revitalize the Chinese Nation," *Selected Works, III*, p. 344.

43. Deng, "One Country, Two Systems," *Selected Works, III*, p. 70.

44. Deng, "Maintain the Tradition," p. 282.

45. Deng, "One Country, Two Systems," p. 70; "We Are Working to Revitalize," p. 345; "We are Confident," p. 316.

46. Deng, "Maintain the Tradition," p. 282; and "Opening Speech at the Twelfth National Congress of the CPC," *Speeches and Writings*, p. 86.

47. Deng, "Urgent Tasks of China's Third Generation of Collective Leadership," *Selected Works, III*, p. 302.

48. Deng, "We are Working to Revitalize," p. 345; "For the Great Unity of the Entire Chinese Nation," June 18, 1986; "Excerpts from Talks"; and "We are Working to Revitalize," *Selected Works, III*, pp. 164, 366, 345.

49. Deng, "A Letter to the Political Bureau of the Central Committee of the Communist Party of China," *Selected Works, III*, p. 313.

50. Deng, "Uphold the Four Cardinal Principles," *Selected Works (1975–1982)*, p. 171; and "Speech Greeting the Fourth Congress of Chinese Writers and Artists," *Speeches and Writings*, p. 79.

51. Deng, "We Shall Draw On Historical Experience," p. 224; "Speech at the Third Plenary Session," p. 95; "Speech at the Third Plenary Session," p. 96; and "We Should Draw On the Experience of Other Countries," p. 261.

52. Deng, "We Shall Speed Up Reform" and "Remarks on the Domestic Economic Situation," *Selected Works, III*, pp. 235, 162; and "Emancipate the Mind, Seek Truth from Facts and Unite as One in Looking to the Future," *Speeches and Writings*, p. 71.

53. Deng, "We Must Rationalize Prices and Accelerate the Reform," *Selected Works, III*, p. 257.

54. Deng, "Seize the Opportunity to Develop the Economy," *Selected Works, III*, p. 351.

55. Deng, "Speech at National Conference on Science," p. 45; "Speech at the Third Plenary Session," p. 96; "We Must Promote Education in the Four Cardinal Principles and Adhere to the Policies of Reform and Opening to the Outside World," *Speeches and Writings*, p. 202.

56. Deng, "Answers to the Italian Journalist Oriana Fallaci," *Selected Works (1975–1982)*, p. 333; "Science and Technology Constitute a Primary Productive

Force," *Selected Works, III*, p. 269; "Speech at the National Conference on Science," p. 41.

57. Deng, "Urgent Tasks of China's Third Generation," p. 303; "Our Work in All Fields Should Contribute to the Building of Socialism with Chinese Characteristics," *Selected Works, III*, p. 33; "Science and Technology," pp. 270, 269.

58. Deng, "Opening Speech at the Twelfth National Congress of the CPC," *Speeches and Writings*, p. 87.

59. See chapter 1 on "Deng Xiaoping's International Strategic Thought," in Jing Xiang and Yao Long (eds.), *Disandai lingxiu waijiao shilu (Record of the Foreign Relations of the Leaders of the Third Generation)* (Beijing: zhongguo yanshi, 1997).

60. Deng, "Speech at National Conference on Science," pp. 45–46, 43, 48.

61. Deng, "Science and Technology," p. 270; "Excerpts from Talks," p. 366; "Speech at the Ceremony Celebrating the 35th Anniversary of the Founding of the People's Republic of China," *Selected Works, III*, p. 79.

62. Deng, "Emancipate the Mind," p. 67; "In the First Decade, Prepare for the Second," *Selected Works, III*, p. 27.

63. Deng, "Our Work in All Fields," p. 33; "Make a Success of Special Economic Zones and Open More Cities to the Outside World," *Selected Works, III*, p. 62; and "Emancipate the Mind," p. 73.

64. Deng, "Excerpts from Talks," p. 362; and "Interview of Deng Xiaoping by Robert Maxwell on Current Affairs," *Speeches and Writings*, p. 97. Obviously, the Chinese Communist Party has decided that the year 2000 is not the time for a wealth redistribution.

65. Deng, "China Will Never Allow Other Countries to Interfere in its Internal Affairs," *Selected Works, III*, p. 347.

66. Deng, "Urgent Tasks of China's Third Generation," p. 304; "Take a Clear-cut Stand," pp. 196, 195.

67. Deng, "The Organizational Line Guarantees the Implementation of the Ideological and Political Lines," *Selected Works (1975–1982)*, p. 199; "With Stable Policies of Reform," p. 307.

68. Deng, "Emancipate the Mind," p. 69; "The Overriding Need Is for Stability," *Selected Works, III*, p. 277.

69. Deng, "We have to Clear Away Obstacles and Continue to Advance," p. 200; "Reform and Opening to the Outside World can Truly Invigorate China," *Selected Works, III*, p. 233; "Take a Clear-cut Stand," p. 196; and "Bourgeois Liberalization Means Taking the Capitalist Road," p. 130.

70. Deng, "China Can Only Take the Socialist Road," *Selected Works, III*, p. 208.

71. Deng, "Speech at a Meeting with the Members of the Committee for Drafting the Basic Law of the Hong Kong Special Administrative Region," *Selected Works, III*, p. 219; "Take a Clear-cut Stand," p. 195.

72. Deng, "The Overriding Need," p. 277; "Take a Clear-cut Stand," p. 196.

73. Deng, "Uphold the Four Cardinal Principles," p. 183.

74. Deng, "In Everything We Do," p. 248; "Emancipate the Mind," p. 66; and "The Present Situation," p. 242.

75. Deng, "Take a Clear-cut Stand," p. 194.

76. Deng, "The Overriding Need," p. 278; "Take a Clear-cut Stand," p. 196; and "We Shall Speed Up Reform," p. 240.

77. Deng, "Let Us Put the Past Behind Us and Open Up a New Era," *Selected Works, III*, pp. 284, 285.

78. Deng, "In Celebration of the Fiftieth Birthday of Comrade Liu Bocheng (1942)," *Selected Works, I*, p. 37.

79. Deng, "Unity Depends on Ideals and Discipline" and "Reform Is the Only Way For China to Develop Its Productive Forces," *Selected Works, III*, pp. 116, 141.

80. Deng, "Excerpts from Talks," p. 361; "Speech at the National Conference of the Communist Party of China," *Selected Works, III*, p. 146; "Unity Depends on Ideals," p. 117; "Speech at the Third Plenary Session," p. 97; "China Can Only Take the Socialist Road," p. 207; and "Reform Is the Only Way," p. 142.

81. Deng, "Speech at National Conference on Science," pp. 52, 149; "Report on the Revision of the Constitution," pp. 27, 33, 6, 5, 28; and "Speech at the National Conference on Science," p. 53.

82. Deng, "Speech at the National Conference on Education," *Speeches and Writings*, p. 58; "Speech at the National Conference on Science," p. 52; "Help the People Understand the Importance of the Rule of Law," *Selected Works, III*, p. 167.

83. Deng, "Excerpts from Talks," p. 368.

84. Ibid.

8

Patriotic Nationalism of the People's Republic

By transforming Marxism into a developmental nationalist ideology, Deng Xiaoping provided the theoretical rationale for the much-needed reforms to resuscitate the moribund Chinese economy. Armed with his "theory of building socialism with Chinese characteristics," the Communist Party in December 1978 initiated the Four Modernizations program.

Agriculture was decollectivized through the introduction of a "contract responsibility system" in which peasant households received usufruct rights to farmland, provided they sold a portion of their harvest to the state. After decades of isolation and hostility, the People's Republic of China opened itself to trade, investment, diplomatic, and cultural linkages with the West. Special Economic Zones (SEZs) and "open cities" along the coast were created to attract foreign investment and technology; newly sanctioned private, collective, and foreign-owned businesses and enterprises flourished; wage incentives to spur production were introduced. The tentacles of the state retreated to afford enterprise managers and local-regional governments a greater measure of autonomy; intellectuals were permitted wider latitudes of thought and dissent so long as they refrained from challenging socialism and Communist Party rule; students in record numbers left China to study at foreign institutions of higher learning. The People's Liberation Army was downsized and its capabilities upgraded through purchases of advanced weaponry and the creation of rapid-response forces and a blue-water navy.

Deng's reforms transformed the economy. From 1979 to 1997, the PRC economy grew at an average annual rate of 9 percent, a rate unprecedented in recent world history. At that rate of growth, a country's GNP more than doubles every ten years.[1] In the 20 years from 1976 to 1996, China's annual per-capita GNP increased 2,100 percent from $139 to $2,935; the agricultural sector grew by 5.5 percent per annum between 1979 and 1982, resulting in an increase of 131 percent in the average annual rural income. Private, collective, and foreign-owned businesses became the engine of growth, bringing prosperity especially to the coastal regions where SEZs are located. Foreign trade more than tripled in volume from 1978 to over $70 billion in 1986, so that by 1995 China became the world's fastest-growing economy and its sixth largest trader. In 1998, it ranked second in the world in foreign exchange reserves that totaled $128 billion. If China sustains its rate of growth, it may very well ascend to superpower status sometime this century.

Attending the economic reforms was the relaxation of the state's iron grip on society, which made possible greater freedom in thought and behavior. In politics, Deng effected some modest improvements, mainly in the Communist Party. The cult of personality was eschewed in favor of a collective leadership; intraparty disputes were resolved in a more rule-governed fashion rather than with violence; political campaigns, while still being mounted, were reduced in frequency and carefully controlled by the state. Where Mao had failed, Deng provided for a younger generation to take over. After two failed attempts with Hu Yaobang and Zhao Ziyang, he successfully groomed Jiang Zemin to take over the reins of government. As for Deng himself, by the end of 1989 he had retired from all public offices, while remaining as his country's unofficial paramount leader until he succumbed to Parkinson's disease on February 19, 1997, at age 92.

For all his achievements, Deng neglected to institute checks and balances on the dictatorial rule of the Communist Party, nor did he reform the inefficient state-owned enterprises, half of which consistently operate in the red, requiring infusions of vast sums in state subsidies. That neglect, together with the unintended consequences of reforms, have spawned increasingly challenging problems of rising crime rates and a swelling mobile population, peasant and labor unrest, overpopulation and environmental degradation, increasing local-regional government autonomy, ethnic separatist movements in Xinjiang and Tibet, pandemic corruption in the party, government, and military, as well as "spiritual pollution" from the West. Not only have these problems troubled the regime, they could threaten the very continuity of the People's Republic.[2]

The Turn to Patriotic Nationalism

It was "spiritual pollution"—the penetration into China of Western values of freedom and democracy—that helped to precipitate a major political crisis in 1989. In April of that year, university students in Beijing demonstrated in Tiananmen Square against political corruption and pressed for greater government accountability, freedom of the press, and the right to organize independent student unions. The students quickly galvanized the support of tens of thousands of demonstrators in cities across China whose ranks included industrial workers, CCP members, and government functionaries. When the demonstrators persisted despite the imposition of martial law on May 20, Deng and other party elders decided to deploy the military. In the predawn hours of June 4, troops in tanks and armored personnel carriers entered the Square, killing 1,000 to 2,500 unarmed civilians.

In the aftermath of the massacre, the government sought to regain control by instigating a campaign of national unity in which young people were singled out for "patriotic education." Calling the democracy movement a "counter-revolutionary rebellion" that had the "black hands" of foreign enemies behind it, the party urged the people to unite under its leadership or China would descend into chaos.[3] In September 1994, the Patriotic Education Campaign was expanded to include the entire populace, followed by the publication in November 1995 of *Selected Works for Instruction in Patriotic Education* containing the writings and speeches of Mao, Deng, and Jiang Zemin on patriotism. The official *People's Daily* admitted that the book was meant "to fill an ideological vacuum" in the Chinese people, who were enjoined to "love their country."[4] Spearheading the campaign was Jiang, who instructed his party to rebuild itself "under the new banner of nationalism" and urged that the masses, especially the youth, be "deeply inculcated" with the values of "patriotism."[5]

Although the Tiananmen incident was the catalyst, Beijing's turn to patriotic nationalism has deeper roots and can be better understood in the larger context of the Communist Party's need to relegitimate its rule. Deng's market reforms had managed to salvage his party's tattered legitimacy from the ruination wrought by Mao and rebuild it upon a pragmatic basis of economic performance. But China's ideocratic political system demands more than pragmatic legitimacy, requiring instead doctrinal legitimation provided by some overarching ideology. Jiang Zemin admitted as much when he said in a speech in 1996 that "Only with resolute theory can our politics be steadfast."[6] And the Communist Party seems to have found its new doctrinal legitimation in Deng's developmental nationalism.

Franz Schurmann once observed that the CCP divides its ideology into two parts: The first is "theory" *(lilun)* comprised of ideas that are claimed to be universally applicable and for all time; the second is "thought" *(sixiang)*, the practical application of universal theory to concrete circumstances of a particular time and place.[7] For much of its history, the CCP considered Marxism-Leninism to be its guiding theory, while the ideas of Mao Zedong served as its thought. In March 1999, however, the party elevated the reformist ideas of Deng to the level of theory when it incorporated "Deng Xiaoping Theory" into the preamble of its constitution. In so doing, the Communist Party appeared to signal its formal adoption of developmental nationalism as its ideology.[8] As observed by *The Economist*, with communism discredited and democracy distrusted, China's leaders have turned to "a new ideology" of "visceral nationalism" to justify their power.[9]

In the case of the People's Republic, nationalism not only is an ideological replacement for an obsolete Marxism, it also functions, in the judgment of some in the academic community,[10] as a unifying force that can hold together a society experiencing the disruptive forces associated with rapid economic development. As expressed by an article in a PRC military journal, nationalism can provide cohesion for China by overcoming and combatting the deleterious effects of economic reform, including "ideological indifference," "a decline in patriotism," and the lamentable and increasing tendency to "worship money."[11]

Contemporary Chinese nationalism is the subject of contentious debate and contrary interpretation. Observers have noted that "No sooner had the debate started than it produced confusion. Equally qualified China scholars are unable to agree on the facts."[12] For some, contemporary Chinese nationalism is antiforeign and aggressive, bent on restoring China to its historical hegemonic position in Asia. Others dismiss this as alarmist, arguing instead that China is a team player that seeks integration into the global economy. Zhang Xudong, for one, sees Chinese nationalism as no different than the positive nationalism that animates most other peoples—one that is the product of emotional links with homeland, territory, language, culture, history, and race. Rather than aggressive and xenophobic, Zhang maintains that China is merely growing into its own as a strong, enlightened, and modernized nation-state that refuses to be a second-class citizen in the world, desiring only to be accorded respect as an equal.[13] Zhao Suisheng dismisses any talk of a rising tide of nationalism altogether. Whatever nationalism there is in China is "exceedingly thin," absent of "collective ideals and shared aspirations . . . coherently expressed in meaningful symbols and myths."[14]

How contemporary Chinese nationalism is interpreted is more than an esoteric academic debate because it bears on U.S. policy toward China and the entire Asia-Pacific region. As such, an understanding of contemporary Chinese nationalism recommends itself—an understanding that should be based on the testimony provided by primary sources. Instead of relying on the opinions and judgments of American academic intermediaries—which are divergent and contradictory to begin with—it may be better to let the inhabitants of the People's Republic speak their own minds. Ideally, those primary sources should be both qualitative and quantitative, comprised of books and journal articles, as well as opinion surveys of PRC citizens on the subject.

The following account of China's patriotic nationalism is an effort to exploit those sources by drawing on the writings and opinion surveys of three groups within China. They are the state-employed intellectuals, the armed forces, and the youth—groups identified by social scientists to be most susceptible to government propaganda and indoctrination.[15] Representing the intellectuals are scholarly books such as *History of the Chinese People* and journals such as *Nationality Studies*. Representing the military are PLA publications, primarily the journal *National Defense*. Representing Chinese youth are popular books such as *China Can Say No* and an opinion survey of university students in Beijing. It is to those materials that we now turn.

Defining Contemporary Chinese Nationalism

Before a portrait of contemporary Chinese nationalism can be drawn, the phenomenon in question should be more precisely identified and defined. Western commentators typically refer to it as nationalism—but that is something of a misnomer. If "nation" refers to a people united by common sympathies and desirous of forming their own government, then whatever passions and sentiments that now animate Chinese on the mainland cannot be nationalism because they already have their own state. Whatever nationalism there is in China today is *reactive*, in the sense of a historical grievance and resentment at the humiliation Chinese endured under Western and Japanese imperialism.[16] Those popular sentiments of reactive nationalism are exploited and amplified by the Communist Party toward its promotion of patriotism: loyalty and devotion to the state. The result is *patriotic nationalism*: a mixture of state-inculcated patriotism and populist reactive nationalism.

The conceptual distinction between nationalism and patriotism is fully recognized in the Chinese language, where nation is *minzu* (people-clan) and nationalism is *minzu zhuyi* (people-ism), while state is *guojia* (country-family) and patriotism is *guojia zhuyi* or *aiguo zhuyi* (love-country-ism). Given China's integral statehood and its multiethnic population, the Communist Party's emphasis on patriotism is a prudent decision.[17] Although ethnic minorities make up only 8 percent of China's population, they occupy 64 percent of the land surface and are concentrated in the "strategically important"[18] border regions. Under these circumstances, ethnic nationalism by any of China's constituent groups would be highly divisive. Jiang Zemin recognized as much when he cautioned that "nationalism, if mishandled, can be deleterious for the unity of the state and of the people."[19] Jiang's warning is elaborated in *A Summary of Nationality Theories and Policies:*[20]

> Protecting the unity of the state requires that we firmly struggle against nationalism that seeks to divide *(fenlie)* and fragment our country. . . . Whether it is big Han chauvinism or the nationalism of localities and regions *(difang),* all are equally harmful to the unity and development of the state and the [Chinese] nation. . . . [This is why] we must prevent and suppress all nationalist movements within China [including] . . . "Pan-Islamism," "Pan-Turkism" . . . and efforts by splittists who collude with international enemies to foment unrest and riots in the name of nation, religion, "democracy, freedom, and human rights."

The Concept of State or Patriotic Nationalism

Instead of ethnic nationalism, the populace in the People's Republic are urged to be animated by "state-nationalism" *(guojia minzu zhuyi)*, defined by a contributor to *Nationality Studies* as "a form of nationalism that is in accord with the interests of the state." The interests of the state, in turn, are defined as "the collective interests of all the ethnic groups" that make up the People's Republic.[21] What the concept of state-nationalism fails to address, however, are the political mechanisms for discerning the "collective interests" of China's constituent peoples. In political systems such as the People's Republic, which lack democratic processes to identify those interests, it is the single-party state that presumes to speak for the general will. In effect, as it is operationalized in China today, state-nationalism is nothing other than a narrow patriotism: loyalty and devotion to the Communist Party-state that claims to represent the will of all the peoples of China. As a

PRC intellectual put it, "Patriotism . . . is love and loyalty for our unified *(tongyi)* multiethnic *(duo minzu) socialist state.*"[22]

The Communist Party argues that only its leadership enabled the Chinese people to triumph over countless obstacles and challenges in the past, which included Japan's war of aggression, the "despotic" Nationalist regime in the 1930s and 1940s, and the West's political blockade of China in the 1960s.[23] It was only with the founding of the People's Republic that Chinese finally "achieved status" and "stood up."[24] Under Deng's leadership, the Communist Party introduced economic reforms that brought dramatic increases in income and GNP. And, it is argued, only with the party's continuing leadership can China adequately defend itself and achieve territorial reunification—and in so doing, fully restore the national honor and dignity so grievously impaired since the Opium War.[25]

At the same time as it is promoting patriotism the Chinese Communist Party is also deliberately blurring the analytic boundaries between nationalism and patriotism so as to exploit the symbiotic relationship between the two. PRC scholars characterize that relationship as one where "national unity" is dependent on the "unity of the people," which is "a necessary condition for the prosperity and development of the state."[26] It is that symbiosis that prompts the regime in China to make the PRC state synonymous with the nation, and to insist to its people that loving the Chinese nation requires fidelity to the Communist Party-state. More than that, in the last analysis, it is the state that is of greater importance and higher priority. As expressed by *History of the Chinese People*, claimed by its authors to be the first published PRC account on the subject, "Nation and state are formed at the same time, with the state as the logical premise *(qianti)* for the existence and development of the nation."[27]

The insistence that nation and state are intimately bound together is repeated and elaborated in other accounts. According to one, "national interests are often bound together with state . . . interests in mono- as well as multinational states."[28] Another account maintains that[29]

Nation and state are born at the same time. . . . Nation is a collectivity *(gong-tong ti)* founded on territory; the state is an organization *(zuzhi)* also founded on territory and property. The formation of the state has an urgency *(boqie xing)* to it . . . and it is the state that molds *(xingzhu)* the nation.

Those assertions are echoed in yet another account:[30]

[N]ation and state are closely related. The relationship between the two is one of mutual inclusiveness and mutual penetration. . . . *In our country, the state's interests are higher than everything else; the interests of the nation must serve those of the state.* ... We, therefore, must unite love for nation with love for our state, ... oppose splittism, and together construct the big family of this great Chinese nation. Only in so doing will [China's constituent] peoples have a future.

Patriotic Nationalism's Attributes

Contemporary Chinese patriotic nationalism is a volatile mix of potentially troublesome attributes that social scientists have identified to have a high propensity toward aggression. Those attributes include an ethnic-racial conception of nationhood; a reactive nationalism that nurses memories of China's historical humiliation at the hands of the imperialist powers; a collective sense of victimhood and insecurity; xenophobic narcissism; a preoccupation with power; cultural-moral relativism; an illiberal worldview; an irredentist resolve to reclaim lost territories; and political authoritarianism.

Racial-Ethnic Conception of Nationhood

An account of contemporary Chinese patriotic nationalism may begin with its conception of what constitutes the Chinese nation. Western scholars of nationalism have observed that nations defined by the primordial law of blood are more disposed to be aggressive and intolerant toward outsiders.[31] In the case of China, although its government has been punctilious in including the ethnic minorities as integral members of China, that does not mean that Beijing has subscribed to a civic conception of nationhood. Chinese nationality is still defined by ascriptive criteria of ethnicity and race. It is just that what is meant by "Chinese" has been broadened to include the ethnic minorities as well as the Han.

This is evident in PRC scholars' conception of "nation" *(minzu)* as a "natural (organic) group" *(ziran zuti)* possessed of a common history, culture, language, territory, economy, "psychology" *(xinli)*, and "self-awareness."[32] Prior to the formation of nations were "blood-related" *(xueyuan guanxi)* groups of "clans" *(shizu)* and "tribes" *(bulo)*. Nations began to make their appearance "at a certain stage in history" when, due to increasing mobility and migration, clans and tribes began to interact and interbreed. At the same time, the primitive economy of tribal communism was replaced by family farms. Gradually, several tribes entered into an "alliance" *(lianmeng)* to form a larger group of nation whose members are now connected less by blood than by the bonds of common territory, language, economics, and psychology. Despite that, it is insisted that within the nation, "common blood remains the real foundation of the alliance."[33]

All of which explains why PRC scholars believe that Han and minority peoples in China are not distinct ethnic groups because, through their cultural and physical assimilation through the ages, they have merged to become a single "Chinese people" *(zhongguo ren)* in a single "Chinese nation" *(zhonghua minzu)*. This Chinese nation is a "large nation-family" *(minzu dajiating)* of "mixed bloodlines" *(hunxue)*—the result of thousands of years of interbreeding and cultural-political assimilation by the more than 50 constituent "blood groups" that make up China. For that matter, the Han people themselves are "the product of interbreeding and assimilation of many peoples *(minzu)* through thousands of years." Furthermore, it is maintained that ever since the Qin dynasty, China has been a unified multiethnic state in which Han and the minorities lived together in "interdependence, interconnectedness, and interactiveness, each making important contributions toward the creation of our ancestral country's *(zuguo)* glorious history and colorful culture."[34]

Through their collective effort in 5,000 years of cohabitation and involvement, the peoples of China created a common culture of traditions and morals. It is claimed that China's entire traditional way of life was founded by the two legendary Emperors Yan and Huang (ca. 2838 B.C. and 2698 B.C., respectively). Emperor Yan discovered medicine and farming, the backbone of the Chinese economy for millennia; Emperor Huang (Yellow) created the code of human relations that served as the moral foundation of Chinese society, as well as some 100 technologies and handicrafts. It is that culture that has kept the Chinese nation together in times of crisis and change, enabling it to survive as the world's oldest continuous civilization.[35] Today, the "soul" *(linghun)*[36] and "spirit" *(jingsheng)* of that millennial culture still define and "bind together" the Chinese nation.[37]

That "spirit" is understood by a contributor to *National Defense* as patriotism, industriousness, perseverance, achievement, collectivism, and "revolutionary enthusiasm";[38] and by *Liberation Army Daily* as loyalty, selflessness, hard work, dedication, and courage—all of which the Communist Party now claims as uniquely "communist sentiments and principles" *(gongchan zhuyi qingcao)*.[39] In addition, it is asserted that certain allegedly traditional Chinese cultural attributes, such as the low esteem for trade and entrepreneurship, are really not representative of China's "mainstream" culture and should not be considered part of its "spirit." Other attributes have been redefined to better suit the party's purpose, especially patriotism. Traditionally understood to mean "loyalty to the emperor" *(gongzhong)*, patriotism is now redefined to mean loyalty not just to China nor even to the Communist Party-state but to the current regime of "socialism with Chinese characteristics," which, it is claimed, truly and best represents the collective interests of all Chinese.[40]

As "the spiritual bond of the Chinese nation" *(Yanhuang wenhua shi zhonghua minzu di jingsheng nuodai)*, it is argued that a revival of traditional culture is needed because only an appeal to the ancient traditions can keep the People's Republic unified. More than that, the commonality of culture can also induce overseas Chinese to contribute their wealth and talent toward China's economic development. It is argued that their common cultural identity will enable Chinese all over the world to survive in an increasingly competitive global environment of emergent regional trading blocs.[41]

All of which could explain why the Chinese government is promoting a revival of traditional culture.[42] China's ancient morals and practices, long vilified by the Communist Party as feudal and hopelessly retrograde, are now recommended as virtues. Jiang Zemin has taken to peppering his speeches with Confucian sayings; ancestor worship is being revived. Historical relics, such as the Great Wall, once considered symbols of feudal oppression, are now embraced. In April 1995, local and overseas Chinese donated $700,000 to refurbish a mausoleum reputedly built for the Yellow Emperor, which *China Daily* promoted as "a place for all Chinese people to worship their ancestors."[43] Institutes and scholarly associations to study "the culture of Emperors Yan and Huang" *(Yanhuang wenhua)* have sprung across China—almost all with government support.[44] Publications on the subject appear with regularity, with the entire country in the grips of a "national study fever" *(guoxue re)*.[45]

The new cultural renaissance is aimed at forging a common national identity out of the nearly 1.3 billion people who inhabit China. Party ideologues now admit that, for 40 years, due to the overweening influence of "leftist" thinking, the CCP was excessively critical of China's traditional culture and, in so doing, overlooked the functional value of tradition for contemporary society. It is now recommended that select elements from Chinese tradition be retained if they enhance economic development and social stability. The classic Confucian virtues—especially *ren* (charity), *li* (propriety), *xiao* (filial piety), and the "five human relations"—are recognized to be timeless and timely for their utility toward social stability. In particular, the virtues of collectivism and patriotism (putatively part of the

"Chinese moral tradition") must be resurrected to combat the rampant corruption, materialism, hedonism, and "extreme individualism" of contemporary society.[46]

More than culture, the Communist Party is also promulgating myths of origins and of descent to promote an ethnic and racial nationalism.[47] It is said that although Han people comprised the "mainstream" of the original Huaxia people who inhabited the central plains of the Yellow River, by the Spring and Autumn Period, Huaxia had "amalgamated" *(yonghe)* with the surrounding ethnic minorities to "gradually form a bigger nation."[48] Through interbreeding, the various *ethnie* in China had merged into a single people—a fact that is allegedly confirmed by scientific studies of blood types in China tracing the bloodlines to a single origin, that is, Emperors Yan and Huang. The latter are the genetic ancestors of both Han and minority peoples, including those in far-flung Qinghai and Tibet. In effect, in the Chinese "civilization family," the distinction between Han and the border peoples is merely one of "varying levels of cultural attainment" *(wenhua shang di xianjin yu luohou zhibie)* rather than of "race" *(zhongzu)*.[49]

Reactive Nationalism

Aside from an ethnic conception of nationhood, another attribute of contemporary Chinese patriotic nationalism is its reactive character. For more than a hundred years beginning with the Opium War of 1840, Chinese suffered repeated humiliation from defeat in wars, unequal treaties, and territorial losses at the hands of the Western Powers and Japan. As a consequence, as one Chinese commentator remarked, the collective memory of this history is "like dry tinder and can easily be inflamed."[50]

That is exactly what the government in Beijing has done. It has published an encyclopedia of abuses by foreign powers since the 1800s and has seized every opportunity "to harp on China's past humiliations and present glory." In 1995 to commemorate the 50th anniversary of the end of World War II, PRC newspapers were "stacked with" articles detailing the wartime violence committed by the Japanese. Busloads of Chinese schoolchildren arrived each day to tour a museum dedicated to the victims in the Rape of Nanjing. The museum's director candidly admitted that the purpose of the exhibit was "to use patriotism as a unifying force."[51] In effect, in the hands of the Communist Party, reactive nationalism has become a touchstone for patriotism. As observed by Hong Kong legislator Christine Loh, "If you don't bear a grudge against China's historical oppressors, then you don't *ai guo* [love your country] enough."[52]

Insecurity and Victimhood

More than a historical grievance about the past, reactive nationalism has been generalized into a sense of contemporary victimhood. Reportedly, Beijing's recitation of past wrongs is meant to arouse the Chinese people's "consciousness of suffering" by channeling their anger against the West, especially the United States. Former U.S. Ambassador to China James Lilley described Chinese nationalism as "a type of anti-Americanism. . . . We are seen as the ones who frustrate their legitimate rights."[53] That sense of victimization could account for China's sensitivity to every criticism and slight, real or imagined. As articulated by the authors of *Behind the Demonization of China*,[54]

> In the past 150 years, Western and Japanese invaders and imperialists had greatly wounded *(chuangshang)* the Chinese people . . . which cause Chinese to become easily enraged whenever the West insults or portrays China in an unflattering light.

Hypersensitivity is accompanied by, and probably stems from, feelings of collective insecurity, which seem to afflict Chinese at the same time as they are self-absorbed and self-congratulatory. An American journalist portrays the Chinese as possessed of a "complicated psyche." Chinese psychology is a mixture of an "insular, self-satisfied" traditional conviction of themselves as the Middle Kingdom, together with a "deep sense of inferiority" that their country is in reality far behind most of the developed world.[55] That mentality is displayed by the five authors, aged 30 to 40, of *China Can Say No*, an immensely popular book that claims to represent a "broad" spectrum of popular opinion in China.[56] In the summer of 1996, it became an instant bestseller with its first print run of 50,000 copies sold out in a few days. More than being popular, the book was lauded by the Chinese Communist Party for its "nationalist purpose" and for being "representative" of the youth's sentiments and experiences. That September, the party bankrolled the production of a television series based on the book.[57] Before the year ended, *China Can Say No* had spawned a sequel and a host of imitators.[58]

As its title implies, the book's main message is that Chinese must stand up to the United States because America is a declining power, whereas China is a rising power whose Confucian civilization is certain to triumph and prevail in the twenty-first century. For all their bravado, however, the authors confess to an insecurity that they trace to their country's "less developed Third World status." Bristling at the manner in which the United

States, mainly through the Voice of America, treats China "like a little country," the authors nevertheless admit that there are times when even they "wonder whether America's brash self-confidence had been fostered by the fearful and insecure demeanor of Chinese like us."[59]

The nagging sense of insecurity can lead to paranoia and a persecution mentality. Both are evident in two other popular PRC books. *Listen to China* insists that many ideas currently in vogue in the world—such as the "China threat," "the clash of civilizations," the supposed global food and environmental crises—are "deliberately manufactured falsehoods . . . directed against China."[60] *Behind the Demonization of China* maintains that American sinologists and mainstream media (such as the *New York Times*, the *Washington Post*, and the major television networks), instead of reporting the truth, deliberately propagate lies and disinformation so as to "demonize" *(yaomo hua)* China. Both books insist that America's China bashing is motivated by racism: *Listen to China* maintains that "two white men with a white supremacist racist attitude" wrote *The Coming Conflict with China*; *Behind the Demonization of China* similarly attributes the U.S. media's prejudice against China to "white supremacist *[bairen zhishang]* racism."[61] What is especially disturbing about *Behind the Demonization of China*, aside from its own racist tone,[62] is its eight authors' claim to possession of a special and objective knowledge about the United States[63] from having spent time as students or visiting professionals in America. To illustrate, the two leading authors, Li Xiguang and Liu Kang, are respectively a former visiting journalist at the *Washington Post* and an associate professor of comparative literature at Pennsylvania State University.

China's siege mentality is also given ample expression in *China Can Say No*. Its authors are convinced that the United States is engaged in a systematic effort to undermine the People's Republic because it fears China as a future competitor. Toward that purpose, Washington has organized an "Anti-China Club" to contain China, "carve up" its territories, and prevent it from achieving greatness. The members of the Club perceive China as a threat to peace and security in the Asia-Pacific region, and include all the Western countries and members of the Association of Southeast Asian Nations (ASEAN) with whom Beijing currently has territorial disputes over rival claims in the South China Sea. Another member of the Anti-China Club is Japan, a country that has made China its "imaginary enemy." The irony, according to *China Can Say No*, is that China has more to fear from the Japanese, who can never be trusted because of their slaughter of "thousands upon thousands" of Chinese when they invaded China.[64]

More distressing still, according to *China Can Say No,* is the phenomenon of Chinese women who have "forsaken" decent "faithful" Chinese men for "the white race." By "throwing themselves into the white man's embrace," such women are no better than dogs who, "as soon as a stranger lets them sniff the sausage in his hands, unhesitatingly abandon their owners to follow the stranger."[65] This suggests that there is a sexual dimension to Chinese reactive nationalism's sense of insecurity. *Behind the Demonization of China* similarly decries women with "Chinese blood" who "smile obsequiously" at "whites" and marry "Chinese-hating" white men. In so doing, those traitorous women are contributing to the "demonized" image of Chinese men as "stupid ... corrupt ... devious" and "sexually impotent"[66] eunuchs.

Xenophobic Narcissism

One way to compensate for and overcome the sense of insecurity is to resort to an exaggerated self-regard. The authors of *China Can Say No* admit as much when they profess their love-hate ambivalence about the United States. During the 1980s, America "captured the imagination" of an entire Chinese "nation." Like countless Chinese young people, the authors forsook China's own culture and tradition to indiscriminately admire everything American—from its popular culture to its democratic ideology. They "worshiped" President Ronald Reagan and wished that someone like him could lead China. It was only when the authors realized that "self-centered" America was interested only in maintaining "world hegemony" did they awake from their "infatuation with America" *(meiguo qingjie)* to embrace "Chinese nationalism."[67]

Narcissistic nationalists are said to be fundamentally incurious and uninterested in the groups they despise except insofar as their behavior confirms their prejudices.[68] In the case of China, Zha Jianying, the author of a PRC book on Chinese popular culture, testifies to his countrymen's insularity and disinterest in other societies when he admits that Chinese "seldom look at other cultures on their own terms, but always compare them to China." China remains "self-centered," being far more interested in itself than in anyone else.[69]

Another characteristic of narcissistic nationalism is the insistence that one's group is *sui generis.* In China's case, its scholars have taken issue with Western anthropologists' claim that human beings, including Chinese, originated in Africa. As an example, an assistant professor of anthropology at Xiamen University takes umbrage at Western scholars who trace the origins of Han people to lands outside of China—variously to Egypt, Babylon, India, or Central Asia. According to him, this kind of "tyrannical" *(badao)* scholarship has "enraged" *(jinu)* the Chinese people because it effectively made Chinese into "bastards" *(sisheng zi)* of other peoples, instead of being "the descendants of the dragon" *(longdi chuanren)* and of Emperors Yan and Huang.[70] Far from being of alien origin, *History of the Chinese People* insists, Chinese are the original man, because fossil remains of precursors to *Homo sapiens* found in China "prove that our country is one of the lands where man originated."[71]

Narcissism has also been described as the systematic overvaluation of the self, which acts as "a distorting mirror" in which one's simple ethnic, religious, or territorial attributes are turned into glorious qualities.[72] Evidence of this narcissistic propensity can be found in PRC elite as well as popular writings.

An example of the former is an article in *National Defense,* entitled "Beloved Motherland, Great Nation," which was an installment in the journal's "Seminars in Patriotic Education." The article begins by reminding the reader that China can claim not just the "four great inventions" of the compass, paper, gunpowder, and printing, but countless other innovations as well. According to the author, Chinese once took the lead in mathematics, being first to calculate the square root and the cube root. A Chinese, Qin Jiushao, first formulated mathematical equations, and "scientist" Zu Chongzhi understood the mathematical concept of pi to be the ratio of a circle's circumference to its diameter some 1,100 years before the ancient Greeks. Ancient China was also notable for the science of astronomy. Chinese were first to record the discovery of a new star, as evidenced by fourteenth-century B.C. inscriptions on a piece of tortoise shell. Chinese were also first to observe sunspots in 43 B.C., more than 800 years before the Europeans, and to record the appearance of Haley's comet in 613 B.C.— the itinerary of which was described in detail in a Jin dynasty (A.D. 265–420) book on astronomy entitled *Jinshu tianwen zhi.*[73]

Chinese were innovators in engineering and hydraulic construction, having constructed the Grand Canal, the Great Wall, and the Dujiang Dam in 251 B.C., considered to be a "miraculous" feat of engineering even by modern standards. Chinese also preceded Europeans in erecting stone arched bridges, the oldest of which in Zhaozhou was designed and engineered by Li Chun during the Sui dynasty (A.D. 589–618). Stone arched bridges would not make their appearance in Europe until some 1,200 years later during the nineteenth century. Chinese can claim humankind's earliest known written script in the form of inscriptions on bones and tortoise shells from the 11th century B.C Their invention of the written script enabled Chinese to record and maintain the peerless *Siku quanshu* of the Qing dynasty, one of the most comprehensive historical chronicles in the world.[74] Chinese can also claim the world's oldest map with distances marked with numbers. Recently discovered by Chinese archaeologists, the 2,300-year-old map of Hebei Province was engraved on copper plate in a scale of approximately one centimeter to five meters (one inch to 42 feet).[75]

More than its human achievements, China is also distinguished by its natural resource endowment. The People's Republic has the world's largest coal reserves and subsoil mineral deposits of siderite, magnetite, and boron. China has wildlife species that are found nowhere else on earth, such as the panda, white dolphin,[76] and lancelet, "the ancestor of all fish." More than 2,000 varieties of edible plants and vegetation can be found across the vast landscape of the People's Republic—more than twice as many as Europe and America combined.[77]

Chinese narcissistic nationalism is also displayed in popular literature such as *China Can Say No*. Its authors are convinced that Chinese represent the epitome of human virtue and attainment. They exult that:[78]

> Every liberation movement in the world was bathed in the sunlight of Chinese thought. Every step towards peace in the world was due to China's achievement. Only the diplomacy of People's China has the rarefied moral character and righteous spirit of a great nation.

Claiming that Chinese have been too "modest and polite" in the past, the authors urge their countrymen "to change our bearing because it is time for us to revel in our beauty as a great nation." Within the authors' lifetime, it is predicted, China will become "a great power" and "the hope of the world." Its "roar will multiply, Chinese thought and ability will deeply affect the world, and we will be the sole force to lead mankind." Given all this, the authors inquire rhetorically: "Why shouldn't we become a superpower and assume leadership of the world?"[79] At the same time, the self-congratulation of narcissists seems to require a concomitant devaluation of others. The authors of *China Can Say No* downplay the accomplishments of other peoples while overvaluing those of China's. As an example, while professing their admiration for Japan, the authors nevertheless insist that Japan owes its achievements to China because "Confucianism was the source of Japan's success, contrary to Japanese national myths."[80]

In some cases, not only do narcissistic nationalists devalue others' achievements, they treat them with outright contempt. The authors of *China Can Say No* reserve their greatest contempt for the United States. According to them, the American "big noses" *(da bizi)* have lost their capacity for independent thought and no longer have new political ideas. America's pluralism of thought and politics has "deluded others into thinking it has cultural depth." The reality is quite different. Contemporary Americans wallow only in "sensationalism," having become "lazy," ill-mannered, ugly, and "closed-minded"—habits of character that come from drinking too much from "the milk of prosperity." By at once "neglecting and indulging" their young, Americans not only "infantilize" their country's politics, thought, and culture, their youth have become decadent drug and sex addicts. This moral decay is not confined to the United States but "corrupts" all who stand within America's "orbit of influence." Everywhere in the world, the United States disseminates its "poison," delivered via Hollywood fantasies, fast food that only gives Chinese "indigestion," and consumer goods such as cigarettes and Coca-Cola with their nicotine and added sugar. All of which are certain harbingers of the decline of human civilization itself. Since Americans have neither "historical conception," "deep thought," "empathy," nor "feelings of pain," the authors wonder how the United States can remain "an advanced nation." Only China can replace America as a great power because great nations, like steel that must be tempered by fire, "are born out of repeated hardships and sufferings."[81]

Preoccupation with Power

More than narcissism, the conviction that China is certain to replace the United States as a great power is also demonstrative of Chinese patriotic nationalism's preoccupation with power. It is said that nations that labor under feelings of insecurity and inferiority tend to be competitive and preoccupied with their standing relative to others—attributes that are strongly correlated with measures of individual aggression such as a readiness to support war.[82]

In the case of the People's Republic, its patriotic nationalism appears to exhibit just such a preoccupation. The authors of *China Can Say No* boast that China, being a rising power, "is sure to win" any future war with the United States. The Korean War was the first war the United States could not win "because of the involvement of Chinese soldiers." Predicting that "the day will come when war with America is inevitable" *(you yitian feida buke)*, the authors warn that "If America insults China on Taiwan one more time," Washington will have to build a memorial even bigger than that for the Korean War so that there will be room enough to "inscribe the names of many more American youth." Even if the United States were to defeat China, the blood shed by Chinese will only inspire others to take their place. Chinese, especially young people, must be "prepared to make war . . . [and] bigger is better than smaller, sooner is better than later"— even at the cost of delaying or damaging China's economic development— because "we must avenge our national humiliation."[83]

More than the rhetoric in popular books, China's preoccupation with power is also exhibited in its determination to become the No. 1 power in Asia. Toward that objective, the city of Chongqing has announced plans to erect what will be Asia's tallest building; Hainan island is constructing Asia's biggest zoo with more than 5,000 animals;[84] and the Three Gorges Dam, when completed, will be the world's largest dam.

It is Chinese preoccupation with national power and prestige that could explain the extraordinary importance accorded to the PRC's performance in international sports. An example was the significance Chinese attached to the selection of the host country for the 2000 Olympic Games—as well as the depths of their bitterness and disappointment when Beijing lost its bid.[85] Another example was their reaction to China's loss to the United States for the Women's World Cup for soccer in 1999. Minutes after the loss, a message was posted on a popular Chinese internet site to "Bomb the U.S. Embassy." In a café in a working-class neighborhood in south Beijing, businessman Wang Jilei yelled at the television to "Put a missile in their net." In other bars, fans shouted expletives at American players; some hurled racial epithets at African-American goal-keeper Briana Scurry. Chinese fans' suspicions were fanned by the propaganda spread by state media outlets leading up to the game—that the American referees were bi-ased, that the PRC team was starved for decent Chinese food, and that tournament organizers exhausted the team by making them crisscross the United States four times in earlier rounds.[86]

Cultural-Moral Relativism

It is said that another nationalist attribute that is correlated with a disposi-tion to be aggressive is an extreme cultural and moral relativism that insists that each ethnic group has the right to follow its separate development, be-cause group identities are comprehensive moral worlds unintelligible to each other.[87] In China's case, its traditional Confucian culture may predis-pose Chinese toward moral relativism. Confucianism is said to lack guide-lines for behavior toward outsiders, especially those pertaining to peaceful modes of conflict resolution, which can lead to excessive violence against outsiders.[88]

In the past, the Confucian propensity to employ violence against perceived outsiders accounted for the often ruthless mob attacks on suspected criminals because conventional restraints against violence are lowered in a mob situation as individual responsibility is diffused to the other participants. After the Chinese Communists came to power, they not only continued but encouraged this traditional practice in the countless "struggle" meetings against landlords, capitalists, and other "enemies of the people." Once an individual was defined as an enemy, he or she became an outsider and a nonperson, against whom violence could be legitimized. All of which accounts for why a vast proportion of violence committed in the People's Republic was undertaken by groups and was unusually excessive and extreme, an example of which was the reported cannibalism in Guangxi Province at the height of the Cultural Revolution in 1968 against fellow villagers suspected of being "class enemies."[89]

Today, by insisting that human rights standards reflect only Western cultural norms and thus are not applicable to the PRC, the Communist Party is continuing China's lamentable tradition of moral-cultural relativism. Given the millions of Chinese who had suffered and perished under the Communist Party's rule, one would think that human rights would be in the interest of every Chinese. Despite that, the authors of popular PRC books seem to have adopted their government's self-serving stance on the matter.

As an example, *Listen to China* maintains that "China has always believed that every country's situation is different, each has the right to choose the system that suits its national conditions."[90] *China Can Say No*, for its part, repeats Beijing's contention that U.S. criticisms of China's human rights record constitute "interference with China's internal affairs." Despite their recognition that human rights conditions in China are "imperfect," the authors blame their country's poverty rather than its abusive government. More than that, they argue that for Chinese to adopt American values would be tantamount to their becoming "slaves" *(nudi)* of "Uncle Sam."[91] Other authors not only reject the universality of human rights, subscribing instead to the notion that morality varies from culture to culture, they are convinced that the West is downright hypocritical in its professed values. *The New World Order and the Outlook for China's Military Strategy* maintains that Western civilization has "the stench of blood" because its industrialization was built on exploitative capitalism and "the plunders of colonialism."[92] *Behind the Demonization of China* insists that the concept of human rights itself is a product of Western "colonialism" and "imperialism," and is nothing more than "white supremacism" and "a new racism."[93]

Illiberal Worldview

China's moral relativism is accompanied and exacerbated by an illiberal Darwinian view of the world. In adopting Deng Xiaoping Theory as its new ideology, the Communist Party has also purchased Deng's worldview of an increasingly competitive environment of dwindling resources where nations are locked in a struggle in which only the "fittest survive."[94] Deng's successor, Jiang Zemin, similarly sees the post–Cold War world as an even more "complex," challenging, and "changeable" arena where[95]

> ideology has decreased in importance as a source of international conflict. *But territorial disputes, racial clashes . . . and nationalist tensions will be increasingly frequent and violent,* causing grave and comprehensive threats to the security of affected countries. A few Western developed countries, intent on dominating the post–Cold War new world order, have obstructed and suppressed China's economic development and international affairs—precipitating a series of clashes and friction. All of this must be considered in formulating China's national defense strategy for the next century.

Echoing Jiang's view of the world, an author for Beijing's Institute of Military Science also sees the world as a battlefield where small and medium-sized wars are regular occurrences, where international relations are defined by conflict instead of cooperation, and where true peace remains a chimera.[96] More than that, as in the nineteenth century, it is a world that remains "controlled" *(zhuzai)* and dominated by the Western powers who persist in presuming that "big countries rule over small countries." In particular, the world is dominated by its sole superpower, the United States, which jealously guards its privileges and regards China as its future rival for world dominance. Prompted by its fears, the United States has "joined hands" with Japan to foment the "groundless" myth of the "China threat"—that the PRC is "the greatest source of instability" in the post–Cold War Asia-Pacific region. That myth is calculated to alienate China from its neighbors who have become "increasingly suspicious" that Beijing is bent on "military expansionism" and will use its military power against Taiwan and to reclaim the Spratlys and the Diaoyu islands. At the same time as the United States is alienating China from its neighbors, it has also induced China to be a signatory to weapons nonproliferation treaties—all of which are seen as only serving America's ultimate objective of "containing and isolating" China.[97]

In a difficult and hostile world, "nation-states remain the fundamental units of development" that could ensure the collective well-being of peoples. In such a world, "there are no eternal friends, only eternal [national]

interests"—all of which "provides the conditions for nationalism to flour-
ish."[98] Deng had instructed that China must "look after [its] own" by safe-
guarding its own interests, sovereignty, and territorial integrity.[99] In the last
analysis, for China to look after itself requires that Chinese be animated by
the "group consciousness" of patriotism, whereby individuals surrender
and sacrifice their selfish interests and concerns for the good and well-being
of the community.[100]

Conclusion

To date, the Chinese Communist Party's Patriotic Education Campaign appears to have been successful. A Chinese commentator observed that ethnic
nationalism has become "the currency of both government and populace."[101] Whatever evidence there is seems to indicate that patriotic nationalism is a widespread phenomenon: Since 1991, up to 10,000 people a day
attend the flag-raising ceremony in Tiananmen Square, described as "a polished, goose-stepping affair."[102] Banners all over Shanghai proclaim: "We
love our motherland! We work to make our country great and rich!"[103]

The campaign appears to be particularly effective with state employees,
young people, and the members of the PLA. As an example, delegates to
China's 1995 National People's Congress reserved their greatest applause
for reactive nationalist themes at the end of Premier Li Peng's speech when
he spoke of the imminent return of Hong Kong to Chinese rule, the anticipated eventual reunification with Taiwan, and a Chinese foreign policy that
"would not allow foreign interference."[104] Former PRC envoys to the
United States, Canada, and Australia are among the authors of a policy paper prepared by an official Beijing think tank that practically exudes national pride. National pride is also evident among Chinese economists in
Beijing, described as convinced that China is returning to its normal position of eminence as first in the world. Even exiled dissidents are not immune from the seductive power of patriotic nationalism. Despite their disagreement with the repressive regime in Beijing, they are among the
quickest defenders of China's accomplishments. As for China's youth, reportedly they are not like the generation who agitated for democracy during the 1980s. Instead, they are less inclined to place the blame for everything with the Communist Party and have impressed many with their
strong sense of patriotism.[105]

Those reports are confirmed by the results of a survey conducted in April
1998 of a nonprobability sample composed of 126 Chinese university stu-

dents in Beijing.[106] The students were asked to respond to 25 statements on a five-point Likert scale, where 5 represents "strongly agree," 4 "somewhat agree," 3 "neither agree nor disagree," 2 "somewhat disagree," and 1 "strongly disagree." The results indicate a strong sense of both nationalism and patriotism on the part of the respondents, as seen in their mean responses of 4.32 and 4.75, respectively, to the statements "I love the Chinese people" and "I love my country, the People's Republic of China."[107] The survey results also seem to validate Beijing's multiethnic conception of the Chinese nation. Although the respondents themselves were Han, they disagreed with the statement that "Real Chinese are Han" with a mean of 1.72, and resoundingly agreed with a mean of 4.40 with the statement that "The Chinese nation includes Han and all the minority nationalities." The respondents also scored highly on the dimension of power. They strongly agreed, with a mean of 4.33, that "China should return to its former status as the greatest power in Asia." At the same time, the students also evinced a moderately strong sense of reactive nationalism against Japan and the United States. The statements that "Japanese are unrepentant about their invasion of China" and "Japanese militarism is reviving" elicited mean responses of 3.89 and 3.81, respectively. Toward the United States, the respondents seemed in agreement (mean of 3.98) with the claim advanced in books such as *China Can Say No* that "The United States is trying to contain China." But, in contrast to the assertions of *Behind the Demonization of China,* the students only somewhat agreed (means of 3.37 and 3.31, respectively) that "the United States demonizes China" and that "America's criticism of China's human rights is unreasonable and imperialistic," and clearly disagreed (mean of 2.24) that "America is racist against China."

The students' survey responses on the dimension of reactive nationalism seem consistent with the available qualitative evidence. One would expect Chinese reactive nationalism against the Japanese to be stronger because of the loss of Chinese territories and lives to Japanese imperialism. Today, China and Japan both claim sovereign ownership over the Diaoyutai islets in the East China Sea, with no resolution in sight. In contrast, Chinese neither were defeated by nor lost sovereign land to the United States, although Chinese do harbor grievances against America. Not only did the United States, for 30 years, withhold diplomatic recognition from the People's Republic of China, in the early 1950s the armed forces of the two countries engaged each other in bloody battle on the Korean peninsula. Today, Washington's continuing support for Taiwan and many Americans' sympathy for an independent Tibet remain sensitive issues. Despite these areas of contention, Chinese resentment against American power is mitigated by their enchantment with the United States. On the one hand, Chinese youth seem to be the most antagonistic toward the United States: A national poll taken by the PRC newspaper *China Youth Daily* in July 1995, found that 87.1 percent of Chinese youth regarded America as the country most unfriendly toward the PRC. At the same time, however, the poll also found that the United States was their country of choice, at a plurality of 35 percent, to visit or move to.[108]

Although patriotic nationalism clearly serves the Communist Party's purpose, it has spontaneous roots in the Chinese people's understandable pride in the measurable progress they have achieved in two decades of economic reform. Economic success has fostered a new collective sense of confidence. The result, as described by the *Wall Street Journal*, is "a new, self-reassuring nationalism."[109] But if Chinese patriotic nationalism were simply a matter of national pride and confidence, it would not pose a potential problem for the world outside of the People's Republic. The fact of the matter is that Chinese patriotic nationalism has a decidedly xenophobic and irredentist flavor.

It is reported that "nationalism with a chauvinistic, authoritarian cast" is gaining credibility within China's elite intellectual circles and their influence is making itself felt within the halls of power.[110] Many former liberals in the People's Republic are disillusioned with the West because of the failure of the 1989 democracy movement and the personal experiences some of them encountered in the West.[111] Those intellectuals have turned inward to embrace a new conservatism[112] as well as a patriotic nationalism that more and more assumes beleaguered and xenophobic overtones. Convinced that neither liberal democracy nor communism is suitable for China, they recall Mao Zedong with "nostalgia"[113] as a "genius" and "godlike" figure.[114] Today, Mao has become a patriotic icon as the founding father of "New China" whose army fought foreign troops to a standstill in the Korean War. Each week, some 20,000 from all across China visit his birthplace in Shaoshan; his destructive policies that led to the deaths of millions are rarely, if at all, mentioned. That could account for Mr. Chen, a Shanghai tourist in Shaoshan, who declared that although "He made mistakes, . . . I don't care" because "Chairman Mao led the Chinese people in liberating all of China."[115] Chen's nostalgia appears to be widespread, if a PRC survey in August 1995 is any indication. The survey found that 94.2 percent of young people approved of the "anti-imperialist, anti-hegemonist" Mao Zedong, while only 48.7 percent approved of the reformist Deng Xiaoping, who had immeasurably improved their lives by opening China to the world.[116]

In June 1996, the Chinese government banned some 2,000 businesses for "undermining national culture" because their names had a "Western-sounding tone."[117] At the same time, in the name of fighting "a slide in cultural values," Beijing imposed new limits restricting prime-time television broadcast of foreign movies to a maximum of 40 minutes every night.[118] The government's overriding message is that calls for democracy and human rights can bring disunity and disorder, thereby "opening the door to foreign aggression and new humiliation." Scenes of turmoil in the former Eastern Bloc are broadcast extensively on Chinese national network and have convinced many that a strong, one-party government is essential for national stability.[119]

Given all this, it was not surprising when Chinese reacted with rage to NATO's ostensibly mistaken bombing of the PRC embassy in Belgrade in June 1999 that killed three Chinese embassy staff. For three days, thousands of Chinese besieged the U.S. embassy in Beijing and its consulates in ten cities across China, pelting the buildings with rocks and bottles. In the city of Chengdu, rioters set fire to the consulate building. It is this potential for PRC nationalism to turn virulent that has become a cause for concern. More than being reactive and xenophobic, Chinese patriotic nationalism also has a profoundly irredentist dimension. That is the subject of the next chapter.

Notes

1. As a point of comparison, during its rapid industrialization in the 19th century, it took the United States almost 50 years to double its GNP.

2. For a more detailed treatment of the post-Mao economic reforms and their unintended consequences, see Maria Hsia Chang, *The Labors of Sisyphus: The Economic Development of Communist China* (New Brunswick, NJ: Transaction, 1998), pp. 93–124, chapters 6 and 7.

3. By "foreign enemies," Beijing was referring to the United States and Taiwan. Nayan Chanda and Kari Huus, "China: The New Nationalism," *Far Eastern Economic Review,* November 9, 1995, p. 20; and Patrick E. Tyler, "China's Campus Model for the 90's: Earnest Patriot," *The New York Times (NYT),* April 23, 1996, p. A4.

4. "China Prints Book to Educate Farmers," *San Francisco Chronicle* (hereafter *SFC*), November 28, 1995, p. A11; Dong Liwen, "Lun zhonggong di aiguo zhuyi (On Communist China's Patriotism)," *Gongdang wenti yanjiu (Studies in Communism)* Taipei, 21:8 (August 1995), p. 26.

5. George Wehrfritz, "China: Springtime Perennial," *Newsweek,* June 10, 1996, p. 17; Quotation by Jiang Zemin, in *Dangdai sichao (Contemporary Thought),* Beijing, no. 1 (1995).

6. See Jiang's speech in *Renmin ribao (People's Daily)*, January 25, 1996.

7. Franz Schurmann, *Ideology and Organization in Communist China* (Berkeley: University of California Press, 1966), pp. 22, 23.

8. The incorporation of "Deng Xiaoping Theory" into the CCP Constitution was preceded by the party's gradual but steadily increasing recognition of the importance of Deng's ideas. In 1992, those ideas were designated by the party as "Deng Xiaoping thought." By the next year, in 1993, it had become Deng's "theory of building socialism with Chinese characteristics" as the "successor and developer of Mao Zedong Thought," eventually becoming "Deng Xiaoping Theory" in 1999. See Maria Chang, *Labors of Sisyphus*, pp. 63–66.

9. "China: Saying No" and "Stay Back, China," in *The Economist*, July 20, 1996, p. 30, and March 16, 1996, p. 15.

10. See, for example, Allen S. Whiting, "Chinese Nationalism and Foreign Policy After Deng," *The China Quarterly*, no. 142 (June 1995), pp. 295–317; and Chalmers Johnson, "Soft Totalitarianism in China," *New Perspectives Quarterly*, 14:3 (Summer 1997), pp. 18–21.

11. Li Hongjun and Zheng Shan, "Dali hongyoung zhonghua mingzu jingshen (Vigorously Promote the Spirit of Chinese Nationalism)," *Guofang (National Defense)* (Beijing: Military Affairs and Learning Periodicals), no. 9 (1993), p. 15.

12. Thomas A. Metzger and Ramon H. Myers, "Chinese Nationalism and American Policy," *Orbis*, 42:1 (Winter 1998), p. 21.

13. Xudong Zhang, "Nationalism and Contemporary China," *East Asia: An International Quarterly*, 16:1–2 (Spring-Summer 1997), pp. 130–147.

14. Suisheng Zhao, *In Search of a Right Place? Chinese Nationalism in the Post-Cold War World* (Hong Kong: Chinese University of Hong Kong, Hong Kong Institute of Asia-Pacific Studies, USC Seminar Series no. 12, 1997), pp. 25, 23.

15. Michael Mann, "A Political Theory of Nationalism and Its Excesses," in Sukumar Periwal (ed.), *Notions of Nationalism* (Budapest: Central European University Press, 1995), p. 55.

16. "Chinese nationalism could be defined as a desire to 'stand up' against its nineteenth century (Britain) and twentieth century (Japan) aggressors." Harvey Sicherman, "Clinton's Many Chinas," Foreign Policy Research Institute *A Catalyst for Ideas E-Notes*, July 7, 1998.

17. Gu Jieshan, "Zhongguo gudai de aiguo zhuyi (China's ancient patriotism)," Part I, *Guofang*, no. 3 (1995), p. 23.

18. Jin Binghao and Zhu Zaixian, *Minzu lilun zhengce gailun (A Summary of Nationality Theories and Policies)* (Beijing: Central National University Press, 1994), p. 180.

19. Weng Jieming, Zhang Ximing, Zhang Tao, Qu Kemin (eds.), *Yu zongshuji tanxin (Conversations with the General Secretary)* (Beijing: Chinese Social Science Publisher, 1996), p. 275.

20. Jin and Zhu, *Summary of Nationality Theories and Policies*, p. 185.

21. Li Xing, "Lun guojia minzu zhuyi gainian (On the concept of state-nationalism)," *Minzu yanjiu (Nationality Studies)*, Beijing, no. 4 (1995), pp. 10, 13, 14.

22. Peng Yingming, "Zailun minzu wenti di hanyi (A reconsideration of the meaning of the national question)," *Minzu yanjiu*, no. 1 (1993), p. 29. Emphasis supplied.

23. Li and Zheng, "Vigorously Promote the Spirit of Chinese Nationalism," p. 18.

24. Deng Xiaoping, "Maintain the Tradition of Hard Struggle," *Selected Works of Deng Xiaoping (1982–1992)* (Beijing: Foreign Languages Press, 1994), p. 282.

25. Weng Shiping, *Junren meide daolu (Introduction to Soldiers' Morality)* (Beijing: Institute of Military Science Press, 1996), pp. 90–91.

26. Jin and Zhu, *Summary of Nationality Theories and Policies*, pp. 184, 183.

27. Jiang Yingliang (ed.), *Zhongguo minzu shi (History of the Chinese People)*, I (Beijing: Nation publisher, 1990), p. 102.

28. He Shutao, "*Luelun minzu dingyi ji minzu gongtongti di xinzhi* (On the definition of nationality and the nature of national communities)," *Minzu yanjiu*, no. 1 (1993), p. 22.

29. Jin and Zhu, *Summary of Nationality Theories and Policies*, p. 28.

30. Peng Yingming, "Reconsideration of the Meaning of the National Question," p. 29. Emphasis supplied.

31. Michael Ignatieff, "Nationalism and Toleration," in Richard Caplan and John Feffer (eds.), *Europe's New Nationalism: State and Minorities in Conflict* (New York: Oxford University Press, 1996), p. 219.

32. Jin and Zhu, *Summary of Nationality Theories*, p. 23; He Shutao, "On the Definition of Nationality," p. 22.

33. Jin and Zhu, *Summary of Nationality Theories*, pp. 23–24, 27.

34. Jiang Yingliang, *History of the Chinese People*, pp. 1–3, 9; Deng Luoqun, "Dangdai yanhuang wenhuare di xingqi jiqi shidai yiyi (The revival and historical relevance of the culture of Emperors Yan and Huang)," *Dangdai sichao*, no. 6 (1994), p. 57; and Qian Zongfan, "Qianlun zhonghua minzu di zuyuan jidui zhongguo lishi wenhua chuantong xingcheng di yingxiang (A brief discussion of the origins of the Chinese people and the effect on the formation of China's historical cultural tradition)," *Xueshu luntan (Academic Forum)*, Guangxi, no. 1 (1995), p. 92.

35. Deng Luoqun, "Revival and Historical Relevance of the Culture of Emperors Yan and Huang," pp. 58, 59.

36. He Shutao, "On the Definition of Nationality," p. 21.

37. Li and Zheng, "Vigorously Promote the Spirit of Chinese Nationalism," p. 15.

38. Ibid.

39. Yao Bolin, "Nianhao gongchan dangren de daodejing (A Careful Study of the Morality of Communists)," *Jiefang junbao (People's Liberation Daily)*, Beijing, 20 November 1996, p. 4.

40. Li and Zheng, "Vigorously Promote," pp. 16, 17.

41. Deng Luoqun, "Revival and Historical Relevance," pp. 60, 61. It is interesting how Deng's ideas mirror those of Joel Kotkin's *Tribes: How Race, Religion and*

Identity Determine Success in the New Global Economy (New York: Random House, 1993).

42. Deng Luoqun, "Revival and Historical Relevance," p. 56.

43. Chanda and Huus, "China: New Nationalism," p. 21.

44. Chen Xi, "Zhongguo zhishi fenzhizhong di minzu zhuyi (Nationalism among Chinese intellectuals)," *Beijing zhichun (Beijing Spring)*, Woodside, NY, no. 39 (August 1996), p. 39.

45. "National study fever" is believed to have begun in 1995 in Beijing University. See Song Xiaoqing, "Jingdai 'guoxue re' di xingshuai (Rise and fall of modern-day 'national study fever')" and Ji Xianlin, "Xifang buliang, dongfang liang (The East, not the West, is bright)" in *Wenhua yanjiu (Cultural Studies)*, Beijing, no. 1 (1996), pp. 55–60, 46.

46. Luo Guojie, "Hongyang zhonghua minzhu youliang daode chuantong (Widely Publicize the Chinese Nation's Excellent Moral Tradition)," *Dangdai sichao*, no. 4 (1994), pp. 2–6.

47. Barry Sautman, "Racial Nationalism and China's External Behavior," paper presented at the annual meeting of the American Political Science Association, San Francisco, August 30, 1996, p. 6

48. Jiang Yingliang, *History of the Chinese People*, p. 3.

49. Deng Loqun, "Dangdai yanhuang wenhuare di xingqi jiqi shidai yiyi (The Revival and Historical Significance of the Culture of Emperors Yan and Huang)," *Dangdai sichao*, no. 6 (1994), pp. 57, 59.

50. Liu Xiaozhu, "Jingti jiduan minzu zhuyi zai dalu qingqi (Beware of the Rise of Extreme Nationalism on the Mainland)," *Shijie ribao (World Journal*, hereafter *WJ)*, San Francisco, April 3, 1994, p. A6.

51. Chanda and Huus, "China: New Nationalism," pp. 20, 21; Tyler, "China's Campus Model for the 90's."

52. N.A., "Shades of Loyalty," *The Economist*, April 13, 1996, p. 80.

53. Marcus W. Brauchli and Kathy Chen, "Nationalist Fervor," *The Wall Street Journal*, June 23, 1995, p. A5.

54. Li Xiguang et al., *Yaomo hua zhongguo di beihou (Behind the Demonization of China)* (Beijing: Chinese Social Science Academy, 1996), p. 27.

55. Seth Faison, "China Exports Its Own Uncertainty," *The New York Times*, October 26, 1997, p. 4.

56. Song Qiang, Zhang Zangzang, Qiao Bian, Yang Zhengyu, and Gu Qingsheng, *Zhongguo keyi shuobu (China Can Say No)* (Beijing: Chinese Industry and Commerce, 1996), p. 1.

57. Jiao Long, "*Zhongguo keyi shuobu* hongdong shijie di qianqian houhou (About the Global Uproar at *China Can Say No*)," *Jiefang jun shenghuo (People's Liberation Army Life)*, Beijing, no. 141 (November 1996), p. 41.

58. The second volume to *China Can Say No* is *Zhongguo haishi neng shuobu (China Can Still Say No)* (Beijing: Chinese Literature, 1996). Some imitators are Jian Qingguo, *Zhonguo bujinjin shuobu (China Not Only Says No)* (Beijing:

Chinese Industry and Commerce, 1996), and Zhang Xueli, *Zhongguo heyi shuobu (Why China Says No)* (Beijing: Hualing, 1996).

59. Song Qiang et al., *China Can Say No*, pp. 24, 30, 20, 48, 15.

60. He Degong, Pu Weizhong, and Jin Yong, *Qingting zhongguo: Xin lengzhan yu weilai moulue (Listen to China: The New Cold War and Future Military Strategy)* (Guangdong: Guangdong People's Publisher, 1997), p. 4.

61. *Ibid.*, p. 5; Li Xiguang et al., *Behind the Demonization*, p. 25.

62. As example, the book pointedly noted that "the owners of America's major news media, such as *New York Times* and *Washington Post*, are all Jews." Li Xiguang et al., *Behind the Demonization*, p. 12.

63. Ibid., p. 2.

64. Song Qiang et al., *China Can Say No*, pp. 61–92, 185, 113.

65. Ibid., pp. 48, 40, 23.

66. Li Xiguang et al., *Behind the Demonization*, pp. 22, 25, 2.

67. Song Qiang et al., *China Can Say No*, pp. 7, 14, 198.

68. Ignatieff, "Nationalism and Toleration," pp. 215, 216.

69. As quoted by Seth Faison, "China Exports its Own Uncertainty."

70. Peng Zhaoyong, "Woshiwo yu wofeiwo (I am me and I am not me)," *Minzu yanjiu*, no. 4 (1994), p. 51.

71. Jiang Yingliang, *History of the Chinese People*, p. 18.

72. Ignatieff, "Nationalism and Toleration," p. 215.

73. Luo Guoliang, "Ke'ai de zuguo, weida de minzu (Beloved motherland, great nation)," *Guofang* (September 1995), p. 18. Luo's claims are reminiscent of those by conservative scholars in the Qing dynasty who claimed that Western science had its origins in China. According to them, Western calendars were derived from the chapter "Yaotian" in the *Book of History;* the essential ideas of Western discussions of the earth were derived from the commentary on the tenth chapter of *Zengzi;* and the formula for computing the circumference of a circle had been figured out and handed down by Zi Chongzhi (429–500); algebra was invented by Li Ye of the Yuan dynasty; other elements of Western mathematics were derived from the ancient mathematical classic *Zhoupi Suanqing.* See Ssu-yu Teng and John K. Fairbank, *China's Response to the West: A Documentary Survey 1839–1923* (New York: Atheneum, 1973), pp. 15–16.

74. Luo Guoliang, "Beloved Motherland, Great Nation," p. 18.

75. "Numbers on the Map," *The New York Times*, November 25, 1997, p. B12.

76. The irony is that both the panda and the white dolphin are now threatened with extinction, in the latter's case because of water pollution.

77. Luo Guoliang, "Beloved Motherland," p. 17.

78. Song Qiang et al., *China Can Say No*, p. 49.

79. Ibid., pp. 50, 51, 30, 35, 39.

80. Ibid., p. 30. What the authors did not explain, of course, was why China lagged behind Japan in economic development, despite being the land where Confucianism originated and flourished.

81. Ibid., pp. 5, 34, 27, 26, 24–25, 28, 46, 13, 33, 34.

82. R. Kosterman and S. Feshbach, "Toward a Measure of Patriotic and Nationalistic Attitudes," *Political Psychology, 10* (1989), pp. 257–274.

83. Song Qiang, et al., *China Can Say No*, pp. 36, 37, 42, 41.

84. Brauchli and Chen, "Nationalist Fervor," p. A5.

85. "I was originally an internationalist. But after I saw how the United States, Britain, and other countries behaved with respect to China's application to host the Olympic Games . . . I slowly became a nationalist *(minzu zhuyi zhe)."* Song Qiang et al., *China Can Say No*, p. 2.

86. "No Shame in 2nd Spot On China's Home Front," *SFC,* July 12, 1999, p. C12.

87. Ignatieff, "Nationalism and Toleration," p. 217.

88. Michael H. Bond and Wang Sung-Hsing, "China: Aggressive Behavior and the Problem of Maintaining Order and Harmony," in Arnold P. Goldstein and Marshall H. Segall (eds.), *Aggression in Global Perspective* (New York: Pergamon Press, 1983), pp. 68, 69, 70.

89. See Zheng Yi, *Scarlet Memorial* (Boulder: Westview, 1996).

90. He Degong et al., *Listen to China*, p. 2.

91. Song Qiang et al., *China Can Say No*, pp. 127, 134, 15, 19, 218.

92. Luo Zhaoyong, *Guoji xinzhixu yu zhongguo zhanlue dazhanwang (The New World Order and the Outlook for China's Military Strategy)* (Guangdong: Guangdong Economics Publisher, 1997), p. 171.

93. Li Xiguang et al., *Behind the Demonization*, p. 26.

94. Chen Xi, "Nationalism Among Chinese Intellectuals," p. 40.

95. Weng Jieming et al., *Conversations with the General Secretary*, p. 233. Emphasis supplied.

96. Weng Shiping, *Introduction to Soldiers' Morality,* p. 86.

97. He Degong et al., *Listen to China*, pp. 8–10.

98. Chen Xiaolu, "Xiandai minzu zhuyi di youlai yu fazhan (Origin and development of modern nationalism," *Minzu yanjiu,* no. 12 (1995), pp. 10–11; and Song Qiang et al., *China Can Say No*, p. 43.

99. Deng Xiaoping, "We are Confident that We Can Handle China's Affairs Well" and "No One can Shake Socialist China," *Selected Works, III*, pp. 316, 318.

100. Gu Jieshan, "China's Ancient Patriotism," Part I, p. 23.

101. Xu Ben, "'Women' shixue? (Who Are 'We'?)," *Dongfang (East)*, Beijing, no. 2 (1996), p. 71.

102. Chanda and Huus, "China: New Nationalism," p. 21.

103. Ian Buruma, "The 21st Century Starts Here," *New York Times Magazine,* February 18, 1996, p. 31.

104. Renee Schoof, "Chinese Premier Wants Crackdown on Corruption," *SFC,* March 6, 1995, p. A9.

105. Brauchli and Chen, "Nationalist Fervor," pp. A1, A5; Chanda and Huus, "China: New Nationalism," p. 21; Tyler, "China's Campus Model."

106. A Chinese-language questionnaire on nationalism was administered to two groups of Chinese university students in Beijing: the first comprised 76 students (30 males, 46 females), ages 19 to 22, at Beijing Language and Culture University; the second group 50 students (10 males, 40 females), ages 20 to 27, from Beijing Second Foreign Language Institute. A few respondents (ranging from one to three) declined to give an answer to some of the questions.

107. But the patriotism of the Chinese respondents is not simple or unidimensional: They seemed to love China much more (mean response of 4.75 to the statement "I love my country") than they were loyal to the Communist Party government (mean response of 3.49 to the statement "I am loyal to my government"). The disparity between their intense love of country and lukewarm loyalty to the government suggests that the Communist Party's efforts to equate itself with China are not entirely successful with the sample group.

108. *WJ,* July 9, 1996, p. A10.

109. Brauchli and Chen, "Nationalist Fervor," pp. A5, A1.

110. Kari Huus, "China: The Hard Edge," *Far Eastern Economic Review,* November 9, 1995, p. 28.

111. Some Chinese intellectuals in the United States have a sense of wounded pride because they feel they were not accorded the respect and dignity commensurate with their professional status. See Chen Xi, "Nationalism Among Chinese Intellectuals," pp. 39–42. Others attribute their negative experiences to America's "white" racism. See Li Xiguang et al., *Behind the Demonization.*

112. Chen Xi, "Nationalism Among Chinese Intellectuals."

113. "Rotten Roots," *The Economist,* February 3, 1996, p. 30. See the many articles lauding Mao in *Dangdai sichao,* no. 1 (1992), pp. 60–62; no. 1 (1994), pp. 26–27; no. 2 (1994), pp. 60–64; and no. 3 (1994), pp. 2–10, 61–62.

114. See the positive regard for Mao in a book that was first published in 1994 in the PRC and became an instant bestseller. Wang Shan, *Disanzhi yanjing kan zhongguo (Looking at China Through the Third Eye)* (Taipei: zhouzhi wenhua, 1994), pp. 45, 48–62, 87, 89–90, 116, 120.

115. Joe McDonald, "Mao's Hometown Cashes in on Legend," *SFC,* August 24, 1999, p. A12.

116. *WJ,* July 9, 1996, p. A10.

117. *SFC,* June 24, 1996, p. A8, citing the PRC's official *China Daily* of June 23.

118. *SFC,* June 25, 1996, p. E3.

119. Chanda and Huus, "China: New Nationalism," pp. 20, 22–23, 21.

9

Chinese Irredentist Nationalism

More than being reactive and xenophobic, Chinese patriotic nationalism is also profoundly irredentist. China's abiding sense of wounded pride and resentment from its "hundred years of humiliation" is particularly acute because its fall from greatness had been so steep. Until the nineteenth century, China was the hegemonic power in Asia, without peer or rival. But the defeat by the British in the Opium War, a war described by *National Defense* as between the forces of "good versus evil,"[1] would begin China's long and precipitous descent.

Irredentism is the desire by an existing state to retrieve lost territories and ethnic kin. It is a post-state phase of nationalism that is activated when a sovereign state is already in existence and has become strong enough to articulate and press its territorial claims.[2] Historically, irredentist impulses have been associated with the presence of certain conditions internal to the retrieving state—those of domestic ambiguity and ideological reexamination.[3] This suggests that irredentist nationalism is susceptible to being used as a tool by political regimes to manage domestic problems in times of transition. And it is irredentism's primeval appeal to human beings' instinctive urge to define their territory that makes possible its manipulation by political authorities.

In the case of China, along with its new sense of confidence and pride, it is poised to resume its historic status as *Zhongguo*, the Middle Kingdom. A Western diplomat in Beijing has described the People's Republic as "maturing" and in the process of "defining its own sphere." Beijing perceives the post–Cold War world to have moved from a bipolar to a multipolar system and intends to be a significant actor in the new world.[4] Another commentator has observed that, unlike Germany and Japan, which have the capabilities but lack the will or self-confidence to

act abroad, China is "a thoroughly traditional great power" that is growing rapidly but uncertainly into a world system in which it feels it de-
serves more attention and honor. It is predicted that in coming years,
China's ambitions are "bound to expand."[5]

While it is understandable that the Chinese people would want to reclaim their traditional status, how they conceive the historical Middle
Kingdom has troubling implications for the Asia-Pacific region. The
gravamen of the problem revolves on China's conception of its national
boundaries.

The Western conception of national boundaries is a complex product of
fairly recent history unique to Europe. Unlike the European states that engaged each other in almost continuous warfare, China has traditionally
been the undisputed hegemonic power in Asia since the Qin and Han dynasties. As described by a contributor to *National Defense*, historic China
was "a giant" that stood "tall and firm"[6] in its known world. For thousands of years relations between China and its neighbors were those between unequals, predicated on the "system of the Celestial Empire" *(tian-
chao tizhi)*—one where the Asian states clearly acknowledged China's
hegemony by adopting its laws and relying on the Chinese emperor to arbi-
trate and settle interstate disputes. Asia was an "integrated cultural system"
(zhenghe de wenhua tixi) dominated by China—a situation quite unlike
that in Europe, where many sovereign and approximately equal states continuously vied for supremacy.[7] As a consequence, China's traditional view
of the world and of its place in that world were quite different from those
of European states. More than that, Chinese historically lacked a firm conception of their territorial boundaries that ebbed and flowed in the course
of China's long history. The Middle Kingdom was an empire comprised of
numerous ethnic groups and nationalities, its expanse was unrestrained by
international treaties and depended solely on the reigning emperor's power
and ambition.

Traditionally, the Chinese Empire was conceived to comprise China
Proper, Outer China, and the tributary territories. China Proper was the
cultural heart of China, being the core of Han settlement. Outer China
comprised buffer territories ruled directly from China Proper but inhabited
almost entirely by non-Han peoples. This buffer zone historically included
all or parts of contemporary Xinjiang, Inner and Outer Mongolia,
Manchuria, Tibet, and, at times, northern Korea and northern Vietnam.
During the Yuan dynasty (1206–1367), Outer China expanded to include
all of Korea, Central Asia, Ukraine, Iraq, Iran, Burma, and Vietnam.
Outside the buffer regions were the tributary territories—China's tradi-

tional client states considered to be voluntary parts of the Chinese Empire that were allowed to have their own rulers as long as their foreign policies were in accord with the Middle Kingdom's. Among them were the peoples of Korea, Taiwan, the East and South China Seas, Vietnam, Laos, Burma, most of the Bay of Bengal, Bhutan, and Nepal.[8] The relationship between China and its clients was that between a suzerain and its vassals. The Chinese emperor provided protection and conferred legitimacy upon their rulers; in return, the latter recognized China's superiority with homage and tributes. The tributary states in effect functioned as buffers for the Chinese Empire. As one PRC author describes it, "With the Ryukyu islands guarding the southeast, Korea guarding the northeast, Mongolia the northwest, and Vietnam the southwest, the Qing empire's borders were secured."[9]

There are reasons to believe that irredentism is an integral component of the Communist Party's promotion of patriotic nationalism. Lending substance to this conjecture are articles that appeared in 1994 in *National Defense*, which described in detail those territories that had been part of the Chinese Empire and those that were lost to the imperialist powers.

One article notes that as early as A.D. 73 during the Han dynasty, Tibet, Qinghai, Xinjiang, and "the region to the west of Xinjiang" were already parts of China. (The "region to the west of Xinjiang" can only mean eastern Kazakhstan.) Chinese troops were dispatched to open political intercourse with Taiwan during the period of the Three Kingdoms (A.D. 221–265). In 589 during the Sui dynasty, troops were sent to the Ryukyu Islands, including Taiwan. Beginning in 618, Jilin, Heilongjiang, southern Siberia, and Mongolia became "subjects" *(chenfu)* of the Tang dynasty. By 627, the dynasty had extended its rule to encompass west Korean Bay, Bohai, Lake Baikal, the Gobi Desert, western Siberia, Mongolia, the Altay Mountains, Lake Balkhash, and the Yenisey River. During the Ming dynasty (1368–1644) China's borders reached the Sea of Japan, Tibet came under Chinese rule through "the system of monk-officialdom" *(sengguan zhidu)*, and "tributary relations" *(zongfan guanxi)* were established with Korea and Vietnam. In 1644, the Ming dynasty was overthrown by the Manchus, who founded the Qing, "stabilized" Tibet, and "reclaimed" Taiwan. At its apex, around the turn of the eighteenth century, the Qing empire stretched across some 13 million square kilometers to the Pamirs Plateau in the west, Lake Balkhash in the northwest, Siberia in the north, the Xing'an Mountains and Lake Khanka (Ku'ye) in the northeast, the Pacific Ocean in the east, Taiwan, Diaoyutai and other islands in the southeast, and the South China Sea in the south. The dynasty's tributary clients included Korea, Nepal, Bhutan, Burma, Laos, and Vietnam.[10]

From that apogee, as a result of the imperialist powers' "military incursions and diplomatic trickery" that included more than 500 humiliating "unequal treaties" *(bu pingdeng tiaoyue)*, the great Chinese Empire was reduced to three-quarters its former size. Although the Qing dynasty had been in decline even before the Opium War, China's ignominious defeat by the British exposed for the first time its weakness and vulnerability and opened the floodgates to its thorough exploitation by the imperialist powers. Hong Kong, "a jewel of the East," was ceded to Britain; Macao was "usurped" *(bazhan)* by Portugal. Malaysia, Burma, and India were "seized" *(zhanling)* by Britain, which also "coveted" *(jiyu)* and "encroached" *(canshi)* on parts of Tibet. France seized Vietnam and Laos and encroached on China's Yunnan Province. Japan, through its defeat of China—its former suzerain—in 1895, managed to colonize Korea and "illegally occupied" *(feifa gezhan)* Chinese territories that included Taiwan, the Diaoyutai islets, and the Penghu islands. Lushun, Jiaozhou Bay, and Guangzhou Bay were leased to the foreign powers.[11]

As for Russia, its "usurpation" *(qinzhan)* of Chinese land began with the Czar's acquisition from the Qing dynasty of more than 1.5 million square kilometers (579,000 square miles) of land in northeastern and northwestern China[12]—the equivalent in area of Germany and France combined—in direct contravention of treaty agreements concluded in the seventeenth and eighteenth centuries.[13] Russian imperialism was continued by the Soviet Union, which, in 1942, "at the most difficult point in China's war of resistance against Japan"—"without even the pretense of an international treaty"—took more than 170,000 square kilometers of land in northern China. This was followed by Moscow's machinations to wrestle Outer Mongolia from Chinese control by urging the 1945 Yalta Conference to "maintain" the autonomy of "the Mongolian People's Republic." In January 1946, in signing a friendship treaty with the Soviet Union, the Chinese Nationalist regime formally recognized "Outer Mongolia's independence," resulting in "another 1.5 million sq. km. of land being carved from the map of China." The cumulative result of this litany of territorial losses was a substantial reduction in the size of the Chinese Empire. From the acme of the Qing dynasty, China was systematically diminished by 3.4 million square kilometers to the present 9.6 million square kilometers of the People's Republic.[14]

Reportedly, PRC school textbooks contain government-issued maps[15] that show three borders for China: the current boundaries; those in 1919; and those in 1840 at the time of the Opium War. Each alienated section is labeled and students are taught how the land was taken. Of the three borders, those in 1840 are the most expansive and include, within them, the Russian Far East, Sakhalin Island, the western half of the Sea of Japan, the Korean peninsula, the Yellow Sea, the East China Sea, the Ryukyu Islands, Diaoyutai islets, Taiwan, Hong Kong, the South China Sea, Vietnam, Laos, Thailand, Cambodia, Burma, Malaysia, the Andaman Sea and Island, Nepal, Bhutan, Kyrgyzstan, the eastern half of Kazakhstan, Russia's Altay and Sayan Mountains, and Mongolia.[16] Chinese school instruction is evidently effective. A 1998 opinion survey of university students in Beijing found them to be in fairly strong agreement (mean response of 4.09)[17] with the statement that "In schools, I was taught that China was much bigger in the Qing dynasty before the Opium War." Similarly, the authors of the sequel to *China Can Say No* observe that "without even considering China at the prime of the Tang dynasty," a cursory look at any map during the reign of Qing Emperor Kangxi (1662–1723) will show that China then was "much larger than that of the People's Republic of China today."[18]

Today, the goal of "national reunification" is an integral part of the Communist Party's Patriotic Education Campaign, as there is nothing in the world "more shameful than losing one's national territory."[19] The Chinese people must be animated by the "consciousness of national defense" *(guofang yishi)*, ever ready to fight for the independence, integrity, and reunification of the ancestral homeland.[20] They are asked to emulate the great patriots in Chinese history, the ranks of whom include those who resisted and fought imperialism, such as the Taiping rebels, Boxers, and Sun Yat-sen,[21] as well as those who unified and enlarged China. The latter included Emperor Qin Shihuang and the Mongol warrior Genghis Khan, who founded the Ming dynasty—the former for his unification of the warring states into a single centralized Chinese Empire; the latter for creating a great empire comprising China, Russia, and most of Asia and parts of Europe.[22] Such patriots are particularly needed today to ensure China's national defense and reunification, as the historic mission of national unification remains unfinished. Only when China becomes fully reconstituted will it regain the dignity that was lost to imperialist predation in the nineteenth and twentieth centuries.

"National defense" is understood by the Communist Party to begin with the preservation and maintenance of the PRC's territorial integrity by preventing the ethnic minorities in the autonomous regions of Xinjiang and Tibet from seceding or "splitting." Beijing's fear of Xinjiang's Muslim separatist movement prompted its diplomatic overtures to the Central Asian republics of Kazakhstan, Kyrgyzstan, and Tajikistan to convince them that it would be in their collective interest not to lend support to a pan-Islamic movement. In 1992 and 1994, those efforts resulted in bilateral communiqués and agreements between China and the three republics to set aside their border disputes in "the spirit of . . . mutual accommodation and mutual understanding."[23] As for Tibet, Chinese maintain that Tibet has been an inseparable part of China from the time of the Yuan dynasty (1280–1368).[24] Given that, to the extent that the U.S. government and people support the cause of Tibetan independence, the United States will be perceived by the People's Republic to be a national security threat. As *China Can Say No* puts it, "The West is active on our soil *(dipan)*. . . . An international conspiracy *(yinmou)* to carve up China's territory is definitely not an alarmist notion." Tibet is not a Chinese colony as Americans allege, but "a member of the big family of the [Chinese] nation."[25]

In 1982, Deng Xiaoping stated that "Sovereignty is not a matter for discussion."[26] Among the land that was lost, the Chinese government as well as its people have been consistent and unequivocal in their determination to reclaim five particular pieces of lost territory. They are Hong Kong, Macao, Taiwan, Diaoyutai islets, and the island groups in the South China Sea.

Hong Kong

Chinese irredentism has succeeded in the return of Xianggang, a British colony since 1843, to the "embrace of the motherland" on July 1, 1997. The day's significance was explained by the director of the Modern History Institute of the Chinese Social Science Academy:[27]

> Since the beginning of history, Hong Kong has been China's inherent *(guyou)* territory. . . . The ceding of Hong Kong island and Kowloon, and the forced leasing of New Territories [to Great Britain] constitutes a page in modern China's grievous and humiliating history. . . . The return of Hong Kong [therefore] cleanses China's hundred years of national shame and humiliation.

A contributor to the PRC magazine *Reunification Forum* also sees Hong Kong's return as "cleansing a hundred years' humiliation" and "greatly contributing" to "the reunification of the motherland and the revival of China."[28] Those sentiments are evidently shared by the Chinese populace. The day before the official celebration in Tiananmen Square, an estimated one million people spontaneously gathered in the Square, surprising and overwhelming the thousands of police charged with maintaining strict security in the capital. A young aircraft mechanic, Mr. Ma, explained: "We are patriotic Chinese and so we came tonight."[29] Zhang Guoping, a 40-year-old construction manager, exulted that "A century's sorrow has been removed. Our own territory has returned to us. . . . This proves the position of our country in the world."[30]

Macao

A Portuguese colony since 1557, Aomen, comprised of a narrow peninsula and two small islands off the southeastern coast of China, was returned to Beijing on December 19, 1999. Just as the return of Hong Kong had been arranged via diplomatic negotiations with London that culminated in the Hong Kong Agreement of 1984, the agreement to return Macao was achieved in a similar manner with Lisbon. It remains to be seen, however, whether disputed sovereign claims over Diaoyutai and the South China Sea, as well as Taiwan's "reunification with the motherland," can be as easily and peaceably resolved.

Diaoyutai Islets

In 1996, controversy reheated between China and Japan over the ownership of eight tiny islands in the East China Sea, which Chinese call Diaoyutai and Japanese Senkaku. Diaoyutai comprises six islets (Diaoyu, Feilai, Beixiao, Nanxiao, Da Beixiao, and Da Nanxiao) and two rocks (Huangwei and Chini) situated approximately 100 nautical miles from Taiwan's northern port of Keelong and, according to Beijing, 120 nautical miles west of Fuzhou within the PRC's Fujian Province.[31]

Chinese maintain that "the preponderance of historical evidence" indicates "there is no doubt" that Diaoyutai has been China's territory "since ancient times," appearing in Chinese maps as early as the Ming dynasty (A.D. 1368–1644). Since that time, the islets were included within China's perimeter of sea defense as islands "appertaining to China's Taiwan." Chinese historical documents indicate that Diaoyutai was never considered to be part of the Ryukyu island chain because the boundary between China and the Ryukyus was marked as the area *north* of Diaoyutai. More than that, fishermen from Taiwan had long been active in the seas around Diaoyutai and had built temples on the islets. When Japan defeated China in 1895, the Treaty of Shimonoseki ceded to Japan the Penghu islands (or Pescadores) and "Taiwan, together with all islands appertaining to Taiwan." After Japan was defeated in World War II, it was divested of all its colonies and war acquisitions including Taiwan, which was returned to China in 1945. In 1948–1949, the defeated Chinese Nationalist government fled the mainland to Taiwan, at which time the island became the Republic of China (ROC) on Taiwan. As for the Ryukyu Islands, considered part of prewar Japan, the United States took control of the archipelago (including its biggest island of Okinawa) until 1971, when Washington, without consulting either Beijing or Taipei, turned over the administration of the archipelago—including Diaoyutai—to Japan. But in making Japan the "administrative authority" over Diaoyutai, the United States "sowed the seeds" for the present dispute because it left ambiguous the matter of sovereign ownership over Diaoyutai.[32]

Although the dispute between China and Japan over Diaoyutai is decades old, the issue took on an urgency in July 1996, when Tokyo extended its exclusive 200-mile economic zone over the islets. At the same time, a Japanese *uyoku* (right-wing group) erected a lighthouse on one of the islets, then placed a Japanese flag and built a stone fort with a door bearing the inscription "Territory of Japan." Though uninhabited, the islets are surrounded by rich fish stocks and potentially large gas and oil deposits.[33]

Such is the power of irredentist nationalism that the dispute mobilized Chinese from disparate communities, igniting a grass-roots movement in mainland China, Hong Kong, Macao, and Taiwan, as well as the overseas Chinese community in the United States and Canada, where demonstrations on September 22, 1996 drew some 4,000 ethnic Chinese in San Francisco and 20,000 in Vancouver, B.C. Even famous PRC dissidents Wang Xizhe and Liu Xiaobo sent an "open letter" to the authorities in Beijing and Taipei, urging the deployment of military force to reclaim the islets.[34] In September 1996, the Japanese coast guard was dispatched to the islets to turn away two groups of Chinese civilian protesters, in the course of which a Hong Kong activist drowned in the stormy sea after leaping overboard to symbolically claim the waters for China. His martyrdom drew more than 50,000 mourners to a candlelit vigil in Hong Kong. On October 1, the PRC's National Day, Premier Li Peng became the highest-level Chinese official to speak out on the issue when he demanded that Japan withdraw its claim.[35]

If *China Can Still Say No* and the Hong Kong newspaper *Mingbao* are indicative of public opinion, the Diaoyutai issue represents something much more than a dispute over a few tiny islands. Writers for *Mingbao* see in the dispute nothing less than the ominous revival of Japanese militarism and the "rising threat" it poses to China. Invoking a domino scenario, they seem convinced that "If China were to lose Diaoyutai, then Taiwan and even China itself are in danger of being swallowed." More than that, the current dispute had been deliberately "incited" *(tiaobo)* by the United States when it returned administrative control of Diaoyutai to Tokyo instead of Beijing—so as to contain China.[36]

For its part, *China Can Still Say No* is convinced that the U.S. occupation of postwar Japan had failed to thoroughly eradicate Japanese militarism, the result of which is that militarism, a sense of racial superiority, and "tyrannical nationalism" *(minzu baquan zhuyi)* have persisted as inherent "structural defects in the Japanese national psychology." All of which explains Tokyo's continuing efforts to whitewash its wartime deeds and its refusal to sincerely apologize to China. The revival of Japanese militarism also lends an added urgency to the Taiwan issue, because the "swift return of Taiwan is the most important chess-piece for the containment of Japan." For it is only when Taiwan is "returned to the motherland" that Beijing can control the Taiwan Strait and thereby "throttle Japan" *(ezhu le riben di bozi)*.[37]

Taiwan

Ever since the Nationalist government of Chiang Kai-shek lost the civil war to the Chinese Communists and fled to the island of Taiwan, Beijing has maintained that the ROC on Taiwan is a "renegade province" that must eventually be reunified with the mainland. That reunification is held to be an integral part of Chinese irredentism. As expressed by a PRC writer, only when "the Taiwan problem is resolved will the complete unification of the ancestral land be realized."[38]

The loss of Taiwan carries special meaning for the People's Republic. A writer for the PRC magazine *Century* explains that Taiwan and Penghu became colonies of Japan in 1895 as a result of "the most unequal of all unequal treaties"—the Treaty of Shimonoseki *(maguan tiaoyue)*. Japan's "seizure" *(juequ)* of Taiwan became the catalyst for the subsequent carving of China into spheres of influence by the Western imperialist powers.[39] A popular PRC book, *Storm Waves Strike the Shores,* similarly views Taiwan's ceding to Japan to be a particularly humiliating chapter in modern Chinese history. More than that, the island's subsequent "occupation" by the Kuomintang is "an open . . . wound in the hearts of the Chinese people, the pain of which is undiminished despite the passage of years."[40]

Beijing has never wavered in its goal of reunifying with Taiwan; only its tactics have varied. In 1958, Mao provoked an armed conflict in the

Taiwan Strait that prompted the United States to dispatch the Seventh Fleet to patrol the Strait—a move described by *Storm Waves* as an act of "interference"[41] in China's domestic affairs. Decades of hostility followed until 1987, when relations between the two sides began to improve, especially in trade and investment. Beginning in the second half of 1995, however, Beijing's demeanor toward Taiwan dramatically hardened.

From the beginning, Beijing insisted that it would not tolerate the creation of an independent Taiwan that would forever be separate from the People's Republic. According to Beijing, such a development would cause it to unleash its military against Taiwan. In mid-1995, Beijing became increasingly perturbed about developments that were transpiring on the island. To begin with, the ROC began to rapidly democratize in 1987—a process that was completed by 1995, resulting in two societies across the Strait that had become even more divergent and dissimilar. Adding to Beijing's concerns were stepped-up efforts on the part of Taipei to gain membership in the United Nations. The proverbial last straw came in June 1995, when Washington approved a visa for ROC President Lee Teng-hui—head of a state that the United States does not recognize—to receive an honorary degree from his alma mater, Cornell University.

All of which deepened Beijing's suspicions regarding Washington's intentions and those of Lee himself, a native-born Taiwanese who had spent his formative years, until age 22, under Japanese colonial rule. Beijing suspects Lee of working surreptitiously for an independent Taiwan that would align itself with Japan and the United States. A contributor to *Century* accuses Lee of having "a profound Japanese and American complex" and for being "devoid of Chinese nationalist feelings." The suspicion extends to Lee's parentage: speculations that he was sired by a Japanese have even been bruited about in mainland publications.[42]

All of this led to a campaign of harassment and intimidation against Taiwan that began in the summer of 1995 and culminated in March 1996. For a week that March, Beijing "test-fired" ballistic missiles that landed barely 20 miles away from Taiwan's biggest ports of Keelong in the north and Kaohsiung in the south. At the same time, the PLA amassed 150,000 troops along the coast facing Taiwan and conducted war-game exercises with live ammunition. In so doing, Beijing effectively imposed a naval and air blockade on the island, over 99 percent of whose export cargo is transported by sea. In response, the United States dispatched two aircraft carrier battle groups to the waters near Taiwan, once again "blatantly interfering in China's internal affairs."[43]

Beijing's saber rattling in the Taiwan Strait not only sent "a *frisson* of fear through the region,"[44] it enjoyed immense popular support on the mainland. Public opinion polls there showed a majority to be in favor of the government's policy of "liberating" Taiwan by force.[45] As an example, *Storm Waves Strike the Shores* declares that the Chinese people are willing to fight a hundred years' war with any alien country or people that "covet" *(ranzhi)* Taiwan and are "maliciously" bent on keeping China divided. In that war, forces that are "anti-China" are "sure" to "have their heads broken and their blood flow." This is because Taiwan's significance transcends that of "the return or loss of a beautiful island," but has to do with "the honor and humiliation of the Chinese nation."[46]

For their part, the authors of *China Can Say No* and its sequel regard Washington's dispatching of two aircraft carrier groups to be nothing less than an act of "international terrorism." They believe that U.S. support for Taiwan is politically motivated as a divided China would be easier for the United States to contain and, thus, less of a threat to America's global hegemony. Taiwan's importance to the People's Republic is likened to that of a man's "private parts" because the island's strategic location makes its re-unification with the mainland "the key" that will determine "whether the Chinese nation survives or dies, prospers or fades." If Taiwan was to become independent and align itself with the United States and Japan, offering itself to them as a military base, Beijing would "have no choice" but to install a blockade by occupying "Taiwan's neighboring islands, so that the normal passage through the Taiwan Strait might then be affected, causing instability in Southeast Asia and the Pacific." In such an eventuality, "the economic dreams of Taiwan and China will be obliterated" and immense sufferings will once again descend on "a crippled Chinese nation." Given Taiwan's importance, the Chinese people are urged to strive for its reunification with "the motherland" even if it means war with the United States, because "Taiwan is part of China, just as two plus two equals four." And in the event that reconciliation with the United States is "impossible," the Chinese people must not hesitate "to retaliate accordingly."[47]

None of this is helped by Taipei's attempt in July 1999 to abandon the "one China doctrine" that had kept alive the political fiction that Taiwan and mainland China are two alienated parts of the same nation-state that would eventually reunify. In a radio interview on July 11, President Lee said that from now on, Taiwan would treat relations with China as "state-to-state" and "nation-to-nation," which meant that "there is no longer any need to declare Taiwanese independence." Lee's somewhat ambiguous remarks were clarified by Su Chi, chairman of Taiwan's Mainland Affairs Council, to mean that Taiwan intended to scrap the "one-China" formula.[48] Making matters even worse was the KMT's loss in the presidential election of March 18, 2000, and the ascension to the presidency of opposition Democratic Progressive Party (DPP) candidate Chen Shui-bian. Since its beginning, the DPP has favored independence for Taiwan, its membership being composed of "native" ethnic Taiwanese (descendants of Chinese who immigrated from Fujian Province some 300 years ago) who do not identify with mainland China.

South China Sea

Chinese irredentist nationalism is also being felt in the South China Sea, a region comprising over 180 islands, rocks, and shoals that the Chinese call the *Nansha* (South Sand or Spratlys), *Xisha* (West Sand or Paracels), *Zhongsha* (Central Sand), and *Dongsha* (East Sand) island groups.[49] Because the region is potentially rich in maritime subsoil or seabed oil and natural gas, it is claimed as sovereign territory not only by Beijing but also by Vietnam, the Philippines, Malaysia, Indonesia, and Brunei.

Containing China, an edited volume with a preface penned by a former PRC deputy foreign minister, describes the South China Sea and particularly the Spratlys as "China's sacred indivisible territory" since "ancient times" when the Spratly archipelago was discovered during Han dynasty Emperor Wudi's reign (140–86 B.C.). By the Song dynasty (A.D. 420), China had "declared authority over" the islands; Chinese fishermen fished in the Sea and used its islands for rest and repair. Maps of China in the Yuan dynasty (1206–1368) included the Spratlys and the Paracels. During the reign of Ming dynasty Emperor Chengzu (1403–1425), when Zheng Ho undertook seven naval expeditions that reached India, Persia, and the eastern shores of Africa, the Spratlys were included within China's naval defense perimeter. In the early years of the Qing dynasty, the Chinese navy regularly patrolled the Sea. By 1733, during the reign of Emperor Yongzheng, the South China Sea was recognized by the countries in the region to be Chinese sovereign territory within the jurisdiction of Guangdong Province's Huizhou prefecture. From that time "until the twentieth century, no country raised any questions regarding China's sovereign rights over the Spratlys."[50]

In 1925, the Chinese Nationalist regime constructed observation posts, custom houses, and lighthouses on some of the Sea's islands. In 1933, the French military "occupied" nine islands in the Spratlys. During World War

II, the South China Sea came under Japanese occupation but was returned to China in 1946, at which time Nationalist troops were dispatched to reclaim the Spratlys and the Paracels: A Chinese flag was erected on Peace Island, and stone markers were placed on other isles. "Many other islands and shoals," however, "became no-man's land." Beginning in the 1950s, the People's Republic entered into conflict with Malaysia, the Philippines, and especially Vietnam over rival claims in the South China Sea. By the mid-1990s, five of the Spratlys were occupied by Malaysia, eight by the Philippines, and 24 by Vietnam. Although neither Brunei nor Indonesia occupies any island, their economic maritime zones overlap by some 40,000 square kilometers with China's.[51]

Beijing has repeatedly expressed a preference for peaceful negotiations to resolve the disputed claims over the Sea. At the same time, it has not hesitated to press its territorial claims by force. PLA naval ships have been cruising the Sea and building armed outposts on its islands and coral reefs. In 1974, Chinese captured the Paracels from a South Vietnamese garrison, followed in 1988 by the capture of six atolls in the Spratly group from united Vietnam. In February 1995, the PLA set up a garrison on Mischief Reef inside the Philippines' 200-nautical-mile exclusive economic zone; controversy also erupted between Beijing and Manila over Huangyan Island in 1997.[52] All of which prompted the Philippine Senate, in May 1999, to partially reverse its expulsion of U.S. forces from Clark and Subic Bay military bases eight years before and conclude a Visiting Forces Agreement with the United States. The agreement not only gives U.S. forces access to Philippine ports and facilities, it also calls for the resumption of major joint military exercises.[53]

The Sea's importance transcends sovereignty and impacts on strategic and resource considerations. Not only are the Spratlys situated in the midst of "a major sea passage" between the Pacific and the Indian Oceans, the archipelago is also "a communications hub" for sea lanes in the East China Sea,[54] commanding the choke points of the Straits of Malacca, Bashi, Sunda, and Lombok. As *Containing China* puts it, "Whoever occupies and controls the Spratlys . . . is sure to become a great maritime power." The South China Sea also contains rich natural resources. Beijing estimates that the Spratlys alone have potential maritime subsoil deposits of 4 to 5 billion tons of oil and over 10 billion tons of natural gas. Additionally, there are countless minerals as well as rich varieties of fish and other seafood.[55]

It is for these reasons that PLA navy deputy commander Zhang Xusan in a talk on naval strategy in 1992 stated that the time had come "for China to alter its naval strategy to reclaim the rich natural resources of the South China Sea."[56] Reportedly, PRC government documents refer to the Sea as China's "living space."[57] PLA navy commander Liu Huaqing, in April 1989, identified the seas to be the loci for future conflicts between the People's Republic and other countries. According to Liu, China is both a continental as well as a maritime power, for whom the "vast expanses" of its seas not only are "natural barriers" of national security but constitute "living space" *(shengcun kongjian)* that could ensure China's economic development and future survival.[58]

In February 1992, the South China Sea was formally designated as part of the People's Republic when its national legislature, the National People's Congress, passed a Territorial Waters Act (TWA) declaring China's "sovereign territory" as including all the territorial and maritime space adjacent to the Chinese mainland, as well as the airspace above. Specifically named territories include Taiwan, Diaoyutai islets, Penghu, the Spratlys, the Paracels, as well as the Dongsha and Zhongsha island groups. Article 14 of the TWA specifies that the PLA navy has the right to pursue and dispel any foreign vessels found within Chinese territorial waters.[59]

Other Territories

After the return of Hong Kong and Macao, explicit Chinese irredentism has been directed at Diaoyutai, Taiwan, and the South China Sea. But there is no logical reason why Chinese irredentist ambitions should remain confined to those areas. As *China Can Still Say No* puts it, "we reserve the right to pursue" all Chinese territories lost since 1662.[60] A meeting of the CCP Military Affairs Commission in 1993 to determine China's post–Cold War military strategy and objectives concluded that, although a new world war was unlikely, medium- and small-scale limited wars were unavoidable. In order of importance, the commission identified the PRC's future military objectives to be gaining control of "First, eastern and southern China's coastal waters; second, the South China Sea; third, the Sino-Indian border."[61]

According to the U.S. Department of Defense in 1995, Beijing has outstanding unresolved border and territorial disputes with at least ten countries. Those countries are Taiwan (over the Pratas Island in the South China Sea, presently occupied by Taipei); Japan (over the Diaoyutai islets); Vietnam (over the Paracel Islands in the South China Sea, occupied by Beijing since 1974); Brunei, Malaysia, the Philippines, Taiwan, and

Vietnam (over the Spratly Islands, six atolls of which have been occupied by Beijing since 1988); the Philippines (over the Mischief Reef in the South China Sea, occupied by Beijing since 1995); India (over two disputed border areas totaling 90,000 square miles left unresolved after the Sino-Indian border war of 1970); and in Central Asia, with Kazakhstan, Kyrgyzstan, and Tajikistan.[62] Of the fourteen countries with whom China shares land borders, Beijing has unresolved boundary disputes with five: Russia, North Korea, Tajikistan, India, and Bhutan.[63] *National Defense* reports that since 1960, Beijing has concluded border treaties with Burma, Nepal, Mongolia, Pakistan, Afghanistan, North Korea, and Laos, which "redrew boundaries" and "satisfactorily resolved border problems." As of the end of 1994, however, the People's Republic still had over 100 pieces of land totaling 160,000 square kilometers and more than 2,000 kilometers of land borders under dispute with Russia,[64] Kazakhstan, Kyrgyzstan, Tajikistan, India, Vietnam, and Bhutan.[65] In addition, Beijing has unresolved maritime border issues concerning the South China Sea islands, continental shelves, exclusive zones, and ocean rights with North and South Korea, Japan, the Philippines, Malaysia, Brunei, Indonesia, and Vietnam.[66] Altogether, according to one estimate, China's territorial interests overlap with those of 24 other countries.[67]

Beijing has expressed a preference for peaceful negotiations to resolve sovereignty disputes, but it insists that any resolution must be "reasonable" by "taking into consideration historical background" so as to construct agreements "on the basis of mutual understanding and accommodation."[68] Despite its rhetoric, future PRC behavior regarding China's lost territories most likely will be determined by practical considerations. These include the success or failure of international diplomacy, Beijing's strategic and foreign policy considerations, the PLA's capabilities and calculations as to the probability of success in employing force, and conditions internal to China that may provoke the regime to use external aggression as a quick but effective way to galvanize domestic unity. Those internal contingencies include population pressures, political fragmentation, social unrest, and resource deficiencies.

Irredentist nationalism serves multiple purposes, only one of which is to provide China with needed land and resources, including energy. Beijing is under enormous pressure to maintain an accelerated rate of economic growth if it hopes to achieve the goal it has set for itself of a GNP of $2.16 trillion by the year 2010, six times the 1993 figure. To do that, China will have to sustain an annual economic growth rate of over 10 percent,[69] significantly expand its existing infrastructure, and increase its power generation. Already, demand for gasoline, fuel oil, and other refined products has outstripped domestic production,[70] so that China became an oil importer beginning in 1994. Control over oil deposits in the South China Sea, estimated by Beijing to be more than 12 percent of the world's oil and natural gas reserves,[71] is not simply a question of extending power but of fueling China's industries and feeding its people in the next century. As one sinologist put it, "So if there is oil in the South China Sea you've got to have it" because Chinese "don't have a lot of spare change to give out."[72]

The "Second National Territory"

The South China Sea is only one portion of an overall policy shift by the Chinese military from a land-based to an ocean defense strategy. An article in *National Defense* in 1995 explains that, "In the past, for a long period of time," humanity primarily relied on land for their survival and development, thinking that "national territory *(guotu)* only meant dry land." But in today's world, due to rapid increases in population and dwindling land and resources, "national territory" must mean more than "land territory" *(lingtu)* but should include "territorial waters" *(linghai)*. This has led nation-states to turn to the "oceans" *(haiyang)*—most of which are still "virgin territory"—in their search for new "living space."[73]

The PRC now conceives oceans to be its "second national territory" *(dier guotu)*.[74] It defines "maritime national territory" *(haiyang guotu)* as "the maritime portion of any land and space belonging to or under the jurisdiction of a coastal country."[75] China's "second national territory" includes 12 territorial seas *(linghai)*, 24 "maritime adjacent regions" *(haili pilian qu)*, 200 maritime economic exclusive zones and continental shelves—totaling more than 3 million square kilometers or one-third of China's land mass.[76]

Defense of its "maritime national territory" requires Beijing to shift its defense strategy from one of "coastal defense" *(jin'an fangyu)* to "offshore defense" *(jinhai fangyu)*.[77] *National Defense* maintains that since "the frontline of maritime national defense lies beyond China's territorial waters . . . there will be times" when China's defense of its seas "may require doing battle in farther maritime regions" including "international waters and seabeds."[78] China's perimeter of "offshore defense" is conceived to include two "island chains." The first chain stretches from the Aleutians to the Kurils, the Japanese archipelago, the Ryukyus, Taiwan, the Philippine archipelago, and the Greater Sunda Islands. The "second island chain" comprises the Bonins, the Marianas, Guam, and the Palau archipelago.[79]

Potential Irredentist Claims

In the future, Chinese irredentism may extend beyond even the oceans to the PRC's far northern borders if *China Can Still Say No* is any indication. Its authors observe that "If certain famous lakes and large water systems in the northwest had not been carved" from China, then "arid Xinjiang would now have sufficient water for beautiful and abundant grasslands." And "If Haisanwei [Vladivostok] were still in our hands, we would have an excellent harbor in the far north." Northeastern China would be greatly enriched from the development of lumber resources as well as trade linkages with Japan and North and South Korea. "Heilongjiang would no longer have to suffer from being an underdeveloped inland border province" because "honest and industrious" Chinese would quickly settle the "expansive" and resource-rich expanse of northeast Asia.[80]

Conclusion

All of the characteristics of irredentist nationalism are descriptive of the People's Republic of China today. The Communist Party is confronted with daunting domestic problems in an environment of ideological uncertainty. To provide itself with a new legitimation, Beijing has turned to patriotic nationalism as a panacea, a nationalism that is reactive and irredentist as evidenced by the qualitative literature from the People's Republic.

The irredentist desires expressed in the qualitative literature are shared by 126 Beijing university students who were surveyed in 1998. The results of the survey show them to be in strong agreement with every statement that pertains to Chinese irredentism. Their mean responses to the statements that "China should recover all the territories that were lost since the Opium War," that "Tibet must not become independent because it is a part of China," that "Diaoyutai belongs to China," and that "The South China Sea and its islands belong to China" were 4.33, 4.52, 4.74, and 4.74, respectively. The respondents' irredentism was so strong that they were prepared to employ military force to press China's territorial claims, as seen in their mean responses of 4.56 and 3.96, respectively, to the statements that "Taiwan must be reunified with the motherland, by force if necessary" and that "China must reclaim Diaoyutai from Japan, using military force if necessary."

In the past, the People's Republic has demonstrated its willingness to go to war over irredentist claims. Examples include the border wars with the

Soviet Union in the 1960s, with India in 1962, with North Korea during the Great Proletarian Cultural Revolution, and with Vietnam in 1979—all over territorial disputes that remain unresolved. As an example, two pieces of border territories totaling 90,000 square miles are still contested by China and India today.

All this has alarmed China's neighbors, who are unnerved by its increasing assertiveness. Already the world's fourth largest, the PLA's defense budget has grown every year since the end of the Cold War. Not only is the Chinese navy transforming itself into a blue-water navy, the PLA is making a major shift from a land-based defense force to a military capable of projecting power throughout the Far East and beyond. That transformation is aided by the purchase and suspected theft of U.S. nuclear and neutron bomb technology and recent purchases of the PRC's first aircraft carrier from Ukraine and advanced fighter aircrafts and destroyers equipped with anti-ship missiles from Russia. By the early part of the new century, China's military capabilities are expected to surpass those of other countries in the Asia-Pacific region. It is this rising concern about China that has led to increased arms spending across the Asia-Pacific region, with the biggest increases undertaken by Japan, South Korea, Taiwan, Thailand, and Singapore.[81]

The possibility of Chinese belligerence has been described as "a nightmare" for Japan because of the latter's strategic dependence on shipping lanes that run near the coast of China and through waters claimed by Beijing.[82] José Almonte, national security adviser to the president of the Philippines, has referred to China's rising nationalism as "ominous." A senior Vietnamese diplomat privately admitted to his country's fear of China's growing power.[83] That is not surprising, given the 1979 Sino-Vietnamese war over contested border territories, not to mention 1,000 years of Chinese rule over northern Vietnam that began in 111 B.C.

The rise of a more assertive China is now described as the main challenge to stability in East Asia.[84] As such, not only is China's irredentist nationalism potentially threatening to its neighbors, it also presents vexing policy dilemmas for the United States. Those dilemmas will be addressed in the next chapter.

Notes

1. An Fengjing (ed.), "'Kuashiji de guofang zhilu' jieshuo ci (Glossary of 'The road to a cross-century national defense')," *Guofang (National Defense)* (Beijing), no. 6 (1994), p. 42.

2. Hedva Ben-Israel, "Irredentism: Nationalism Reexamined," in Naomi Chazan (ed.), *Irredentism and International Politics* (Boulder: Lynne Rienner, 1991), pp. 32, 34.

3. Naomi Chazan, "Irredentism, Separatism, and Nationalism," in Chazan (ed.), *Irredentism and International Politics,* p. 150.

4. Marcus W. Brauchli and Kathy Chen, "Nationalist Fervor," *The Wall Street Journal,* June 23, 1995, p. A1.

5. Fareed Zakaria, "Speak Softly, Carry a Veiled Threat," *New York Times Magazine,* February 18, 1996, pp. 37, 36.

6. Luo Guoliang, "Ke'ai de zuguo, weida de minzu (Beloved motherland, great nation)," *Guofang* (September 1995), p. 17.

7. Hsu Cho-yun, "Preface," *Wanguo gongfa (Elements of International Law)* (Taipei: Chinese International Law Association, 1998), pp. 1–4. This book is a reprint of a Chinese translation of Henry Wheaton's *Elements of International Law,* China's first book on international law, published in 1864.

8. "The Dragon Awakes," *Browning Newsletter,* 20:2 (February 21, 1996), p. 5. This is an investment newsletter for stockbrokers, published in the United States.

9. Mao Yuanyou, "Zhongguo bantu di xingcheng yu bianqian (Formation and Changes in the Map of China)," *Guofang,* no. 3 (1994), p. 34. Chinese historical chronicles often referred to Japan as *Liuqiu* (Ryukyu). Thus, the reference here could either be to the Ryukyu Islands or to Japan.

10. Ibid., pp. 33–34.

11. Ibid., p. 34; An Fengjing, "Glossary of 'The Road to a Cross-Century National Defense'," p. 42.

12. Mao Yuanyou, "Formation and Changes in the Map of China," p. 34.

13. An Fengjing, "Glossary of," p. 42. The Nibuchu (Nerchinsk) Treaty of 1689 and the Bulianqisi (Kiakhta) Treaty of 1727 demarcated the Sino-Russian border with the Er'guna River and the Shabinayi Mountains, and determined that Chinese sovereignty began south of the outer Xing'an Mountains and extended eastward from the Gorbitsa and Argun Rivers to the Pacific Ocean to embrace the basins of the Heilong(jiang) and Ussuri Rivers. Du Renhuai, "Kang Qian shengshi shiqi de bianfang (Emperors Kangxi and Qianlong's border defense at the height of the Qing dynasty)," *Guofang,* no. 7 (1994), pp. 33–34.

14. Mao Yuanyou, "Formation and Changes," p. 34.

15. This map is included in a PRC textbook, *A Brief History of Modern China,* published in Beijing in 1954. "The Dragon Awakes," p. 4.

16. Ibid.

17. On the survey, a score of 5.0 represented "strongly agree," and 4.0 represents "moderately agree."

18. Song Qiang, Zhang Zangzang, Qiaobian, Yang Zhengyu, and Gu Qingsheng, *Zhongguo haishi neng shuobu (China Can Still Say No)* (Beijing: China Culture Alliance, 1996), p. 356.

19. Li Zeshun, "Guanyu kaizhan guoqi jiaoyu de sikao (Thoughts on Developing a National Shame Education)," *Guofang,* no. 5 (1994), p. 14.

20. Xiang Wenrong, "Guofang yishi yu aiguo zhuyi (Consciousness of National Defense and Patriotism)," *Guofang,* no. 9 (1996), p. 32.

21. Guo Jishun and Gao Yong, "Bainian xuelueshi buxiu zhonghuahun (China's Soul Survives a Hundred Years' History of Blood and Tears)," *Guofang,* no. 5 (1995), pp. 21–31.

22. Gu Jieshan, "Zhongguo gudai de aiguo zhuyi (China's Traditional Patriotism)," Part I, *Guofang,* no. 3 (1995), p. 23.

23. M. Drozdov, "Novyy Vzglyad Na Sholkovyy Put," *Politicheskiy Izvestnik,* November 15, 1995.

24. Tibetans, for their part, insist that they have "always been a distinct nation" that was effectively independent from 1912 until the Chinese Communist "liberation" in 1950. See James D. Seymour, "Zhongguoren kandai xizang wenti di lishixing zhuanlie (A Historic Turning Point in Chinese Perception of the Tibetan Problem)," *Zhongguo zhichun (China Spring)* (Alhambra, CA), no. 154 (July 1996), p. 89.

25. Song Qiang et al., *Zhongguo keyi shuobu (China Can Say No)* (Beijing: Chinese Industry and Commerce, 1996), pp. 31, 33, 40.

26. Zhang Haipeng, "Zhongguo jindai yongru cuoyao (Important points concerning modern China's glory and shame)", *Guofang,* no. 7 (1997), p. 14.

27. Ibid., pp. 12, 13.

28. Cao Jun, "Dui haixia liangan guanxi fazhan di yingxiang (Effects on the developing relations across the Taiwan Strait)," *Tongyi luntan zhazhi (Reunification Forum),* no. 6 (1996), p. 17.

29. "Huge Crowd Celebrates in Beijing," *San Francisco Chronicle* (hereafter *SFC),* June 30, 1997, p. A12.

30. Henry Chu and David Holley, "156 Years of 'Disgrace' Wiped Away," *SFC,* July 1, 1997, p. A8.

31. *Diaoyutai: Zhongguo de lingtu! (Diaoyutai: China's Territory!)* (Hong Kong: Mingbao, 1996), p. 2.

32. Ibid., pp. 2, 21, 55; Hungdah Chiu, *An Analysis of the Sino-Japanese Dispute Over the Tiaoyutai Islets* (University of Maryland School of Law: Occasional Papers/Reprints Series in Contemporary Asian Studies), no. 1, 1999, pp. 10, 6.

33. *Diaoyutai: China's Territory!,* p. 12; *WJ,* September 24, 1996, p. A13.

34. *WJ,* September 23, 1996, p. A1; and October 1, 1996, p. A2.

35. "In an Ocean of Controversy," *Time,* October 7, 1996, p. 30; "China Premier Warns Japan on Islets," *SFC,* October 1, 1996, p. A14.

36. *Diaoyutai: China's Territory!,* pp. 14, 17, 2–22.

37. Song Qiang et al., *China Can Still Say No,* pp. 91, 84, 123, 148, 77, 79–80, 89.

38. Cao Jun, "Effects on the Developing Relations Across the Taiwan Strait," p. 18.

39. Chen Changfu, "Wuwang guochi (Forget Not Our National Shame)," *Shiji (Century)* (Shanghai), no. 11 (February 1995), pp. 4, 5.

40. Yang Fang, *Jingtao po'an (Storm Waves Strike the Shores)* (Fuzhou, Fujian: Haixia wenyi, 1997), p. 1.

41. Ibid.

42. See Li Xiaozhuang, "Jie Li Denghui dipai (Lifting Lee Teng-hui's Bottom Card)," parts I & II, in *Shiji*, no. 15 (November–December 1995), pp. 10–15; and no. 16 (January–February 1996), pp. 14–18.

43. Yang Fang, *Storm Waves*, p. 5.

44. "Terrific Pacific," *The Economist*, July 20, 1996, p. 29.

45. "Against the Wind," interview of Liu Binyan with Kari Huus, in *Far Eastern Economic Review*, November 9, 1995, p. 26.

46. Yang Fang, *Storm Waves*, pp. 4, 5.

47. Song Qiang et al., *China Can Say No*, pp. 248, 73, 221, and *China Can Still Say No*, pp. 248, 71, 73, 295, 298, 300, 38, 221.

48. Seth Faison, "Taiwan Drops 'One China' Doctrine," *SFC*, July 13, 1999, p. A1.

49. Ding Zongyu, "Lun zhonggong yu nanhai zhoubian guojia lingtu di fenzheng (On the Territorial Disputes Between Communist China and the Countries Bordering on the South China Sea)," *Gongdang wenti yanjiu (Studies in Communism)*, Taipei, 21:4 (April 1995), p. 39.

50. Sun Keqin and Cui Hongjian (eds.), *Ezhi zhongguo (Containing China)* (Beijing: China True Speech, 1996), pp. 741, 743; Ding Zongyu, "On the Territorial Disputes," pp. 48, 43.

51. Ding, "On the Territorial Disputes," pp. 43–44, 39; Sun and Cui, *Containing China*, pp. 744, 745.

52. Nayan Chanda, Rigoberto Tiglao, and John McBeth, "Territorial Imperative," *Far Eastern Economic Review*, February 23, 1995, p. 14; *Huaxia wenzhai (China News Digest)*, 27 April 1997, p. 1.

53. Benjamin Pimentel, "U.S. Military Invited Back," *SFC*, July 6, 1999, p. A4.

54. *China: An Inside Look Into the Chinese Communist Navy*, Foreign Broadcast Information Service, July 16, 1990, p. 12.

55. Sun and Cui, *Containing China*, pp. 740–741; see also *Zhongguo dili zhishi (Geography of China Handbook)* (Kowloon, Hong Kong: Knowledge, 1973), p. 15.

56. Ding, "On the Territorial Disputes," p. 43.

57. Nayan Chanda and Kari Huus, "China: The New Nationalism," *Far Eastern Economic Review*, November 9, 1995, p. 22.

58. *1995 Zhonggong nianbao (1995 China Yearbook)* (Taipei: zhonggong yanjiu zazhishe, 1995), section 6, p. 41.

59. "Zhonghua renmin gongheguo linhai ji pilianqu fa (The People's Republic of China's Territorial Waters and Adjacent Territories Act)," in *1995 China Yearbook*, section 6, pp. 36–37.

60. Song Qiang et al., *China Can Still Say No*, p. 356.

61. Ding, "On the Territorial Disputes," p. 47.

62. See map on "Boundary and Territorial Disputes in East Asia," in *United States Security Strategy for the East Asia-Pacific Region* (Washington, DC: Department of Defense, February 1995), p. 19.

63. Zakaria, "Speak Softly, Carry a Veiled Threat."

64. In April 1999, a Sino-Russian committee declared it had successfully resolved the bulk of border disputes between the two countries, except for two islands in the Ussuri River and an island in Argun River. See *WJ*, April 28, 1999, p. A11.

65. As for Bhutan, the PRC recently claimed that at least half of Gangkhar Puensuum, the world's highest virgin mountain, is actually in Tibet. See "Enter the Dragon Kingdom," *San Francisco Examiner Magazine*, March 14, 1999, p. 10.

66. Mao Yuanyou, "Formation and Changes in the Map of China," p. 34.

67. Zakaria, "Speak Softly."

68. Mao Yuanyou, "Formation and Changes," p. 34.

69. Lin Chung-cheng, "Spread the Risk," *Free China Review*, 46:3 (March 1996), p. 52.

70. Craig S. Smith and Mary Scott, "Demand for Refineries is High in China," *The Wall Street Journal*, December 26, 1995, p. A4.

71. Ding, "On the Territorial Disputes," p. 41.

72. Quote by Andrew Nathan, in Chanda and Huus, "China: New Nationalism," p. 22.

73. Wu Xiangshun and Wang Shengyong, "Haiyang, haiyang guan, haishang changcheng (Oceans, oceanic perspective, oceanic great wall)," *Guofang*, no. 10 (1995), p. 4.

74. Song Yan, "Womeng di 'dier guotu' (Our 'second national territory')," *Guofang*, no. 4 (1994), p. 41.

75. Wu and Wang, "Oceans, Oceanic Perspective, Oceanic Great Wall," p. 5.

76. Song Yan, "Our Second National Territory," p. 41.

77. *1995 China Yearbook*, section 6, pp. 39–40.

78. Wu and Wang, "Oceans," p. 5.

79. *1995 China Yearbook*, section 6, p. 38; and Alexander Chieh-cheng Huang, "The Chinese Navy's Offshore Active Defense Strategy," *Naval War College Review*, XLVII:3 (Summer 1994), p. 18.

80. Song Qiang et al., *China Can Still Say No*, p. 357.

81. "Asia's Arms Racing," *The Economist*, February 3, 1996, p. 29.

82. Steven Butler et al., "Refocusing in Asia," *U.S. News and World Report*, April 22, 1996, p. 49.

83. Chanda and Huus, "China: New Nationalism," p. 22.

84. "Terrific Pacific."

10

The Other Face of Janus

The testimony from both qualitative and quantitative evidence points to contemporary Chinese nationalism's possession of every trait that, according to the social science literature, is indicative of a propensity toward collective violence. Chinese, at an elite as well as popular level, seem preoccupied with national power and status; their conception of nationhood is ethnic and racial; they are narcissistic but insecure. China's modern history is scarred with the trauma of defeat that left an abiding sense of victimhood and aggrievedness; its morally relativistic culture, exacerbated by the toxic legacy of the Maoist era, lacks the guidelines that can prevent the abuse of outsiders; the People's Republic is profoundly irredentist. Last but not least, because of the incompleteness of Deng Xiaoping's reforms, China remains an authoritarian state. Such states typically are intolerant of outsiders and historically prone to aggressive nationalism. [1]

Political Authoritarianism

In the lethal brew of attributes that singly and collectively dispose a people toward aggressive nationalism, none is as potent as political authoritarianism. For in the last analysis, it is the state that is the ultimate gatekeeper to all the other attributes of aggressive nationalism.

The state can choose to attenuate or suppress its people's propensity toward aggression with appropriate legislation, or by channeling, redirecting, and educating them toward more constructive methods of problem solving. In political systems that provide for freedom of speech and of the press, the people also benefit from the airing of diverse opinions and alternative solutions. In authoritarian polities, in contrast, instead of being the voice of reason and restraint, the state may actually orchestrate nationalist sentiments to serve its own ends by adopting an exaggerated patriotic nationalism as its legitimating ideology. In the process, the prosaic nationalism that animates every community is fanned into an inferno.

The historical examples of Nazi Germany and Imperial Japan are instructive. In both cases, nationalist passions were inflamed and manipulated by their governments' systematic manipulation. In both, it was the totalitarian state that exploited myths of origins to promote the narcissistic conviction, disseminated via the machinery of government propaganda, that Aryans and Japanese were biologically superior "races" who deserved to rule over, and even eliminate, "lesser" peoples. In both, it was the state that capitalized on its people's reactive nationalism and historical grievances[2] so as to transform their resentment into a determination to exact revenge. In both, it was the state that subscribed to a pseudo-Darwinian worldview where moral considerations were not extended to those deemed inferior. The latter were subhumans who could be abused and killed with impunity, their women forced into sexual servitude, as their homelands were absorbed into the Third Reich and the Imperial Japanese Empire. And it is also in both cases that nationalism, though it sprang from the primal impulse to ensure the collective well-being of Germans and Japanese, ultimately brought immense sufferings upon both peoples. In the end, patriotic racial nationalism almost destroyed both countries.

Today, more than two decades after the initiation of economic reforms, the People's Republic of China remains an authoritarian state, caught in transition between Maoist totalitarianism and an uncertain future. China is increasingly capitalist but remains a political dictatorship. The Communist Party has loosened its suffocating control on the economy, but inefficient state-owned enterprises still hobble productivity. Famous dissidents Wei Jingsheng and Wang Dan are freed, but nameless multitudes still languish in *laogai* prison camps.[3] Christians and labor union activists are still persecuted, and Tibet remains a police state. Rather than the hoped-for ripple effects of liberalization, President Clinton's visit to China in the summer of 1998 seemed only to have precipitated a new wave of repression. Leaders of the embryonic opposition China Democracy Party were arrested and imprisoned;[4] progressive newspapers, magazines, and journals were censored.[5] The avowedly apolitical Buddhist sect Falun Gong, with a membership of perhaps 100 million, was suppressed and vilified as a "devil cult"[6] for having organized a peaceful demonstration on April 25, 1999 in Beijing. That day, 10,000 to 16,000 sect members took the authorities by surprise when they appeared before the Communist Party headquarters at Zhongnanhai to ask that their sect be accorded legal recognition.

Although the Chinese masses enjoy greater freedoms in their daily lives, the Communist Party does not hesitate to bring all the brutal power of the state against any and all who step beyond its confines of tolerance.[7] Despite the proliferation of private businesses and entrepreneurs since 1979, China still lacks a civic culture from which democracy can grow. Today, more than 20 years after the death of Mao, the People's Republic has neither a civil society nor genuinely competitive elections. Instead, there is only the space vacated by the silencing, deportation, and disappearance of political dissidents; the intellectuals have been cowed by repression and the masses are either apathetic or tranquilized by the fruits of economic growth.

Civil Society

Political theorists have long argued for the crucial importance of civil society as a force to provide the organizational basis for democracy. As it is used, the term "civil society" has two meanings. The first refers to the presence of autonomous voluntary associations in society—social organizations that are neither organized nor supervised by the state, but are created by private citizens to serve and protect their interests. A secondary meaning of civil society refers to the democratic institutions of civil rights, representation, and the rule of law.[8]

Two decades after China opened itself to intercourse with the West and, presumably, to the liberalizing influence of Western thought and culture, an impressive number and variety of societal groups and associations have emerged. But beginning in 1989, after it violently suppressed the democracy movement in Tiananmen Square, the Communist Party government began to rein in those groups and associations. Its Department of Civil Affairs instituted a centralized system of compulsory registration and control of social organizations, the express purpose of which is to thwart the creation of autonomous associations by excluding those deemed unacceptable.[9] Once approved, a group's registration would be reviewed every year. In October 1998, new regulations were introduced to further tighten the registration procedures.[10]

According to Gordon White, four types of societal groups and associations are discernible in China today. The first is a "caged sector" comprising traditional CCP mass organizations that serve as the party's organized base of social control and support and, as a consequence, have virtually no organizational autonomy. Examples include the All-China Federation of Trade Unions, the Women's Federation, and the Young Communist League.[11]

A second type of societal association includes those that belong to an "incorporated sector"—groups that have not been organized by the Communist Party but owe their existence and continual operation to the government because they are registered with and approved and supervised by the state. In 1997, registered groups that were national in scope numbered more than 1,800[12] and included chambers of commerce, business and trade associations, academic societies, professional associations, women's aid groups, and sports, recreational, and cultural clubs. Each group is linked with a specific government agency that acts as the group's official sponsor and supervisor by appointing its leaders and mandating "official" tasks to the group.[13]

A third type of societal group in the People's Republic belongs to the "interstitial limbo world"—associations that are not explicitly political and, therefore, are mostly tolerated by the Communist Party but are nevertheless subject to its periodic harassment.[14] Examples include the environmental Green China Association, founded in 1993; intellectual salons; traditional associations based on kinship, geography, and ethnicity; and state-sanctioned religious groups of Christians, Muslims, Daoists, Buddhists, and until recently, Falun Gong.

The fourth type are groups that belong to the "suppressed sector." These are genuinely autonomous groups that operate underground in defiance of the state and, as a consequence, are targeted for active suppression. They include the following: opposition parties, such as the China Democracy Party and the Democratic Justice Party; independent labor unions; independent religious organizations, such as the China Christian Association and the China Catholic Association; separatist ethnic-regional groups, such as the Xinjiang Justice Party and the Independent Party of Inner Mongolia; criminal organizations; and secret societies.[15] While all these groups operate in secrecy by necessity, the secret societies may be the least known but arguably the most interesting, given their historically prominent role in China's dynastic changes. The PRC Ministry of Public Security estimated in 1992 that some 30,000 individuals belonged to more than 1,830 secret societies, some of which had international connections, especially with the Triads in Hong Kong. Not surprisingly, Beijing regards the societies as dangerous because of their overseas connections, criminal activities, and sporadic political involvement.[16] An example of the latter was when the societies reportedly gave refuge to and helped smuggle out of China some of the student leaders of the 1989 democracy movement.

Among the new groups that have appeared in the People's Republic since 1979, Western academics and policymakers accord special importance to the burgeoning class of industrial and commercial entrepreneurs because that class played a pivotal role in the West's own democratization. As one U.S. academic-cum-official put it, "The Chinese Communists are living on borrowed time; economic liberalization is going to create pressure for political freedom."[17] It is said that ownership of their own businesses has given Chinese entrepreneurs a measure of autonomy as they are "no longer at the mercy of the state." That new class has made Chinese society "much more vibrant and autonomous," resulting in the rise of a nascent civil society.[18]

That conclusion is at once optimistic and premature. To begin with, although there were nearly 30 million entrepreneurs in China in 1998, they nevertheless constituted only 3 percent of a total population of almost 1.3 billion.[19] More than their small portion in the population, the entrepreneurs constitute a class that seems uninterested in political change and whose most firmly held belief seems to be that "getting rich is glorious."[20] The voluntary associations formed by the entrepreneurs are also not encouraging. Among China's chambers of commerce, the larger ones are composed of owners of big businesses, most of whom are family members of Communist Party officials. Their intimate connection to the party suggests that the large chambers of commerce most likely have been coopted by the party-state. The medium-sized chambers of commerce comprised of small and medium businesses are more independent of the state but, as a consequence, are also more subject to its interference.[21] All of which led one sinologist to observe that much of autonomous activity in the People's Republic depended upon the tolerance of the authorities, for there were still no well-institutionalized legal or other guarantees protecting civil society from the state.[22] Another sinologist similarly averred that it is difficult to find in China an ideal-type civil society organization that fully embodies the principles of voluntary participation, separation from the state, and self-regulation.[23]

In effect, among the many groups and associations spawned by economic reforms, only those in the suppressed sector can be considered genuinely autonomous. They constitute whatever civil society China has. But that incipient civil society comprises groups that are diverse but fragmented, restive but unorganized—presenting an overall picture of potential anarchy instead of budding democracy.

State repression of the suppressed sector has been sufficiently successful so that independent churches operate furtively, and the opposition parties and illegal labor unions remain embryonic and ineffective. As a consequence, China has neither a church nor a labor union comparable in power and influence to communist Poland's Catholic Church or Solidarity. More than that, not all the underground groups are democratic or desirous of political democracy for China—among them are criminal organizations, separatist groups that aim to secede from the People's Republic, and nostalgic Maoist groups. The very secrecy of the groups in the suppressed sector compels them to be undemocratic in their internal structure and operations, which makes it problematic and unlikely that such groups can play much of a role in building a democratic China. All of which suggests that civil society in its current form in China may be more an obstacle than a force for democratization, prompting one observer to compare the present situation to "a boiler building up a dangerous level of steam pressure."[24]

The Limits of Political Reform

Although China's post-1979 reforms have been mainly economic, that does not mean that the years after Mao were entirely devoid of political reforms. As examples, there were efforts to introduce a measure of stability and institutionalization to the Communist Party through the eschewal of charismatic one-man rule and vicious intraparty factional struggles. Other political reforms are meant to create what the party conceives to be a "rule of law." Toward that purpose, new legislations were introduced, especially business laws governing foreign trade and investment. In 1979–1980, a series of laws was passed that included the Arrest and Detention Act, Criminal Law, Criminal Procedure Law, Organic Law for the Courts, Organic Law for the Procuratorate, and the Provisional Law on Lawyers. In 1982, a new state constitution—the PRC's fourth[25]—was put into place, followed in 1986 by the passage of a civil code.[26]

While these political reforms represent a decided improvement from the lawlessness of the Maoist era, they have not transformed China into a polity that provides for civil rights, representation, and the rule of law. Instead of democratizing the People's Republic, it can be argued that the reforms have merely made the authoritarian system more rule-governed and efficient. This is nowhere more evident than in the PRC Constitution.

Civil Rights

In its Chapter Two, China's constitution prescribes an array of civil rights (as well as duties) that should make the People's Republic the object of envy across the world. To begin with, there are all the standard individual rights and liberties of Western democracies, including equality before the law, the right to vote and stand for election, freedom of speech, the press, assembly, association, procession, demonstration, and religious belief, as well as freedom from arbitrary arrest, detention, and unlawful search of person and home.[27] In addition, there are other rights and liberties, some of which remain forlorn aspirations even in the United States. They include the following:[28] freedom and privacy of correspondence; the right to criticize and make suggestions to any state organ or functionary;[29] the right to work, and of working people to rest, retirement, and a secure livelihood; the right of the old, ill, or disabled to material assistance; the right to receive education; the freedom to engage in scientific research, literary and artistic creation and other cultural pursuits; and equality of rights between men and women.

But this impressive panoply of individual rights and liberties are circumscribed and effectively neutered by Article 51 of the same Constitution, which stipulates, "The exercise by citizens of the People's Republic of China of their freedoms and rights may not infringe upon the interests of the state, of society and of the collective."[30] And in a political system such as China's, where political power remains the exclusive purview of a single party, it is the Communist Party that determines exactly what are "the interests of the state, of society and of the collective," as well as what constitutes an "infringement" of those interests.

Rule of Law

When none other than the state constitution—the supreme law of the land—is compromised, the Communist Party's proclamations of having institutionalized a rule of law can only sound hollow. As Franz Michael aptly put it,[31]

> There is no better illustration of the contempt in which the Chinese Communists hold law than the frequency with which new constitutions have been adopted in the PRC. . . . All this shows that the party is the real sovereign authority that controls the government; the party can write and rewrite state constitutions at will. When rewriting is inopportune, constitutions can be ignored.

The constitution is not the only important body of law that is compromised. China's criminal code is likewise problematic. Adopted by the National People's Congress on July 1, 1979, the Criminal Law and Criminal Procedure Law became effective at the beginning of the next year.

While having a criminal code is better than not having one, the PRC Criminal Law is written in such vague and ambiguous language that its usefulness to citizens is doubtful.

There are many examples of the law's vagueness and ambiguity. Among them is Article 10's specification that "acts that endanger society are crimes ... but if the circumstances are *clearly minor* and the harm is *not great,* they are not to be deemed crimes." Article 17 states that "Criminal responsibility shall be borne where legitimate defense *exceeds the necessary limits* and *causes undue harm.*" Article 95 stipulates that "Ringleaders in armed mass rebellion ... whose crimes are *monstrous* are to be sentenced to life imprisonment. . . ." Article 103 specifies that "Whoever commits any of the crimes of counterrevolution[32] . . . may be sentenced to death when the harm to the state and the people is *especially serious* and the circumstances *especially odious.*" As if these articles have not already perverted the criminal code, the catch-all elastic Article 79 should remove any doubt. According to that article, "A crime that is not expressly stipulated in . . . this Law may be determined and punished according to the *most closely analogous* article of . . . this Law."[33]

It appears that the primary function of law in the People's Republic is as a tool of power for the Communist Party. That is made evident in the state constitution's preamble, which stipulates that the PRC is to be governed by "the leadership of the Communist Party" and "guided by Marxism-Leninism, Mao Zedong Thought, and Deng Xiaoping Theory."[34] Similarly, the purpose of the Criminal Law and Criminal Procedure Law is "to use criminal punishments ... to defend the system of the dictatorship of the proletariat"[35]—the proletariat being "represented" by the Chinese Communist Party. All of which could explain the adoption by China's national legislature of a new law that specifically targets Falun Gong. In October 1999, three months after the government banned the sect as a threat to Communist Party rule and social stability, the legislature revised the criminal code so as to label Falun Gong a "cult"—thereby making its leaders liable for prosecution for murder, fraud, "endangering national security," and other crimes. The revision enables the government to sentence Falun Gong members to more than the two- to seven-year prison terms previously mandated by the code for "cultists."[36] On December 26, 1999, four individuals identified to be among the sect's "principal organizers" were sentenced to up to 18 years in prison at a one-day trial.[37]

If law in the People's Republic turns out to be a political tool of the Communist Party, the phenomenon of administrative sanctions renders even more dubious a rule of law in China. Today, in the People's Republic, the executive branch of government—represented by local public security officials—can impose administrative sanctions on anyone without benefit of judicial review, effectively bypassing the entire judicial system. Through the Security Administrative Punishment Act, the police can independently issue warnings, impose fines, confiscate property, and detain individuals for up to 15 days. Through the 1979 Re-education Through Labor Act, individuals can be imprisoned for one to three years, after which their imprisonment can be extended for another year solely at the discretion of local officials.[38]

Despite the Communist Party's efforts to introduce a rule of law, some of the worst features of the Maoist era still persist in China today, albeit diminished in scale and intensity. Unlike the days of Mao when the masses were urged to mete out mob justice, the party now eschews mass mobilization, preferring to target select individuals. But just as in the Maoist era, there are still labor reform camps and due process is still violated. Public trials and summary executions are still put on for ostensibly didactic and prophylactic purposes. There are still dossiers and informants; and China still has a network of some 100,000 neighborhood committees, charged with helping the state to buttress the crumbling household registration system *(hukou)*, enforce population control, and maintain a close eye on residents.[39]

Political Representation

According to the PRC Constitution, the National People's Congress (NPC) is conceived to be the seat of popular sovereignty, being the repository of political representation at the national level. As such, the NPC has the following functions and powers: to amend and supervise the enforcement of the constitution; to enact and amend basic statutes pertaining to criminal offenses, civil affairs, and state organs; to elect and recall the president and vice-president of the PRC; to approve the PRC president's nominations for heads of the executive branch, including the premier, vice premiers, and ministers; to elect the chairman and other officers of the Central Military Commission; to elect the heads of the Supreme People's Procuratorate and Supreme Court; to examine and approve the state budget and the plans for China's economic and social development; to approve the establishment of regional government units, including special administrative regions such as Hong Kong; to decide on questions of war and peace; and to "exercise such other functions and powers as the highest organ of state power should exercise."[40]

Leaving aside the suspect identity of the NPC as a legislative body (it is highly doubtful that a genuine legislature can complete its lawmaking tasks by convening once a year for only a week), we can raise questions regarding the representativeness of that body. The NPC comprises some 3,000 delegates, each of whom serves a five-year term. With the exception of those delegates who represent the People's Liberation Army, Hong Kong, and Taiwan,[41] most NPC delegates are drawn from the 31 provinces and autonomous regions across China, having been elected to the NPC by lower-level People's Congresses (PCs). At the lowest level, some 650 million citizen voters elect 2.5 million delegates to represent them at village-township PCs. Those delegates then select 600,000 to 700,000 from among themselves to district-county PCs; the district-county PC delegates, in turn, choose the delegates for 31 provincial-municipal-autonomous region PCs. The latter delegates—together with PLA PC delegates, 120 delegates ostensibly representing Taiwan "province" and 424 Hong Kong delegates—eventually determine the delegates to the National People's Congress.[42]

In effect, the system of People's Congresses forms a pyramid of *indirect* election and representation. In this system, popular participation occurs only at the lowest tier, when the Chinese people vote to select those individuals who will presumably represent their interests at the village-township People's Congresses. Even here, the representativeness of the delegates is questionable. To be eligible as candidates in PC elections, individuals must be either approved by the government or nominated by ten or more PC delegates—a process that effectively ensures that only the politically orthodox could survive the arduous screening process. The experience of a factory worker, Yue Changqing, who attempted to compete in Shaanxi's provincial PC election in 1998 is instructive. Yue had been active in the 1989 democracy movement, for which he was imprisoned for half a year. Although he was nominated by 60 of his co-workers, Yue was denied candidacy and was threatened by the factory manager.[43]

The culmination of this pyramidal process is a parliament more in name than in actuality. Despite a marginal increase in recent years of dissenting votes,[44] the National People's Congress remains a rubber-stamp institution for decisions that have already been made by the leaders of the Communist Party. This is the extent of political representation in the People's Republic. As Yan Jiaqi concludes, the electorate in China "have virtually no impact on Chinese politics."[45]

Village Elections

Among the political reforms undertaken since 1979, one in particular has become something of a beacon of hope to China watchers. This is the phenomenon of village elections in the People's Republic.

In his treatise on the discouraging status of civil society in China, Gordon White concluded that "a successful transition towards democracy, if indeed it can be achieved, will need to be sponsored and organized by reformist elements within the current political elite."[46] A small step toward that transition seemed to have been undertaken by precisely those reformist elements within the PRC's Ministry of Civil Affairs, when they managed to persuade the Communist Party leadership to allow direct popular elections for village committees.[47]

The impetus for village elections was the collapse of the People's Communes that had been installed in the late 1950s during Mao's Great Leap Forward. The communes were more than agricultural production units; in addition to their many other functions, they were also political administrative units for rural China, with each commune comprising three to four former villages encompassing some 5,000 households. Even before the Communist Party began to reform agriculture in late 1978, some of the communes had already disintegrated. With the introduction of the contract responsibility system, which revived the rural household as the basic production unit in the countryside, whatever communes that remained were dismantled—leaving in their wake an administrative vacuum in the 930,000 villages across rural China.

That eventually led to the adoption, in November 1987, by the NPC Standing Committee of the Organic Law of Village Committees. The law mandates that every three years, the chairman, vice chairmen, and members of village committees would be directly elected by the village residents. Implementation of the Organic Law began in 1989 in select experimental villages. By the next year, 74.6 percent of rural residents in a nationwide survey reported that their villages had conducted elections—increasing to 75.8 percent in 1993[48] and 90 percent in 1998.[49] By that time, some villages had gone through four to five election cycles.

The significance of village elections seems to be in the eye of the beholder. To those disposed to see the glass as half full, the elections represent "unmistakable signs" of important positive changes pointing to the growth of grass-roots democracy in China.[50] Others less sanguine are more restrained in their enthusiasm. One observer allowed that across China, "in a low-level and uneven way," an election sensibility is starting to germinate.[51] For another, the flawed elections are a "first step on a long march" in expanding choices for the country's 900 million rural people.[52]

For elections to be considered democratic in a meaningful sense, they should meet certain criteria. The election must be free (voting is completely voluntary and not a result of coercion), equal (each vote counts as much as any other vote), fair and competitive (anyone who desires to stand for election has the opportunity to do so, with no candidate enjoying a preferential advantage, so that voters can choose from among candidates who hold a range of views). Finally, the act of voting itself must be anonymous and secret, so that the voter is able to make choices without fear of reprisal.

Although the Organic Law of Village Committees does provide for a secret and individual ballot, multiple candidates for each position, and a transparent and publicly monitored count, it is unclear whether elections actually meet these criteria. What empirical data we have are spotty and skimpy; the elections witnessed by international observers are a nonrepresentative sample and so few that they are statistically insignificant. There is also considerable variation from village to village, with many local elections that are flawed and even precooked.[53] As an example, the number of ballots that were cast in a village election in Shenzhen in 1999 exceeded the total number of voters in that village![54] One Western observer remarked that even "model villages" made mistakes.[55] Another commented that many essential elements of elections, such as the secret ballot, are hard to inculcate in a populace that still remembers the Cultural Revolution.[56] An official of China's Ministry of Civil Affairs in charge of promoting village elections admitted in April 2000 that elections were corrupt or failed to follow the rules in some 40 percent of villages. He estimated it would take 50 years until 90 percent of the villages conducted their elections properly.[57]

Among the irregularities noted by outside observers is the lack of genuine competition among candidates. The example of Banqiao, a hamlet in Sichuan Province, which was observed by a U.S. delegation from the Carter Center, is illustrative. In that election, all four candidates on the ballot had been picked by the Communist Party.[58] That seems to be what is meant by electoral competition in the People's Republic—that there are more candidates than seats, even if all the candidates have been approved by the party-state. Worse yet, a nationwide survey in 1993 found that 48.4 percent of respondents said that their villages' elections were not competitive at all.[59]

Banqiao's experience was confirmed by an in-depth study by a Taiwan scholar of the electoral process in Hope (Xiwang) village. From 1996 to 1998, Chen Shunbin visited the village three times and interviewed government officials at the local, township, county, provincial, and central levels, as well as party cadres, scholars, and peasants. As described by Chen, the election process begins with the nomination of candidates. In theory, anyone can be nominated, but that does not mean that the nominees will actually become candidates on the ballot. The task of compiling an initial list of nominees is left to a "village election leadership small group," comprising five to seven individuals who have been appointed by the local Communist Party secretary. Members of the small group are also members of the local party committee and CCP mass organizations (the Communist Youth Corps, the Women's Federation, and the militia). The small group undertakes a background investigation of the nominees on their respective age, work history, work performance, "cultural level," and "political qualifications." In this manner, the initial round of nominees is pared down to a more selective second list that is forwarded to higher-level officials for their scrutiny and approval, the result of which is a third and final list of candidates. It is that list that is made public to the village residents three days before the election.[60]

During those three days, the candidates actively campaign with speeches and appearances before town hall meetings. At the same time, party cadres go door to door to register voters and encourage their turnout, in the process of which cadres have been known to lobby for their favorites. On election day, beginning at 7:30 in the morning, cadres visit each household carrying ballot boxes into which the residents cast their anonymous ballots. In some cases, the cadre would vote for an individual who is illiterate or away at work. All the ballots are then brought to a central location, where they are publicly recorded and tallied.[61]

As it is described, the electoral process in Hope village displays several problematic features. To begin with, the nomination of candidates is less than free and competitive because of the veto power of local and higher-level party and government officials. The result is that village residents have almost no effect on the nomination process, their role confined to that of being notified, consulted, and persuaded. Moreover, villagers may also be pressured into voting because of the cadres' aggressive voter registration and mobilization. Most egregious of all is the practice of cadres casting ballots for absentee voters. All of which led Chen to conclude that voting becomes almost a mere formality because it has lost its competitive and democratic meaning—which could account for the villagers' apathy, disinterest, and "pervasive lack of civic-mindedness."[62]

Even if village elections met every democratic criterion, that does not mean that self-government has been instituted in rural China. In the first place, the primary function of village committees is to be the local agents of the state to assist Beijing in enforcing policies and ensuring citizen compliance with those policies—specifically those concerning tax collection, population control, and the mandatory sale of agricultural produce to the state.[63] Therefore, it should not be surprising that, being local agents of the state, the village committees are secondary in power to the local party committees. Each village has both an elected chief and an appointed CCP secretary, and it is the latter who has the greatest political clout.[64] Village elections were never conceived by the Communist Party leadership as a liberalizing step toward greater democracy, but began as a pragmatic device to fill the administrative vacuum left by the demise of the communes. Later, party leaders thought the elections could help with the increasingly unmanageable problem of pandemic corruption by party and government officials. Allowing the peasants to vote out corrupt leaders, it is hoped, will dissipate some of their frustration and disaffection.[65]

In effect, the significance of village elections in China revolves around whether they are conducted in accordance with democratic principles and criteria. More than that, even if village elections were conducted in a democratic manner, by themselves they will not lead to the democratization of the whole country. In the last analysis, for local elections to be meaningful, the present glass ceiling must be broken so that the selection of government personnel for China's counties, municipalities, provinces, autonomous regions, and the central government in Beijing will also be determined by popular elections. Whether village elections will progress on to the county level will entirely depend on the central leadership.

The attitude of that leadership, in the person of Jiang Zemin, is not encouraging. On the one hand, he was reported on July 4, 1997, to anticipate that "China will institute widespread democracy when it has become sufficiently economically developed."[66] A year and a half later, in December 1998, in a speech to an assembly of party elites, the same Jiang Zemin vowed that the present system "must not be shaken, weakened, or discarded" and that the People's Republic will never adopt a Western-style democratic system.[67] In March 1999, his trusted adviser Liu Ji declared that, "So long as the PRC constitution exists, China will forever be ruled by a single party."[68]

In effect, whatever political reforms that are undertaken have resulted only in the People's Republic's transition from communism back to authoritarianism. The cumulative result of more than 20 years of post-Mao reforms is a China that more and more resembles the traditional bureaucratic despotic state. In past and present China, state power stops at the county level, leaving the villages to self-rule by the gentry (past) or elected chiefs (present). Just as in days of old, the upper crust of Chinese society is composed of an overlapping political-economic elite: the mandarin-gentry-landlord class in the past; the CCP–big business elite today.

Despite its bankrupt ideology and endemic corruption, the Communist Party is determined to hold onto its absolute power and seems unable to adapt peacefully to the demands of a rapidly changing society. With no one in charge of helping the country navigate a transition from totalitarian communism to a stable democratic future, political change risks becoming chaotic. In an increasingly chaotic environment, the Communist Party seems to have retreated into a siege mentality, as exemplified by Jiang's admonition to his colleagues "against infiltration, subversive activities and separatist activities of international and domestic hostile forces."[69] Efforts are undertaken to police the internet, used by more than 9 million Chinese. The U.S. cable Cartoon Network has been banned from television for one year, its broadcast of Bugs Bunny and Daffy Duck replaced by Chinese cartoons that feature patriotic themes—all in the interest of preventing "subversive ideas" from invading the country.[70]

U.S. Policy Implications

Like the mythical Janus, nationalism is said to have two faces: a peaceable herbivorous face and an aggressive carnivorous face. Which face of Janus is worn by Chinese patriotic nationalism is a question that has potentially grave implications for regional stability as well as U.S. policy. China's wounded pride, historical resentment, and irredentism—when coupled with its rising power and political authoritarianism—make for a volatile and potentially dangerous mix. All of which points to the unsettling conclusion that the patriotic nationalism of the People's Republic may well bear the carnivorous other face of Janus.

If China is not deterred in its irredentism, there will be untold implications for Asia and the Pacific. The United States still has bilateral security treaties with a number of countries in Asia, including Japan, the Philippines, and Thailand, as well as a congressional act on Taiwan. Thus, the United States would likely be involved should conflict erupt between the PRC and the Philippines in the South China Sea, between the PRC and Japan over Diaoyutai, or between the PRC and Taiwan. In the case of Taiwan, the United States has a substantial economic stake in the island: In 1997, U.S. foreign direct investments in Taiwan were roughly equal to those in the PRC ($4.944 and $5.013 billion, respectively). More than that, despite the abrogation of the 1956 Mutual Defense Treaty, the 1979

Taiwan Relations Act has committed the United States to the maintenance of Taiwan's peace and security. As for Japan, the renewed U.S.-Japan Security Treaty contains a reference to Japan's "associated territories" that can be interpreted to include Taiwan and Diaoyutai.

Given the circumstances reviewed here, Washington's policy of "constructive engagement" with China may bear rethinking. That policy was initiated by the Carter administration in 1978 for the express purpose of using China to counterbalance the Soviet Union. Despite the latter's collapse in 1991, successive U.S. administrations—Republican and Democratic—have continued to "engage" China, hoping that U.S. relations will eventually transform it into a democracy. That hope, however, may be built on a dubious premise: that the capitalist transformation of China's economy will spill over to democratize its political system. But capitalism does not inevitably lead to democracy: One needs only recall the historical examples of capitalist but totalitarian Nazi Germany, Fascist Italy, and Imperial Japan. Today, Iraq is a capitalist dictatorship, Saudi Arabia a capitalist monarchy, and Singapore is a capitalist pseudo-democracy.

Instead of wishful thinking, *The Federalist* recommended that foreign policy and relations should be constructed on mutual interests[71] that China and the United States may lack. America's market is open to Chinese goods; China, being a developing country, is disinclined to be a mass consumer market for U.S. exports, except for needed items such as food grains, high technology, and advanced weaponry. The incompatibility in economic interests mainly accounts for America's ever-growing trade deficits with China, from $0.37 billion in 1985 to $63 billion in 1998 (and an expected $70 billion in 2000)—an increase of 17,000 percent in 13 years—so that China has replaced Japan as the largest deficit trading partner of the United States.

Regionally, China intends to return to its traditional role as Asia-Pacific's hegemonic power and is resolved to reclaim some of its lost territories, especially Taiwan, Diaoyutai, and the South China Sea—which threatens the security of America's allies and friends. Politically, as with NATO's 1999 military campaign in Kosovo, Washington and Beijing more often than not are on opposing sides. China is an ally of North Korea, and is suspected of having supplied nuclear technology, reprocessed uranium, Silkworm missiles, and biochemical weapons to countries unfriendly to the United States, including Iran, Iraq, Libya, and Myanmar. As for human rights, Beijing rejects the notion that there are universal moral principles, insisting instead that moral principles are culturally dependent. Thus Beijing suppresses political dissidence and freedom of religion and enforces involuntary abortion and sterilization—all of which Americans find repugnant.

The release in 1999 of the House of Representatives' Cox Report on China's suspected theft of U.S. nuclear and neutron weapons technology might give cause for a sober reassessment of China policy. Instead of democracy, it seems that 20 years of "constructive engagement" with China have brought as many years of tireless Chinese espionage. Jean-François Revel once counseled that we must refrain from acting so as to rescue totalitarian systems from their failures and "thus preserve them from a necessary liberalization."[72] So long as China remains a dictatorship, it may not be in U.S. interests to enhance its military capabilities, either through sales of advanced technology, or inadvertently through laxness in nuclear lab security.

Conclusion

In resorting to irredentist reactive nationalism, the Chinese Communist Party may well come to discover that the cure is worse than the disease. For patriotic nationalism is a double-edged sword: It can rally support for the regime, but it can also prompt adventurism.

Populist Chinese irredentism may exceed that of the government, if the survey of Beijing university students is any indication. The respondents in the survey seemed to think that their government has been "too soft" on Tokyo over the Diaoyutai islets dispute.[73] To secure popular support, the Communist Party might find itself increasingly pressured to take military action against its neighbors over contested territories. Like Pandora's box, once opened, the passions of reactive and irredentist nationalism may prove difficult to contain and may lead China to military conflict—and possible defeat—against its neighbors and the United States. Like Nazi Germany and Imperial Japan, China may find that aggressive patriotic nationalism is ultimately self-destructive.

Today, more than ever, voices of prudence in the People's Republic should be heeded, but they are a minority. One such voice is that of Li Zeshun, who reminded his countrymen that the real meaning and purpose of Chinese revolutions in the twentieth century, including the Communist revolution, was national regeneration, not revenge. As he put it:[74]

> The fundamental way to cleanse our national shame is to achieve economic prosperity and a strong defense. [The purpose of patriotic education] is not . . . to instill a narrow sense of national revenge. The purpose . . . is rather to increase the Chinese people's self-respect and self-confidence. . . .

244 • The Other Face of Janus

Power becomes dangerous when it refuses to let self-pity go. Much as the Chinese people suffered grievously from foreign imperialism in the nineteenth and twentieth centuries, the reality is that China today is no longer the object of abuse and mistreatment. Nor is it subject to the will of others, as the People's Republic amply demonstrates—being a sovereign, strong, and integral nation-state.

The rise and fall of great civilizations has its own logic. It may be that China's time as the Middle Kingdom that once commanded the Asia-Pacific region was in the past and may never be restored. It may be that China can reclaim its historical status as a great power only if it forsakes a reliance on the use of force. So long as China continues to be ruled by a government that refuses to respect human freedom and the inalienable dignity and sanctity of its own people, its quest to be restored as the great and glorious Middle Kingdom will remain frustrated and unfulfilled. For the great Chinese Empire of old was not created by military conquest and force. As Chinese themselves constantly reiterate, in the last analysis, the Middle Kingdom was great because of the appeal of its demonstrably superior culture and civilization. As a new century dawns, the challenge before the children of the dragon is to reconstruct themselves as a great civilization that commands respect by virtue of their overriding humanity.

Notes

1. See Michael Ignatieff, "Nationalism and Toleration," in Richard Caplan and John Feffer (eds.), *Europe's New Nationalism: State and Minorities in Conflict* (New York: Oxford University Press, 1996), p. 221; and Michael Mann, "A Political Theory of Nationalism and Its Excesses," in Sukumar Periwal (ed.), *Notions of Nationalism* (Budapest: Central European Press, 1995), p. 62.

2. Germans resented being defeated in World War I, as well as the punishment exacted by the Treaty of Versailles. The Japanese nursed a resentment against the historical domination of China and against the Western Powers' imperialism that began with U.S. Admiral Perry's forced opening of Tokugawa Japan, in 1854.

3. In fact, the evidence seems to indicate that it is precisely the unknown who are imprisoned and abused. The more famous an individual, the more likely the Communist Party will be constrained in its behavior. This suggests that the outside world, including governments and nongovernmental organizations (NGOs) such as Amnesty International, can have an important impact on the fates of those caught in Beijing's maw.

4. As examples, Xu Wenli, Wang Youcai, and Qin Yongmin were sentenced to 13, 12, and 11 years, respectively. They were part of a group of several hundred activists, who, beginning in June 1998, tried to register the China Democracy Party in

14 provinces and cities. John Pomfret, "China Widens Its Crackdown on Speech," *San Francisco Chronicle (SFC),* December 24, 1998, p. A10.

5. Two newspapers that were suppressed in December 1998 were *Cultural Times* and *Southern Weekend*—the first was closed, the second censored. In January 1999, the Communist Party suspended the operations of China Today Publishers, one of China's boldest and most influential book publishers. In March 1999, two journals identified with the reformist faction were suppressed: *Strategy and Management* was censored; *Procedure (Fangfa)* ceased publication. Erik Eckholm, "Quiet Chinese Campaign Results in Tighter Controls on Liberal Publications," *SFC,* January 19, 1999, p. A8; and *Shijie ribao (World Journal* or *WJ),* March 19, 1999, p. A11.

6. The Chinese Communist Party's estimate was 2 million; Falun Gong claimed a total membership of 100 million, most of whom were in China. Charles Hutzler, "Falun Gong Accuses Police of Torture," *SFC,* October 29, 1999, pp. A1, A7.

7. An example is the arrest in March 1998 of a construction engineer, Liu Kangxiu, for writing an as yet unpublished book on political reform. *WJ,* March 30, 1998, p. A7.

8. Gordon White, "The Dynamics of Civil Society in Post-Mao China," in Brian Hook (ed.), *The Individual and the State in China* (Oxford: Clarendon Press, 1996), pp. 196, 198.

9. Ibid., p. 206.

10. John Leicester, "'Green' Movement Arising in China," *San Francisco Examiner,* November 29, 1998, p. A22.

11. White, "Dynamics of Civil Society in Post-Mao China," p. 208.

12. *WJ,* January 27, 1997, p. A10.

13. White, "Dynamics of Civil Society," pp. 209–211.

14. Ibid., pp. 212–214.

15. Ibid., pp. 214–215.

16. Ibid., p. 216.

17. Comment by Stanford University Professor Condoleezza Rice, who was the Bush administration's National Security Council aide on Soviet affairs. As quoted in Jacob Heilbrunn, "The Unrealistic Realism of Bush's Foreign Policy Tutors," *The New Republic,* September 27, 1999, p. 24.

18. Jing Ling, *The Opening of the Chinese Mind: Democratic Changes in China Since 1978* (Westport, CT: Praeger, 1994), pp. 134, 142, 141.

19. *WJ,* March 31, 1998, p. A11.

20. Emblematic of that attitude is 52-year-old businessman Wu Z. S., who thought that political dissidents "wouldn't get much support from the general population" because Chinese understood human rights to mean "the right to make a living, the right to work." For 30-year-old office clerk Wang L. L., not only was he unaware of the recent crackdowns, he maintained that "Elections and democracy aren't important . . . as long as we have a good living." Indira A. R. Lakshmanan, "Many in China Unaware of Recent Crackdowns on Democracy Activists," *SFC,* January 16, 1999, p. A12.

21. See David L. Wank, "Civil Society in Communist China? Private Business and Political Alliance, 1989," in John A. Hall (ed.), *Civil Society: Theory, History, Comparison* (Cambridge, MA: Polity Press, 1995), pp. 56–79.

22. Martin K. Whyte, "Urban China: A Civil Society in the Making?", in Arthur Lewis Rosenbaum (ed.), *State and Society in China: The Consequences of Reform* (Boulder: Westview, 1992), pp. 93–94.

23. White, "Dynamics of Civil Society," p. 207.

24. Ibid., p. 219.

25. The 1982 constitution was preceded by its 1954, 1975, and 1978 counterparts.

26. Franz Michael, "Law: A Tool of Power," in Yuan-li Wu, Franz Michael, John F. Copper, Ta-ling Lee, Maria Hsia Chang, and A. James Gregor, *Human Rights in the People's Republic of China* (Boulder: Westview, 1988), p. 46.

27. See Articles 33–39 of *The Constitution of the People's Republic of China* (Beijing: Foreign Languages Press, 1983), pp. 31–33.

28. Articles 40–48 in *Constitution of the PRC*, pp. 33–38.

29. On February 26, 1998, political dissident Yang Qinheng was sentenced to three years of "labor reeducation" for exercising precisely this constitutional right. In an open letter to the National People's Congress, he had asked the Congress to pay heed to the plight of unemployed workers. *WJ*, March 28, 1998, p. A11.

30. *Constitution of the PRC*, p. 39.

31. Michael, "Law: A Tool of Power," p. 45.

32. The term "crimes of counterrevolution" was replaced by "crimes endangering the national security" in the 1998 Criminal Law.

33. *The Criminal Law and The Criminal Procedure Law of China* (Beijing: Foreign Languages Press, 1984), pp. 12–13, 14, 36, 38–39, 32. Emphasis supplied.

34. *Constitution of the PRC*, p. 5. "Deng Xiaoping Theory" was added to the Preamble by an amendment in 1999.

35. Articles 1 and 2 of *Criminal Law and Criminal Procedure Law of China*, p. 9.

36. N.A., "China Uses New Law Against Falun Gong," *SFC*, November 1, 1999, p. A11.

37. Charles Hutzler, "Organizers of Sect Sentenced in China," *SFC*, December 27, 1999, p. A1.

38. Michael, "Law: A Tool of Power," p. 50.

39. Frank Langfitt, "Capitalism Starts At Home in China," *SFC*, December 17, 1998, p. C7.

40. *Constitution of the PRC*, pp. 47–50, 45.

41. The PLA, Hong Kong, and Taiwan are represented by 270, 36, and 13 delegates, respectively.

42. Yan Jiaqi, "Xuanmin toupiao dui zhongguo zhengju di yingxiang (The effect of the electorate's vote on Chinese politics)," *Zhongguo zhichun (China Spring)*, no. 173 (1998), pp. 3–4.

43. *WJ,* January 7, 1998, p. A11.

44. As an example, at the 1998 meeting of the NPC, out of a total of 2,949, there were 200 delegates who dissented on the appointment of Li Peng to the premiership; 36 delegates opposed Jiang Zemin being both president of the PRC and chairman of the Central Military Commission. *WJ,* March 16, 1998, p. A1.

45. Yan Jiaqi, "Effect of the Electorate's Vote," p. 4.

46. White, "Dynamics of Civil Society," p. 221.

47. See Tianjian Shi, "Village Committee Elections in China: Institutionalist Tactics for Democracy," *World Politics,* 51 (April 1999), pp. 385–412.

48. Ibid., pp. 385–386.

49. Jaime A. FlorCruz, "Village Voices," *Time International,* 150:31 (March 30, 1998), p. 24. According to another account, however, only 60 percent of villages had conducted village committee elections by 1998. *WJ,* August 25, 1998, p. A12.

50. Henry S. Rowen, "The Short March: China's Road to Democracy," *The National Interest,* 45 (Fall 1996), p. 61.

51. FlorCruz, "Village Voices."

52. Robert A. Pastor, "Seems Legit," *Time International,* 150:31 (March 30, 1998), p. 27.

53. Jaime A. FlorCruz, "Eyewitness: An Experiment in Voting, If Not Democracy," *Time,* 153:14 (February 1, 1999), p. 34.

54. *WJ,* August 27, 1999, p. A11.

55. Pastor, "Seems Legit."

56. FlorCruz, "Village Voices."

57. Renee Schoof, "Chinese Taste Democracy Only At Lowest Level For Now," *San Francisco Examiner,* April 9, 2000, p. C–13.

58. FlorCruz, "Eyewitness." Despite that lack of choice, the five-term incumbent, a high school principal, was voted out.

59. Shi, "Village Committee Elections in China," p. 386.

60. Chen Shunbin, "Dalu nongcun di cunmin zizhi zhidu (Mainland Chinese Villages' Village Self-Rule System)," *Zhongguo dalu yanjiu (Mainland China Studies),* 41:10 (October 1998), p. 43.

61. Ibid., pp. 44, 51.

62. Ibid., pp. 50, 51, 54.

63. Village committees are also responsible for dispute mediation, public affairs, public welfare, law and order, rural cooperatives, and collective landownership. Ibid., p. 53; and Song Jiayi, "Zhongguo dalu di minzhu zhicun (Mainland China's Democratic Village)," *Shijie zhoukan (World Journal West),* May 18, 1997, pp. S–1, S–5.

64. FlorCruz, "Village Voices." See also *WJ,* March 16, 1998, p. A7.

65. FlorCruz, "Village Voices."

66. *WJ,* July 5, 1997, p. A11.

67. Henry Chu, "Chinese Leader Gives Anti-Democracy Address," *SFC,* December 19, 1998, p. A15.

68. *WJ*, March 22, 1999, p. A9.

69. Chu, "Chinese Leader Gives Anti-Democracy Address."

70. Steven Roback, "Bugs Bunny and Daffy Duck No Laughing Matter to China," *SFC*, April 16, 2000, p. 7.

71. *The Federalist* (New York: Charles Scribner's Sons, 1864), p. 30.

72. Jean-François Revel, *Does Communism Have a Future?* (New York: Orwell Press, 1989), p. 6.

73. The mean response to the survey statement that "The Chinese government has been too soft on Diaoyutai" was 3.89. A score of 4.0 means "somewhat agree".

74. Li Zeshun, "Guanyu kaizhan guoqi jiaoyu de sikao (Thoughts on Developing a National Shame Education)," *Guofang (National Defense)*, no. 5 (1994), pp. 15–16.

Index